Marvels of
Nature

Published by Reader's Digest Children's Books
Reader's Digest Road, Pleasantville, NY, U.S.A.10570-7000 and
Reader's Digest Children's Publishing Limited, The Ice House
124-126 Walcot Street, Bath UK BA1 5BG

Reader's Digest Children's Books is a trademark and Reader's Digest
is a registered trademark of The Reader's Digest Association, Inc.

Conceived and produced by Weldon Owen Pty Limited
59 Victoria Street, McMahons Point, NSW, 2060, Australia
A member of the Weldon Owen Group of Companies
Sydney • San Francisco • Auckland

© 2003 Weldon Owen Inc.

WELDON OWEN PTY LTD
Chairman: John Owen
Publisher: Sheena Coupe
Creative Director: Sue Burk
Design Concept: John Bull
Editorial Coordinator: Jennifer Losco
Production Manager: Caroline Webber
Production Coordinator: James Blackman
Vice President International Sales: Stuart Laurence

DINOSAURS
Author: Paul Willis
Consultant: Michael K. Brett-Surman, Ph.D.
Illustrators: Jimmy Chan, Lee Gibbons/Wildlife Art Ltd, Ray Grinaway,
Gino Hasler, David Kirshner, Murray Frederick, David McAlister, James McKinnon,
Luis Rey/Wildlife Art Ltd, Peter Schouten, Peter Scott/Wildlife Art Ltd,
Marco Sparaciari, Kevin Stead
© 1999 Weldon Owen Inc.

EARTHQUAKES AND VOLCANOES
Author: Lin Sutherland
Consultant: Thomas L. Wright
Illustrators: Richard Bonson/Wildlife Art Ltd, Chris Forsey, Ray Grinaway,
James McKinnon, Stuart McVicar, John Richards
© 2000 Weldon Owen Inc.

INSECTS AND SPIDERS
Author: Matthew Robertson
Consultants: Louis N. Sorkin, B.C.E.; Dr. David Grimaldi
Illustrators: Sandra Doyle/Wildlife Art Ltd, Christer Eriksson, Ray Grinaway,
Ian Jackson/Wildlife Art Ltd, James McKinnon, Rob Mancini,
Steve Roberts/Wildlife Art Ltd, Chris Shields/Wildlife Art Ltd, Kevin Stead
© 2000 Weldon Owen Inc.

ISBN 0-7944-0351-4

Color Reproduction by Colourscan Co Pte Ltd
Printed by Imago Productions (F.E) Pte Ltd
Printed in Singapore

10 9 8 7 6 5 4 3 2 1

A WELDON OWEN PRODUCTION

A NOTE TO READERS AND PARENTS
This publication contains the opinions and ideas of its writers and is designed to provide useful information
to the reader on the subject matter covered. When engaging in any activities which may be suggested in or
relate to the subject of this publication, always exercise caution, and children should always be under adult
supervision. Any references in this publication to any products or services do not constitute or imply an
endorsement or recommendation. The publisher and the author specifically disclaim any responsibility
for any liability, loss or risk (personal, financial or otherwise) which may be claimed or incurred as a
consequence, directly or indirectly, of the use and/or application of any of the contents of this publication.

Reader's Digest
Pathfinders

Marvels of
Nature

Reader's
Digest
Children's Books™

Pleasantville, New York • Montréal, Québec

Dinosaurs

Contents

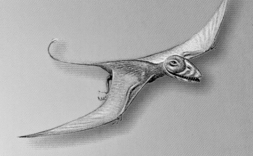

Introducing Dinosaurs 8

What Is a Dinosaur? 10
Triassic Times 12
Jurassic Giants 14
Cretaceous Conditions 16
The Two Hip Groups 18
What's Cool? What's Hot? 20
Survival 22
The Next Generation 24
Sharing Dinosaur Space 26

The Dinosaur Parade 28

The Meat-Eaters 30
The Plant-Eaters 32
The Long Necks 34
The Head Cases 36
The Armored Division 38
Big and Small 40
The Tough Guys 42
The Fast Movers 44

The Dinosaur Puzzle 46

Fossil Evidence 48
Following Fossil Clues 50
Famous Finds 52
Hunting for a Dinosaur 54
Reconstructing a Dinosaur 56
Brought Back to Life 58
When the Dinosaurs Died 60
Dinosaur Relatives Today 62

Glossary .64
Index 66

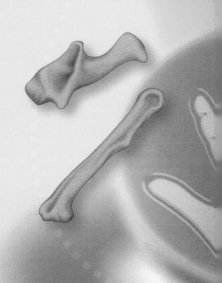

Pick Your Path

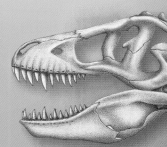

OPEN *DINOSAURS* AND slip back through time on a journey like no other to the prehistoric world of these amazing creatures. Start by learning just what makes a dinosaur a dinosaur, then read straight through to the end and puzzle over why they disappeared from Earth. Or follow your own interests. Want to read about some of the scariest meat-eating dinosaurs? Jump straight to "The Tough Guys" and move through the book from there.

You'll find plenty of other discovery paths to choose from in the special features sections. Read about great dinosaur moments in "Inside Story," or get creative with "Hands On" activities. Delve into words with "Word Builders," or amaze your friends with fascinating facts from "That's Amazing!" You can choose a new path with every reading—READER'S DIGEST PATHFINDERS will take you wherever *you* want to go.

INSIDE STORY
Big Dinosaur Moments

Share the excitement of Paul Sereno and Fernando Novas when they dig up the earliest dinosaur ever found. Join David Gillette as he discovers the remains of the biggest animal ever to walk on Earth. Imagine you're with John Horner when he comes upon 15 nests of fossilized dinosaur eggs and babies—the first evidence that dinosaurs looked after their young. INSIDE STORY lets you feel what it's like to make a discovery and contribute to our knowledge of how the dinosaurs lived and died.

HANDS ON
Create and Make

Find out how many steps you would have to take to keep up with a running *Tyrannosaurus*. Put a chicken's skeleton back together to learn how paleontologists reconstruct dinosaur skeletons. Go hunting for real fossils in the field. Prove to yourself why dinosaurs with long necks had such tiny heads. HANDS ON features experiments, projects, and activities that make the dinosaur world come to life.

Word Builders

What a strange word! What does it mean? Where did it come from? Find out by reading **Word Builders**.

That's Amazing!

Awesome facts, amazing records, fascinating figures—you'll find them all in **That's Amazing!**

Pathfinder

Use the **Pathfinder** section to find your way from one subject to another. It's all up to you!

Ready! Set! Start exploring!

Introducing Dinosaurs

Journey back in time and meet the dinosaurs and the Earth that they ruled for 165 million years. Learn how to tell a dinosaur from a non-dinosaur, and go on a tour of the dinosaurs' world during the Triassic, Jurassic, and Cretaceous periods. Then it's time to get to know dinosaurs a little better—their unique features, their tactics for survival, and their methods of bringing up their babies. Finally, meet the other creatures that lived alongside dinosaurs.

page **10**

How do you tell a dinosaur from a dinosaur look-alike?

Go to WHAT IS A DINOSAUR?

page **12**

When did the dinosaurs first walk on Earth?

Why doesn't this look like the world that you know?

Go to TRIASSIC TIMES.

page **14**

When did the dinosaurs really flourish? Why?

Can you recognize any plants from dinosaur times that are still around today?

Go to JURASSIC GIANTS.

page **16**

When was *Tyrannosaurus* terrorizing Earth?

Go to CRETACEOUS CONDITIONS.

page **18**

What could dinosaurs do that no other animal before them could do?

Go to THE TWO HIP GROUPS.

page **20**

How did dinosaurs survive in cold weather?

Go to WHAT'S COOL? WHAT'S HOT?

page **22**

Why would a dinosaur have stripes like a tiger?

Go to SURVIVAL.

page **24**

Did dinosaurs care for their young?

Go to THE NEXT GENERATION.

page **26**

If dinosaurs ruled the land in the Mesozoic era, what creatures ruled the seas? The skies?

What animals were small and furry and first appeared with the dinosaurs?

Go to SHARING DINOSAUR SPACE.

MAGIC DRAGON
People have been digging up dinosaur bones for thousands of years but didn't always know what they were. The Chinese once thought they were dragon bones with magical properties.

What Is a Dinosaur?

WHEN YOU THINK about dinosaurs, you may imagine huge, ferocious creatures—still frightening even though they have been extinct for millions of years. But not all dinosaurs were large. Not all were scary. In fact, an amazing thing about these animals is how different they were from one another. There were some dinosaurs larger than a bus, who romped along on four legs. Others were no bigger than a chicken and cruised about on two legs. Some lived by themselves or in pairs. Others lived in herds of a thousand or more.

Despite their differences, though, dinosaurs had many things in common. They all laid eggs, and they walked with their legs directly under their bodies. Most had scaly skin, like present-day lizards and crocodiles, although some may have had feathers. Dinosaurs can be divided into two groups—those called lizard-hipped and those called bird-hipped, depending on the shape of their hipbones.

Millions of years before our first human ancestors appeared, dinosaurs ruled the Earth. The Age of Dinosaurs lasted 160 million years, during the Mesozoic era. This era is divided into the Triassic, Jurassic, and Cretaceous periods.

DINOSAUR HUNTING GROUNDS
The best places for hunting buried dinosaur bones are the badlands. That's where rivers and streams have eroded layers of rock, making it easier to find the fossils. Dinosaur-rich badlands can be found in the Rockies in the United States and Canada. The badlands in Mongolia are also filled with dinosaur remains.

DEFINITELY NOT A DINOSAUR
The Mesozoic dinosaurs are all dead, so don't let this Komodo dragon fool you. It's the world's largest living lizard. Unlike a dinosaur, it walks with its legs spread out to the side.

EARTH TIME
The history of Earth is divided into eras and periods of time. Different plants and animals were alive at different periods of time. Dinosaurs lived during the Mesozoic era.

Precambrian Time	Cambrian	Ordovician	Silurian	Devonian
			Paleozoic	
4,600 million years ago 550	505		435	408

Word Builders

The word **dinosaur** means "a fearfully great, or terrible, lizard." Sir Richard Owen created the term in 1842 from two ancient Greek words, *deinos* and *sauros*. He needed a name for a new group he had discovered— animals that were often huge, with bodies that looked like lizards.

That's Amazing!

Today we know about more than 800 different types of dinosaurs, and a new type is discovered every seven weeks. Paleontologists think we will eventually find more than 1,000. But there are many dinosaurs that we will never know anything about—they are the dinosaurs that left no fossils behind to tell us about themselves.

Pathfinder

• How were the bird-hipped dinosaurs different from the lizard-hipped dinosaurs? Go to pages 18–19.
• Were dinosaur eggs the biggest eggs ever? Go to page 25.
• How do you start your own fossil collection? Go to page 55.

SPOT THE LOOK-ALIKES

Dinosaurs did not live in the sea. That was the home of marine reptiles. Synapsids, mammal-like reptiles, lived before dinosaurs. Dinosaurs couldn't fly. Pterosaurs, or flying reptiles, did that.

Peloneustes, marine reptile

Dimetrodon, synapsid

Pteranodon, pterosaur

ONE OF MANY

A *Dilophosaurus* lunches on a lizard. This meat-eater of the Jurassic period was almost 20 feet (6 m) long, but it was light and could sprint after prey on its strong back legs. With its fancy head crest, it might have attracted a mate or frightened off a rival.

INSIDE STORY

The Dinosaur Experts

Do you like studying rocks? Have you ever seen a fossil and wondered what it looked like before it became a fossil? Do you love dinosaurs and their prehistoric world? Then becoming a dinosaur expert someday may be just right for you.

You can start now by reading books about dinosaurs and creating your own fossil collection. Fossils are the bits left behind by animals and plants of the past. Most fossils are found in sedimentary rocks.

Dinosaur experts are called paleontologists. They study dinosaur fossils. First they dig the dinosaur fossils up carefully, like these paleontologists. Then they take the fossils to a laboratory where they clean and preserve them. Finally, they study the fossils and discover more about the dinosaurs and the prehistoric past.

Carboniferous	Permian	Triassic	Jurassic	Cretaceous	Tertiary	Quaternary
			Mesozoic		Cenozoic	
360	286	248	208	144	65	2 0

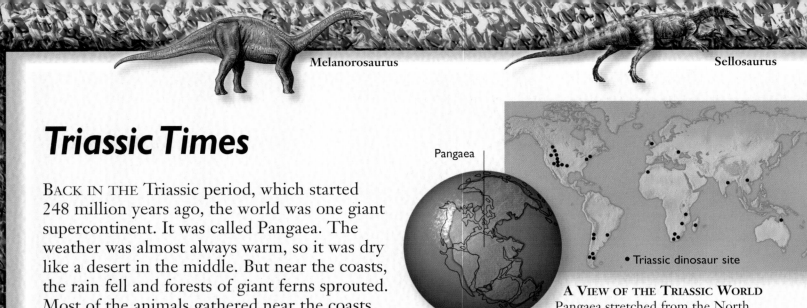

Triassic Times

BACK IN THE Triassic period, which started 248 million years ago, the world was one giant supercontinent. It was called Pangaea. The weather was almost always warm, so it was dry like a desert in the middle. But near the coasts, the rain fell and forests of giant ferns sprouted. Most of the animals gathered near the coasts, because that's where they could find plenty of insects and reptiles to eat and plenty of water to drink.

The first dinosaurs appeared about 228 million years ago. They were small meat-eaters that probably evolved from animals no bigger than rabbits. Although they were small, they had one big advantage. Their two back legs let them stand upright and run much faster than the animals they hunted. These speedy killers soon ruled the Triassic world, taking over from the reptiles that had ruled Pangaea before them. Then the first plant-eating dinosaurs started appearing, and they were as big as a pickup truck. By the end of the Triassic period, dinosaurs had spread all over the world. They were bigger and faster and could move more easily than anything else around. And there were no oceans to stop them from spreading across the world.

Pangaea

• Triassic dinosaur site

A VIEW OF THE TRIASSIC WORLD

Pangaea stretched from the North Pole to the South Pole. Triassic dinosaurs could go anywhere they liked in Pangaea without getting their feet wet. Today, the fossils of Triassic dinosaurs have been found on all continents except Antarctica. It's possible to uncover fossils of the dinosaur *Massospondylus* in two such faraway places as southern Africa and Arizona, U.S.A.

A PILE OF OLD BONES

How do scientists find out the age of dinosaur bones? First, scientists identify the type of rock in which the bones were found. Then they compare the bones with other fossils whose age they already know. Last, they find volcanic rock near the bones and measure the rate of decay of the radioactivity in the rock. Scientists used high-tech equipment to determine that these *Coelophysis* bones are about 225 million years old.

Word Builders

The word **Pangaea** comes from ancient Greek and it means "all Earth." Pangaea was the only continent in the Triassic period, so all the land in the world was a part of it. The continents we know today—North and South America, Europe, Asia, Africa, Australia, and Antarctica—were joined together in this single, huge landmass.

That's Amazing!

Coelophysis dinosaurs were cannibals. When paleontologists found a big group of *Coelophysis* skeletons at Ghost Ranch in New Mexico, U.S.A., some of them had tiny baby *Coelophysis* skeletons inside their bellies. The babies were the last thing the adults had eaten. But dinosaurs are not the only animals that ate their young. Many other animals still do today.

Pathfinder

• What animals ruled the Triassic seas and skies? Go to pages 26–27.
• What did plant-eating dinosaurs like to eat? What did the meat-eaters eat? Go to pages 30–33.
• Exactly how did dinosaurs end up as fossil bones? Go to pages 48–49.

OTHER INHABITANTS

ON THE GROUND

Animals such as *Kannemeyeria* dominated the first half of the Triassic period. They were synapsids, which were pre-mammals that functioned like reptiles. They survived the dinosaurs' arrival by becoming smaller.

INSIDE STORY

The Earliest Dinosaur

In 1993, a team of American and Argentinian scientists, led by the famous paleontologists Paul Sereno and Fernando Novas, went looking for the earliest dinosaur. They were searching the harsh badlands of northwest Argentina. As they searched, one of the team was about to throw away a rock when he noticed that it had teeth. He took a second look. The rock contained a fossil skull. Soon he and his colleagues were on the ground, digging up a whole skeleton of an animal that none of them had ever seen before. They knew it was a dinosaur. But how old was it? Was it the first dinosaur?

After months of study, the paleontologists knew it really was the earliest dinosaur ever to be found. They called it *Eoraptor*, meaning "dawn stealer." It was a meat-eating dinosaur, barely as tall as a German shepherd dog, and it lived 228 million years ago.

UP IN THE AIR

The earliest creatures to swoop through the world's skies were flying reptiles called pterosaurs. They appeared soon after the first dinosaurs. *Eudimorphodon* was about the size of a large gull. It had wings of skin, like a bat's. It flew over what is now northern Italy.

LIVING SIDE BY SIDE

A plant-eating *Plateosaurus* munches on some ferns in a scene from the late Triassic world. It is about 28 feet (8.5 m) long and has little to fear from two nearby *Coelophysis*. Although they are meat-eaters, the much smaller *Coelophysis* are more interested in catching lizards.

UNDER THE SEA

The oceans were full of marine reptiles like this *Nothosaurus*. Scientists have found fossils of *Nothosaurus* mothers with their babies. The babies were probably born alive, instead of hatching from eggs.

Eoraptor

Herrerasaurus

Jurassic Giants

THE JURASSIC PERIOD started 208 million years ago. This was when the supercontinent Pangaea split in two. The seas rushed in to make two smaller supercontinents, Laurasia and Gondwana. The weather changed, too. It got slightly cooler and rained a lot more. Forests grew thick with tree ferns, cycads, and conifers. This was good food for the plant-eaters, and a good stalking ground for the meat-eaters.

Jurassic conditions were just right for dinosaurs. Many new types flourished. Giant sauropods lifted their long necks to eat from the tallest trees. Armored stegosaurs lumbered about on all fours. Ornithopods no bigger than dogs feasted on undergrowth. Meat-eaters three times as big as an elephant hunted the huge sauropods, while the little meat-eaters scurried after insects and small reptiles.

Dinosaurs were living all over the two continents by the end of the Jurassic period. Those in Laurasia were beginning to look different from those in Gondwana. Most dinosaur groups existed on both continents, but the species were different. Plated *Stegosaurus* roamed North America, while its close relative *Kentrosaurus* lived in Africa.

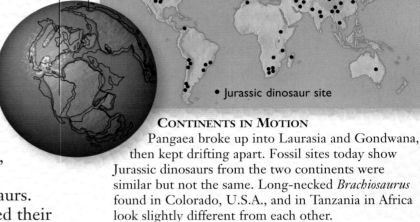

Laurasia

Gondwana

• Jurassic dinosaur site

CONTINENTS IN MOTION
Pangaea broke up into Laurasia and Gondwana, then kept drifting apart. Fossil sites today show Jurassic dinosaurs from the two continents were similar but not the same. Long-necked *Brachiosaurus* found in Colorado, U.S.A., and in Tanzania in Africa look slightly different from each other.

COULD THEY COME BACK?
Dinosaurs are alive again, and some are tracking down tasty humans to eat. That's what happened in the movie *Jurassic Park*. But could it ever happen in real life? The answer is no. The scientists in *Jurassic Park* brought the dinosaurs back to life with a technique called genetic engineering. But to use it, you need dinosaur DNA. We don't have any dino DNA and probably never will. So it seems we won't end up as dino food.

Diplodocus   **Camptosaurus**

Word Builders

• **Gondwana** means "land of the Gonds." The Gonds were a tribe of people who lived in India (a long time after the Jurassic period, of course).
• **Laurasia** comes from two words, Laurentia—an area on the St. Lawrence River in Canada—and Asia. Laurasia included both Laurentia and Asia.

That's Amazing!

There are Jurassic dinosaur bones buried in Utah, Colorado, and Wyoming, U.S.A., that you can find with a Geiger counter, a machine that clicks when it comes across anything radio-active. It clicks at the Jurassic bones because they contain uranium—but only a small amount, so they're safe.

Pathfinder

• How did meat-eaters kill much larger prey? Go to pages 30–31.
• How big could the Jurassic giants grow? Go to pages 34–35.
• Is it easier for a soft thing like a leaf or a hard thing like a bone to turn into a fossil? Go to pages 48–49.

INSIDE STORY

Plant People

Plants were behind the dinosaur dynasty. Without plants, there would have been no plant-eaters. And no plant-eaters would have meant no meat-eaters. Plants even affected where a dinosaur lived—a big dinosaur couldn't squeeze into a thick forest.

Some plants from the Mesozoic era still grow on Earth today, but most of them haven't been seen for millions of years. The people who know about these vanished plants are paleobotanists such as Bruce Tiffney from the University of California, in Santa Barbara, U.S.A. He is especially interested in the plants that dinosaurs ate and the kinds of environments that plants created for dinosaurs.

He studies fossils like this fossilized hazel leaf to learn about the vanished plants from the world of the dinosaurs.

GROUP ATTACK

A mother *Barosaurus* rears up to protect her baby from an *Allosaurus* attack. The *Barosaurus* could rise up as tall as 50 feet (15 m), and then crash back down to Earth, flattening anything that got in the way of her huge front feet. This scene takes place in a conifer forest of the Jurassic period.

A DINOSAUR DIET

There was plenty of dinosaur food in the Jurassic world. Meat-eaters that didn't eat other dinosaurs gobbled up turtles, crocodiles, lizards, and insects. Plant-eaters liked to nibble on the leaves from ferns and trees. They had many plants to choose from.

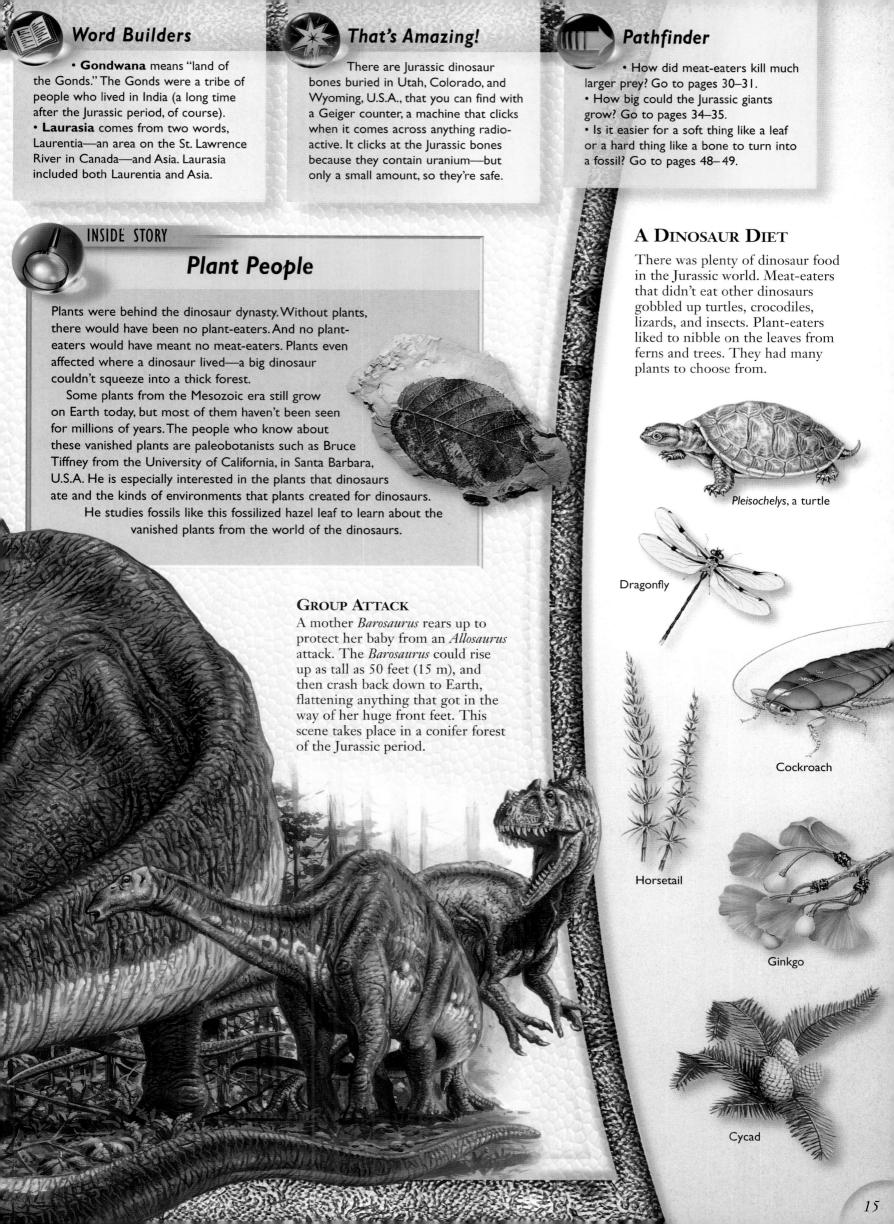

Pleisochelys, a turtle

Dragonfly

Cockroach

Horsetail

Ginkgo

Cycad

15

Cretaceous Conditions

THE CRETACEOUS PERIOD started 144 million years ago. During that period, the supercontinents of Laurasia and Gondwana kept moving apart, and Gondwana started breaking up into smaller continents. The weather became more seasonal. Summer was warm and wet. In winter, it got chilly. The first flowering plants appeared. By the late Cretaceous period, oaks, magnolias, and hickories covered parts of the Northern Hemisphere. This abundance meant there were more types of dinosaurs than ever before.

Dinosaurs went through many changes during this period. Some, such as the stegosaurs, died out, but armored ankylosaurs took their place. The huge, long-necked sauropods became less common, and new plant-eaters thrived. These included hadrosaurs, with their amazing headgear, and ceratopsians, which looked like rhinoceroses with up to seven horns. And with so much food to feast on, meat-eating theropods like *Tyrannosaurus* appeared.

But after 80 million years, the dinosaurs were all gone. A mass extinction occurred at the end of the Cretaceous period. About 60 percent of all animals died out, including the dinosaurs. It was the end of the Age of Dinosaurs.

• Cretaceous dinosaur site

THE BIG BREAKUP

Laurasia and Gondwana started splitting up into smaller chunks of land. It was harder for dinosaurs to travel between continents. Dinosaurs living in Asiamerica looked more and more different from dinosaurs in Euramerica. There were also more of them than ever before. Finds of Cretaceous dinosaurs are the most common dinosaur fossil sites today.

HANDS ON

Create an Imaginary Dinosaur

Dinosaurs came in some pretty strange shapes. Some of them looked as if they were stuck together from bits of different animals. Have you ever thought about creating your own imaginary dinosaur? What would a *Giraffeodon* look like? How big would an *Elephantosaurus* be?

❶ You will need plain paper and colored pencils to create your imaginary dinosaur. If you need some ideas, look at picture books of birds, reptiles, animals, and dinosaurs.

❷ Draw your imaginary dinosaur on the paper. Take features from real dinosaurs and combine them with characteristics from living animals. Decide what color your dinosaur should be, and then color it in.

❸ Give your dinosaur a name. If you like, write a short history of its life— what it ate, where it lived, and what other dinosaurs lived with it.

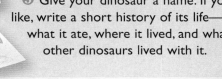

Word Builders

- The **Cretaceous** period gets its name from bright white chalk deposits that you can see in the cliffs of southern England. *Creta* is Latin for "chalk," and these chalk cliffs were formed in the Cretaceous period.
- The name **Jurassic** comes from rocks found in the Jura Mountains in southern Germany. These particular rocks date back to the Jurassic period.

That's Amazing!

Cockroaches existed long before dinosaurs, and they're still scuttling around today. That makes them living fossils. A living fossil is an animal or plant that looks the same today as it did when it first appeared in prehistoric times. Some types of crocodiles, lizards, frogs, and turtles are living fossils that first appeared in the Age of Dinosaurs. Some sharks go back even further in time.

Pathfinder

- Do you want to see more hadrosaurs similar to *Corythosaurus*? Go to pages 36–37.
- How did a ceratopsian like *Chasmosaurus* attack? Go to pages 38–39.
- Teams of paleontologists went back to the Gobi Desert in the 1980s. Did they excavate any more dinosaurs? Go to page 52.

PART OF THE SCENE

FIRST FLOWERS
Members of the magnolia family were among the first flowers on Earth. They look almost the same today as when they appeared in the late Cretaceous period. Plant-eating dinosaurs probably ate early flowering plants.

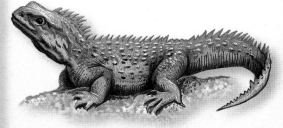

LIZARD LIFE
Lizards and the first snakes were common inhabitants of the Cretaceous period. *Polyglyphanodon* was about the size of a rabbit. It was a food source for small, meat-eating dinosaurs in North America.

ANCIENT MAMMALS
The early mammals were common by now. Mammals never got any bigger than cats during the Cretaceous period. One was *Crusafontia*, which made a tasty snack for smaller, meat-eating dinosaurs.

INSIDE STORY

Going into the Gobi

Because of its extreme temperatures, the Gobi Desert in Mongolia is one place you probably wouldn't want to live, but it's a great place to visit if you're after dinosaur fossils. Roy Chapman Andrews led four expeditions there between 1922 and 1925 for the American Museum of Natural History. Andrews and his crew drove a caravan of camels and cars, packed full of supplies. They fought off bandits, battled sandstorms, and found hundreds of dinosaur fossils. They dug up a nest of dinosaur eggs, the first ever found. They also discovered dinosaurs such as *Oviraptor*, *Protoceratops*, *Saurornithoides*, and *Velociraptor*. The fossils were taken to the Museum for study and are on display there today.

HERD APPROACHING
A herd of crested *Corythosaurus* and horned *Chasmosaurus* thunders across a plain in North America. These plant-eating dinosaurs are making their annual migration in search of new food. A herd could have had more than 10,000 dinosaurs. Meat-eaters such as *Tyrannosaurus* lurked behind, ready to attack any weak or sick animals.

Pachycephalosaurus

Lizard-hipped **Apatosaurus**   *Bird-hipped* **Wuerhosaurus**

The Two Hip Groups

A DINOSAUR COULD belong to one of two different groups, depending on what type of hips it had. The saurischian group had hips that looked like a lizard's, so they are called the lizard-hipped dinosaurs. Ornithischians had birdlike hips. They're the bird-hipped dinosaurs.

All the meat-eaters belonged to the lizard-hipped group. Some plant-eaters also belonged, such as the long-necked sauropods and their smaller ancestors, the prosauropods. All the other plant-eaters were bird-hipped. They had a pubis bone in their hips that pointed backward. That left more space for a big stomach and intestine, which they needed to digest the plants they ate.

Although saurischians and ornithischians had different hips, their hipbones connected to their leg bones in exactly the same way. A right-angled joint meant that they could walk with their legs straight under their bodies, instead of sprawling—the first animals ever able to do this. They used up less energy than the sprawling animals so they could grow bigger, walk farther, and run much faster than anything else around. The straight-walking stance of the dinosaurs was the secret of their success.

LEGS OUT
Lizards sprawl when they walk. They have to twist their whole body and lift each leg one at a time. This takes a lot of energy and can be used only for short bursts of speed.

UNDER OR OUT
Young crocodiles have an upright stance for walking. But once they have grown, crocodiles sprawl their legs out like other reptiles.

HANDS ON

A Skeleton Puzzle

When paleontologists have a pile of dinosaur bones and want to put them together, it's like solving a jigsaw puzzle. If they put the bones together correctly, they get a dinosaur skeleton. You can put together a skeleton, too, next time you have cooked chicken.

❶ Keep all the chicken bones. Ask your parents to boil them so they are clean. Then place the bones on a flat surface.

❷ Look at the bones. Think about how they go together to form a skeleton. The legs and wings are long, straight bones. Curved ribs form a cage in the chest. The hipbones are flat, a platform for the legs. The back has many small, squarish bones called vertebrae. Can you solve the puzzle and put the chicken skeleton back together again?

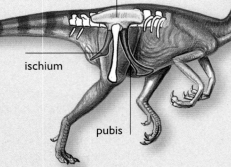
ilium

ischium

pubis

DIFFERENT HIP BITS

A dinosaur's hips had three bones. The pubis and ilium supported leg muscles, and the ischium supported tail muscles. The two types of dinosaur hips are easy to tell apart. In the lizard-hipped group, the pubis pointed forward, and in the bird-hipped, it pointed backward.

LIZARD-HIPPED
Oviraptor was a meat-eating dinosaur and a typical saurischian. Its pubis pointed forward, sticking out by itself to make a triangle with the other two pelvic bones, the ilium and ischium.

Word Builders

Certain parts of words keep popping up in dinosaur names. If you know what the parts mean, you can work out many new words.
• *Sauro* means "lizard," and *ischian* means "hip." Join them together to get **saurischian**, or "lizard-hipped."
• *Ornitho* means "bird," so **ornithischian** means "bird-hipped."

That's Amazing!

Birds evolved from dinosaurs—not from bird-hipped dinosaurs, as you're probably thinking. Scientists now believe that birds evolved from lizard-hipped dinosaurs. They aren't trying to play a trick. The system of grouping dinosaurs by their hip shape was worked out long before scientists knew that birds came from dinosaurs.

Pathfinder

• How do paleontologists put a dinosaur skeleton back together again? Go to pages 56–57.
• Why did dinosaurs like *Lambeosaurus* have head crests? Go to pages 36–37.
• Dinosaurs could move faster than all the other animals on Earth in the Mesozoic era. Could they have run faster than humans? Go to page 44.

INSIDE STORY

A Group of Their Own

Therizinosaurs were the odd ones out. This group of dinosaurs may have been related to meat-eating theropods or long-necked sauropods. They had a funny mix of features. Therizinosaurs such as *Segnosaurus* and *Erlikosaurus* lived in the late Cretaceous world. A few fossils have been found in Mongolia and Canada, but they are extremely rare. This makes it very difficult to understand what therizinosaurs were like, how they lived, and how they fit in with the other dinosaurs. Scientists have some suggestions, though. Perhaps they were meat-eaters that ripped open and ate nests of termites. Or they swam in lakes, hunting for fish. They might even have preferred plants, and not eaten meat at all.

LEGS UNDER
A dinosaur's legs were tucked under its body and swung backward and forward when the dinosaur walked or ran.

ON TWO OR FOUR FEET
Lambeosaurus was a bird-hipped plant-eater. It could stand up on its back legs or keep all four feet on the ground. Standing on the back legs was good for running away from predators or for reaching leaves high up in the trees. Its fours legs were perfect for browsing, with its head near the ground and low-growing plants.

ilium
ischium
pubis

BIRD-HIPPED
Hypsilophodon was a small, plant-eating ornithischian dinosaur. Its pubis pointed backward and lay just below the ischium and the backbone.

ilium
ischium
pubis

HUMAN-HIPPED
Your hips are completely different from dinosaur hips. But they are still made up of the same three bones—the pubis, ilium, and ischium.

What's Cool? What's Hot?

IF ANIMALS GET too hot or too cold, their bodies can't work properly. Animals feel best when their body temperature is just right. They regulate their body temperature in two different ways. Cold-blooded animals, such as lizards and snakes, get their body heat from outside. They sunbathe until they warm up, then they move into the shade. Warm-blooded animals, such as humans and other mammals, generate heat inside their bodies. They convert energy from the food they eat into heat to keep warm.

It seems that the dinosaurs did it both ways. Some dinosaurs were probably "cold-blooded." They lived in warmer climates, where it was easy for them to keep warm. Their huge bulk held heat in to get them through cold days. Some had sails, plates, and frills—good for soaking up the Sun, then cooling off again. The long-necked dinosaurs had lots of skin to let off steam fast so they didn't overheat.

Small dinosaurs were more likely "warm-blooded." Warm-blooded dinosaurs were able to live in cold or hot places, so long as they could get enough to eat. That's the way they fueled their internal fires, keeping warm and busy by eating plenty of food.

DINOSAURS IN THE DARK
Leaellynasaura lived in southern Australia during the Cretaceous period. The days would have been dark and freezing cold during the winter months. *Leaellynasaura* was too little to migrate. It must have been warm-blooded to survive in a place where the Sun didn't shine.

STAYING COOL
Spinosaurus was a big, meat-eating dinosaur. Because it lived in a hot place, it had no trouble getting warm. But keeping cool would have been a problem without the sail on its back. It may have acted like a built-in cooling plant. When things got too hot, the dinosaur may have stood in the shade and pumped warm blood into the sail, where the blood cooled down before going back into the body.

INSIDE STORY

Not So Slow After All

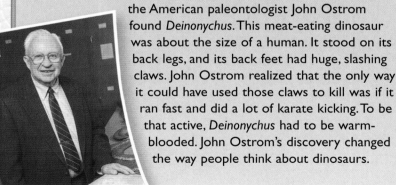

All dinosaurs were big, dumb, cold-blooded creatures that thudded along slowly. That's what everyone used to think, until the American paleontologist John Ostrom found *Deinonychus*. This meat-eating dinosaur was about the size of a human. It stood on its back legs, and its back feet had huge, slashing claws. John Ostrom realized that the only way it could have used those claws to kill was if it ran fast and did a lot of karate kicking. To be that active, *Deinonychus* had to be warm-blooded. John Ostrom's discovery changed the way people think about dinosaurs.

BONES UNDER THE MICROSCOPE
Warm-blooded and cold-blooded animals have different growth patterns. You can see the differences in their bones if you use a powerful microscope. Paleontologists look for these differences in dinosaur bones, too.

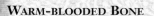

WARM-BLOODED BONE
This microscopic picture of a dinosaur bone looks similar to pictures of mammal bones. So maybe this dinosaur was warm-blooded like modern mammals.

Word Builders

- An **ectotherm** is an animal that gets its heat from outside its body. This name comes from *ektos*, meaning "outside." Ectotherm is one technical name for a cold-blooded animal.
- An **endotherm** is an animal that generates heat inside its body. *Endon* means "within." Endotherm is a term for warm-blooded animals.

That's Amazing!

Feathers and fur are so soft, they hardly ever get preserved as fossils. But scientists recently dug up some dinosaur fossils in China and found small, meat-eating dinosaurs that had feathers. Maybe they were warm-blooded, like birds, and the feathers helped keep them cozy.

Pathfinder

- Do you want to see a *Deinonychus* ready to attack? Go to pages 30–31.
- Just how fast could warm-blooded dinosaurs travel? Go to pages 44–45.
- What would have happened to the dinosaurs if the weather had gotten too hot or too cold? Go to page 61.

Thin skin allowed heat to spread quickly.

Long bones held up the huge back sail.

Blood vessels filled the sail, letting blood cool down.

HANDS ON
Warming Up on a Cold Day

You can get some idea of how long it would have taken a cold-blooded dinosaur to warm up, compared to a warm-blooded dinosaur. All you need is a watch to time yourself. Then bundle up and go outdoors on the next cold but sunny day.

1 First, pretend you're a slow, cold-blooded dinosaur that can't find a sunny spot. Stand still in the shade. How long does it take to feel warm? Or do you feel colder the longer you stand there?

2 Now stand still in a sunny spot. Do you get warm? How long does it take?

3 Run around outside, like an active, warm-blooded dinosaur would. Stop when you're nice and warm. Check how long it takes. How much energy do you use? That's another thing you can check: Are you very hungry, a little hungry, or not hungry at all?

HOT PLATES
Stegosaurus had back plates packed full of blood vessels. It may have turned its plates to face the Sun to warm its blood before it was pumped to the rest of the body. To cool the blood, *Stegosaurus* may have turned the thin edge of its plates to the Sun.

Bony core of plate

Thin skin covering

Blood vessels

QUICK-GROWING BONE
Birds and mammals have bones like this dinosaur bone. Such bones form those parts of the skeleton that grow quickly when the animal is young.

COLD-BLOODED BONE
The rings in this dinosaur bone are like those in reptile bones. Rings form because cold-blooded animals grow more slowly in winter, as their temperature drops.

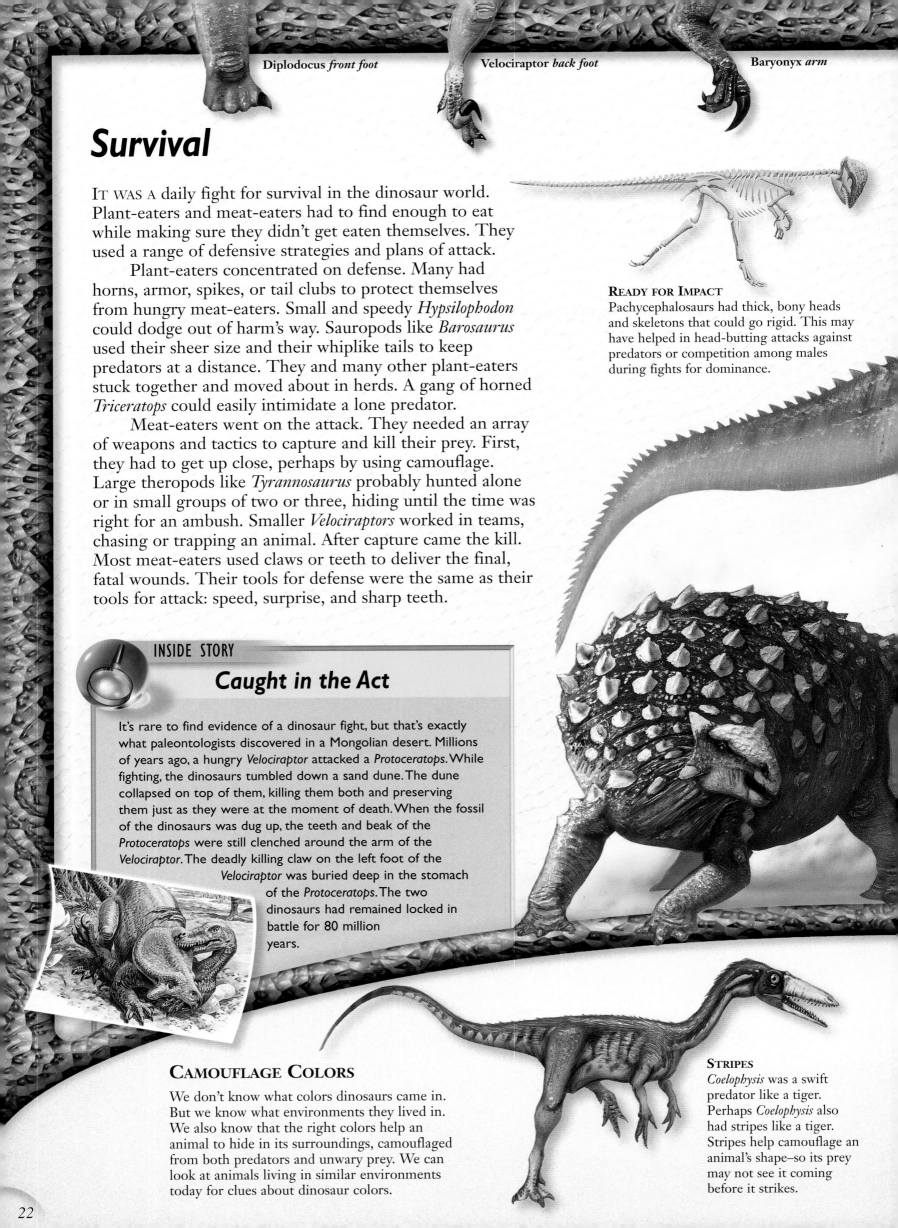

Diplodocus *front foot*

Velociraptor *back foot*

Baryonyx *arm*

Survival

IT WAS A daily fight for survival in the dinosaur world. Plant-eaters and meat-eaters had to find enough to eat while making sure they didn't get eaten themselves. They used a range of defensive strategies and plans of attack.

Plant-eaters concentrated on defense. Many had horns, armor, spikes, or tail clubs to protect themselves from hungry meat-eaters. Small and speedy *Hypsilophodon* could dodge out of harm's way. Sauropods like *Barosaurus* used their sheer size and their whiplike tails to keep predators at a distance. They and many other plant-eaters stuck together and moved about in herds. A gang of horned *Triceratops* could easily intimidate a lone predator.

Meat-eaters went on the attack. They needed an array of weapons and tactics to capture and kill their prey. First, they had to get up close, perhaps by using camouflage. Large theropods like *Tyrannosaurus* probably hunted alone or in small groups of two or three, hiding until the time was right for an ambush. Smaller *Velociraptors* worked in teams, chasing or trapping an animal. After capture came the kill. Most meat-eaters used claws or teeth to deliver the final, fatal wounds. Their tools for defense were the same as their tools for attack: speed, surprise, and sharp teeth.

READY FOR IMPACT
Pachycephalosaurs had thick, bony heads and skeletons that could go rigid. This may have helped in head-butting attacks against predators or competition among males during fights for dominance.

INSIDE STORY

Caught in the Act

It's rare to find evidence of a dinosaur fight, but that's exactly what paleontologists discovered in a Mongolian desert. Millions of years ago, a hungry *Velociraptor* attacked a *Protoceratops*. While fighting, the dinosaurs tumbled down a sand dune. The dune collapsed on top of them, killing them both and preserving them just as they were at the moment of death. When the fossil of the dinosaurs was dug up, the teeth and beak of the *Protoceratops* were still clenched around the arm of the *Velociraptor*. The deadly killing claw on the left foot of the *Velociraptor* was buried deep in the stomach of the *Protoceratops*. The two dinosaurs had remained locked in battle for 80 million years.

CAMOUFLAGE COLORS

We don't know what colors dinosaurs came in. But we know what environments they lived in. We also know that the right colors help an animal to hide in its surroundings, camouflaged from both predators and unwary prey. We can look at animals living in similar environments today for clues about dinosaur colors.

STRIPES
Coelophysis was a swift predator like a tiger. Perhaps *Coelophysis* also had stripes like a tiger. Stripes help camouflage an animal's shape–so its prey may not see it coming before it strikes.

Word Builders

• If something is ankylosed, it is fused together. **Ankylosaurus** means "fused lizard." It's the name of the dinosaur with an armor of bone that was fused together to protect its body.
• **Pachycephalosaurus** means "thick-headed lizard." It gets its name from the Greek words *pachys*, meaning "thick," and *kephalos,* or "head." This dinosaur had a thick, bony head.

That's Amazing!

How long could a dinosaur live? We don't know for sure, but it helps to look at animals alive now. If dinosaurs lived and grew at the same rate as crocodiles, the biggest dinosaurs would have lived over 300 years. If they were like elephants, then the biggest probably lived to 100. Small dinosaurs would have lived only about five years.

Pathfinder

• How did *Velociraptor* hunt in a pack? Go to page 31.
• Do you want to see a whole range of dinosaurs with horns, spikes, clubs, and armor? Go to pages 38–39.
• How do scientists know what color dinosaurs were? Go to page 58.

FOSSIL FIGHT
A *Dromaeosaurus* attacks a *Lambeosaurus*. These two skeletons have been reconstructed in this realistic pose to show what would have been a fight to the death.

WHIPPED
Diplodocus had a tail that was almost as long as a tennis court and that worked like a whip. *Diplodocus* used its tail to lash out at attackers with stinging blows.

ON THE ATTACK
The *Ankylosaurus* stands its ground and takes a swipe at an attacking *Tyrannosaurus* with its tail. One direct hit to the ankles by the massive bony club on the end could cripple the *Tyrannosaurus*. Sharp studs and slabs of bone protect the back of *Ankylosaurus*, but one bite to its soft underbelly from the powerful meat-eating jaws of *Tyrannosaurus* would finish it off.

SPIKED
Tuojiangosaurus had a serious set of tail spikes. With one swing of its tail, this plant-eater could puncture a predator's belly.

SPOTS
Dryosaurus was a small plant-eater that lived in forests, as many deer do today. Deer have light spots on a darker background, similar to the dappled light in forests. *Dryosaurus* perhaps had spots, too.

PLAINS COLORS
Edmontosaurus lived in herds and migrated across continents, the same way antelopes do today. Antelopelike colors may have helped *Edmontosaurus* blend in on the open plains.

The Next Generation

DINOSAURS LAID EGGS, like birds and most reptiles. The first dinosaur eggs were found in France in 1859. Then nests full of eggs were uncovered in Mongolia in the 1920s. But what about the parents? Paleontologists decided that dinosaurs didn't stay around to look after their young. They just built the nests, laid the eggs, then left—the same as most turtles, lizards, and snakes today.

That thinking changed in 1978, when John Horner dug up a duck-billed dinosaur nursery near Choteau, in Montana, U.S.A. The nests full of *Maiasaura* eggs were built close together, but there was enough space for the parents to move about, guard the nest, and not squash anything. The babies had worn-down teeth, and the eggshells they had hatched from were broken up. This meant they must have stayed in their nests, being fed and cared for by their parents, until they were ready to leave.

Paleontologists have found more fossil eggs, from giant sauropods and small meat-eaters like *Oviraptor* and *Troodon*. Each dinosaur had its own type of eggs and nests and way of doing things. But most of them were more like birds than reptiles when it came to caring for their young.

OVIRAPTOR EGG
This long, thin egg belongs to an *Oviraptor*. Shallow grooves run along its length. Millions of years ago, it got squashed somehow and fossilized that way.

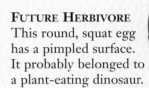

CHICKEN EGG
This chicken egg helps to show the size of the dinosaur eggs.

FUTURE HERBIVORE
This round, squat egg has a pimpled surface. It probably belonged to a plant-eating dinosaur.

FEEDING TIME
A mother *Oviraptor* returns to her nest of hungry babies. She has a freshly killed baby *Velociraptor* for their dinner. *Oviraptor* means "egg thief," because the first *Oviraptor* fossil was found near a nest of eggs. Scientists initially thought that the nest belonged to another dinosaur and that the *Oviraptor* had been stealing the eggs to eat. But now we know that the nest actually belonged to the *Oviraptor*. She was looking after her unhatched babies.

INSIDE STORY

The Egg Man

Baby dinosaurs are extremely rare. So when John Horner, field paleontologist at the Museum of the Rockies, came across a baby dinosaur fossil in a rock shop in Montana, U.S.A., he went looking for where it had come from. He and his team ended up in the badlands of Montana, uncovering a nest of crushed eggshell and 15 duck-billed babies, each about 3 feet (1 m) long. The team eventually found a whole breeding ground that contained 15 nests of *Maiasaura* eggs and babies— and the first evidence that dinosaurs looked after their young.

The discoveries didn't stop there. At Egg Mountain, Dr. Horner found nests and eggs of *Orodromeus*. These babies needed less care than *Maiasaura* babies. He and his team have found more than 500 dinosaur nests, plus a herd of 10,000 dinosaurs that died in a volcanic eruption. And he's still out there looking.

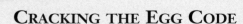

CRACKING THE EGG CODE

THE LINEUP
Dinosaurs had different ways of laying their eggs. Some small meat-eaters laid pairs of eggs side by side to form two lines. The eggs were usually half-buried in the nest.

IN AN ARC
The sauropods laid their eggs in an arc across the ground. They laid the first egg, then moved their back legs around a little (their front legs always stayed in the same spot) to lay the next egg, and so on. They don't seem to have built any nests.

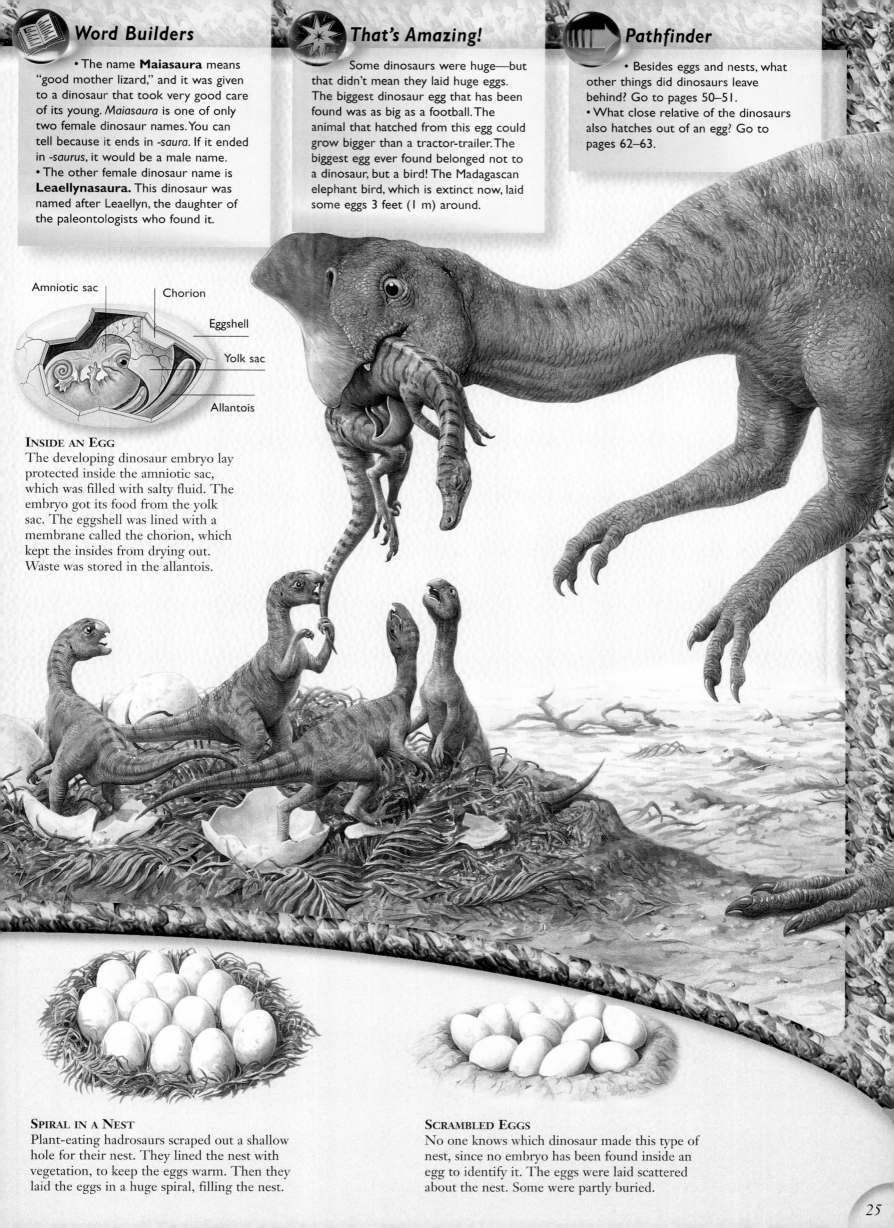

Word Builders

- The name **Maiasaura** means "good mother lizard," and it was given to a dinosaur that took very good care of its young. *Maiasaura* is one of only two female dinosaur names. You can tell because it ends in *-saura*. If it ended in *-saurus*, it would be a male name.
- The other female dinosaur name is **Leaellynasaura**. This dinosaur was named after Leaellyn, the daughter of the paleontologists who found it.

That's Amazing!

Some dinosaurs were huge—but that didn't mean they laid huge eggs. The biggest dinosaur egg that has been found was as big as a football. The animal that hatched from this egg could grow bigger than a tractor-trailer. The biggest egg ever found belonged not to a dinosaur, but a bird! The Madagascan elephant bird, which is extinct now, laid some eggs 3 feet (1 m) around.

Pathfinder

- Besides eggs and nests, what other things did dinosaurs leave behind? Go to pages 50–51.
- What close relative of the dinosaurs also hatches out of an egg? Go to pages 62–63.

Amniotic sac
Chorion
Eggshell
Yolk sac
Allantois

INSIDE AN EGG

The developing dinosaur embryo lay protected inside the amniotic sac, which was filled with salty fluid. The embryo got its food from the yolk sac. The eggshell was lined with a membrane called the chorion, which kept the insides from drying out. Waste was stored in the allantois.

SPIRAL IN A NEST

Plant-eating hadrosaurs scraped out a shallow hole for their nest. They lined the nest with vegetation, to keep the eggs warm. Then they laid the eggs in a huge spiral, filling the nest.

SCRAMBLED EGGS

No one knows which dinosaur made this type of nest, since no embryo has been found inside an egg to identify it. The eggs were laid scattered about the nest. Some were partly buried.

Dimorphodon

Pterodaustro

Sharing Dinosaur Space

DINOSAURS DOMINATED THE land during the Mesozoic era, leaving the air and the oceans to other creatures. Flying reptiles soared through the skies. Marine reptiles patrolled the seas. Some of these reptiles might have looked a bit like dinosaurs, but they were only very distant cousins.

Before birds there were the pterosaurs, the flying reptiles of the Mesozoic era. They could be as small as a seagull or as big as a biplane. Their very fine bones kept their bodies light enough to fly. They glided or maybe even flapped about on wings of skin, their large eyes on the lookout for fish and small animals to eat.

Under the oceans it was just as busy. Different types of marine reptiles competed to feed on fish, small sea creatures, and each other. The dolphinlike ichthyosaurs were fast predators, torpedoing through the water. The plesiosaurs swam more slowly, using four flippers to push their barrel-like bodies along. Their small heads flicked from side to side on their long necks as they searched for fish. The pliosaurs had much larger heads and short necks. They were the killer whales of the Mesozoic seas. Turtles, sea crocodiles, and sea dragons, or mosasaurs, were there too. Their relatives are still around today.

ICHTHYOSAURUS
With its dolphinlike shape, this fishlike reptile could swim at high speeds.

LIOPLEURODON
This typical pliosaur had a long head and short neck.

BERNISSARTIA
Crocodiles like this were the cousins of the dinosaurs, and were common at this time.

INSIDE STORY

65-Million-Year-Old People?

A man rides a *Barosaurus* to work. Kids slide down a *Diplodocus*'s tail. People live side by side with dinosaurs. You've probably seen it in *The Flintstones*, or read about it in *Dinotopia*. But it never happened. The last dinosaur died 65 million years ago. The first humans didn't appear on Earth until some time during the last million years.

Our distant relatives were there during the Mesozoic era, though. The early mammals were no bigger than cats and they looked a little like rats, but they were the dinosaurs' next-door neighbors. And there are some descendants of the dinosaurs living with us humans today—the birds. But there's no confusing a turkey with a *Tyrannosaurus*.

Elasmosaurus, *a plesiosaur*

Kronosaurus, *a pliosaur*

Word Builders

• *Plesio* means "similar" or "close to," so **plesiosaur** means "similar or close to a lizard." This group got its name because scientists used to think plesiosaurs were closely related to crocodiles. Now we know they're not.
• *Ptero* means "wing." **Pterosaur,** meaning "winged lizard," is the name of the group of reptiles that could fly.

That's Amazing!

Quetzalcoatlus was a pterosaur, the biggest animal ever to fly through the air. It had a wingspan as wide as 45 feet (14 m). That's wider than the wingspan of many small planes! *Quetzalcoatlus* probably didn't flap its wings of skin to get about. Instead, it would have stretched them wide to soar on air currents, like a glider.

Pathfinder

• Why is a plesiosaur not a dinosaur? Go to pages 10–11.
• Birds didn't evolve from pterosaurs. How did they evolve? Go to pages 62–63.

EVOLVING AT THE SAME TIME
The Mesozoic world had other creatures living alongside the ruling reptiles.

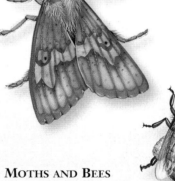

SNAKES AND LIZARDS
Pachyrhachis was one of the earliest known snakes. It lived in what is now Israel during the Cretaceous period. Snakes as well as lizards developed during the Mesozoic era.

BUILT FOR FLIGHT
This fossil of *Rhamphorhynchus* shows how lightly built the bodies of pterosaurs were. You can also see the wings of skin, which stretched from its body to the very tip of its incredibly long fourth fingers.

MOTHS AND BEES
While many groups of insects had already evolved, tiny moths and small social bees were two groups that first appeared with the dinosaurs.

DANGER ON ALL SIDES
A *Scaphognathus* dive-bombs through late Jurassic skies over what is now Europe. It is headed for the same school of *Pholidophorus* fish that a 13-foot (4-m) plesiosaur, *Cryptoclidus*, is after. The end of *Scaphognathus*'s long tail was shaped like a leaf. It probably acted like a rudder, helping *Scaphognathus* steer through the air. You can still find fossils of these creatures in rocks in southern England.

MAMMALS
Warm-blooded mammals got their start in the Age of Dinosaurs. But they stayed small for most of that time, like the *Alphadon* above.

Archelon, *a turtle*

Platecarpus, *a mosasaur*

The Dinosaur Parade

From a safe distance, you can see the many different dinosaurs that crashed or scurried through the Age of Dinosaurs. First view meat-eaters, the fierce killers who dominated the dinosaur world in their search for prey. Then look at all the different plant-eaters—some with long necks and others with strange headgear or spikes, clubs, and plates of bony armor. Stop to take in the biggest and smallest, and finish up with the fiercest and fastest among all the dinosaurs.

page **30** What did meat-eaters eat, apart from other dinosaurs?

Go to THE MEAT-EATERS.

page **32** What does this skull tell us about how its owner ate?

Go to THE PLANT-EATERS.

page **34** This is a young *Barosaurus*. How does it compare in size with its mother?

Go to THE LONG NECKS.

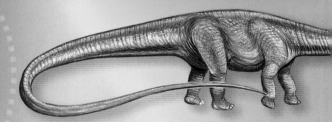

page **36** How did boneheaded dinosaurs such as *Stygimoloch* fight?

Go to THE HEAD CASES.

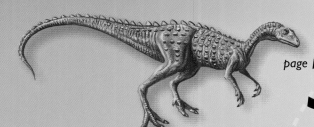

page **38** Would a dinosaur such as *Scutellosaurus* usually stand and fight, or make a run for it?

Where was the one soft spot in *Sauropelta*'s bony armor?

Go to THE
ARMORED DIVISION.

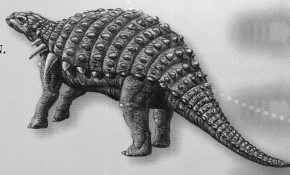

page **40** This shows a boy compared to the smallest meat-eater. How would the boy compare to the biggest meat-eater?

Go to BIG AND SMALL.

page **42** What dinosaur had a huge mouth with more than 50 stabbing teeth?

One dinosaur's killer claws had a special feature. What was it?

Go to THE TOUGH GUYS.

page **44** Who would win the race between the fastest human in the world and the fastest dinosaur?

How do we know that this dinosaur could run at 40 miles (64 km) per hour?

Go to THE FAST MOVERS.

The Meat-Eaters

MEAT-EATING DINOSAURS WERE lean, mean, killing machines. Their bodies were designed to capture, kill, and tear apart prey. They gave chase on two strong back legs, and some grabbed their prey with their hands. If there was a struggle, the large, curved claws on their hands and feet could pierce skin to get a grip on slippery flesh. For the final kill, most carnivorous dinosaurs chomped down with their mouthful of murderously sharp teeth, then used those same teeth to tear their food into bite-sized pieces.

Meat-eating theropods dominated the dinosaur world in the quest for food. Some ate other dinosaurs, usually plant-eaters. Some liked meals of small mammals, lizards, or insects. The dinosaur's diet depended a lot on its size.

Theropods such as *Tyrannosaurus* and *Allosaurus* grew as big as a dump truck. They hunted alone or in groups of two or three, perhaps stalking herds of plant-eaters until they spotted a weak animal. Other theropods, like *Compsognathus*, were no bigger than a chicken. But they didn't let their size stop them from terrorizing the neighborhood. *Deinonychus* and *Velociraptor* probably hunted in packs to make a meal of an animal more than four times their size.

MEAT-EATERS DON'T NEED FALSE TEETH

With so much munching on flesh and bone, meat-eaters were always breaking or wearing out their teeth. But sharp, new teeth always grew in. You can see some new teeth ready to replace the old ones in this theropod jaw.

KILLER KICK

Deinonychus kicks out at its next victim. The claws on its back feet could slash open an animal's stomach. Its hands, tipped with more claws, would hold the animal down while it bit out a mouthful of flesh. *Deinonychus* may have had feathers, not for flying but to keep warm. Birds evolved from dinosaurs like this one.

Troodon

Daspletosaurus

STEAK-KNIFE TEETH

Carnosaur teeth had curved edges lined with little bumps called serrations. The serrations are clear on the *Troodon* tooth above. The *Daspletosaurus* teeth also have serrations, but they are too small to see.

 HANDS ON

Meat-Eaters Near You

What are the meat-eaters in your neighborhood like? Dogs and cats have some features in common with carnivorous dinosaurs. You can see this particularly in their teeth, legs, and claws.

Many dogs can run fast after their quarry on their long legs. They have sharp, stabbing teeth in the front of their mouth. These are designed to hold their prey down while their back teeth shear and slice the meat into small pieces. The dogs you know probably don't get their food this way, but remember that dogs in the wild, such as wolves, still do.

Cats have similar teeth to dogs, and they use them in much the same way. They also have sharp, curved claws on their paws to grab their prey and then hold on to it. Many dogs' claws are different, because dogs don't use their claws or paws for attack or defense.

Word Builders

If you want to know what an animal eats, check whether it's called a carnivore, a herbivore, or an omnivore.
• *Carni* means "meat" or "flesh." *Vore* means "eater." **Carnivores** eat meat.
• *Herbi* means "plant." **Herbivores** feed on plants.
• *Omni* is Latin for "all." **Omnivores** eat both meat and plants.

That's Amazing!

Most families have one member who is just a little unusual. Theropods had *Carnotaurus*. This 25-foot (7.6-m) predator had a short face like a bulldog's, with a pair of horns over the eyes. Its arms were so stubby that they couldn't have been much use. Its skin was studded with lumps. Scientists are still trying to figure out what this creature from the late Cretaceous period did and how it fit in.

Pathfinder

• What was the biggest meat-eater? What was the smallest? Go to pages 40–41.
• Which dinosaurs were the scariest of them all? Go to pages 42–43.
• Which meat-eater could run at 50 miles (80 km) per hour? Go to page 44.

DIFFERENT DINNER TOOLS

QUICK HANDS
Compsognathus was a very small coelurosaur that used its hands to catch and eat its lizard dinners. Its cutting teeth sliced easily through flesh, but it didn't chew its food much.

BIG MOUTH
Tyrannosaurus's teeth were stabbing pegs, up to 6 inches (15 cm) long. The teeth could not cut or chew. *Tyrannosaurus* ripped off chunks of meat and swallowed them whole.

NO TEETH
Some theropods didn't have teeth. Instead, they had sharp, narrow beaks, perfect for catching the food they liked. *Gallimimus* probably snapped up insects, small animals, or eggs that it could swallow in one gulp.

FISHING HOOK
Scientists have found fish scales in the stomach of *Baryonyx*. It probably speared slippery fish with the huge hook on its hand. Then it held the fish in its long jaw before swallowing.

INSIDE STORY

Ganging Up

A pack of *Velociraptors* cruises through the forest. Each is about as big as a goat, and when they spot a much larger *Pinacosaurus*, they all break into a run. The *Pinacosaurus* takes off, but the *Velociraptors* soon overtake it. A few of the smaller *Velociraptors* crowd the *Pinacosaurus* as it runs, tormenting and nipping at it. When the larger animal finally stops, exhausted, the pack of *Velociraptors* encircles it. The strongest *Velociraptors* take turns distracting the *Pinacosaurus* while the others attack from behind, jumping and kicking, slashing with their claws, leaping away as it twists to retaliate. They keep attacking until the *Pinacosaurus* gives up. Then the *Velociraptors* close in. When one rips open the belly of the *Pinacosaurus*, it sinks down dead. This is one of the ways we think that *Velociraptors* hunted prey.

Velociraptor

Ceratosaurus *skull*

31

Conifer pine fossil *Ginkgo fossil* *Cycad fossil*

The Plant-Eaters

THERE WERE HUNDREDS, probably even thousands, of different plant-eating dinosaurs. In fact, most dinosaurs ate plants rather than meat. It's not easy to survive just on plants because they aren't as nutritious as meat. But in the warm, wet Mesozoic era, plants grew so thickly that dinosaurs had plenty to choose from.

All plant-eaters didn't eat the same things. Their diet depended on what plants they could reach and what their mouths, teeth, and stomachs could handle. Small plant-eaters, such as *Heterodontosaurus* and *Hypsilophodon*, nibbled at low-growing cycads and tree ferns, eating the most nutritious bits—the young leaves and seeds. Hadrosaurs and ceratopsians, such as *Corythosaurus* and *Triceratops*, had rows of teeth and strong chewing muscles. They ground up the tough leaves from cycads and tree ferns, and then let the digestive system do the rest. The huge sauropods, such as *Diplodocus*, stretched their long necks up to the tops of tall conifer trees. They couldn't chew their food, so they swallowed it whole, and then brewed it into a nutritious mixture in their stomachs. All these dinosaurs had the right tools to make the most of the Mesozoic world's plants.

Mouth open   Mouth closed

EATING ACTION
When an ornithopod dinosaur such as *Iguanodon* closed its mouth to chew, the action forced its upper jaw to swing outward. The teeth in the upper jaw and the teeth in the lower jaw then ground against one another. Any food caught in the middle was shredded like a carrot in a grater.

NOSE TO THE GROUND
Two *Stegosaurus* feed on some low-growing ferns. These dinosaurs' front legs were much shorter than their back legs, making it easier to keep their heads down by the food. They had weak teeth, so maybe their narrow snouts picked out only soft things to eat. They didn't chew their food. Instead, they swallowed bundles of plants whole, and broke them down in their large gut. That's why their bodies needed to be so big.

INSIDE STORY
An Earthshaking Fossil Find

Imagine finding the remains of one of the biggest animals ever to walk on Earth. David Gillette, the state paleontologist for Utah, did just that when he discovered *Seismosaurus*. This sauropod was probably 140 feet (42.7 m) long, and it lived 150 million years ago. It was so big that Gillette and his team needed eight years to excavate it. There may still be some bones buried at the site in New Mexico, U.S.A. During the excavation, the team discovered 231 gastroliths, or stomach stones, in the rib cage of the *Seismosaurus*. It had swallowed the stones to help digest food in its stomach. Most of the stones were about the size of a peach, but one was as big as a grapefruit. David Gillette thinks that maybe this larger gastrolith had gotten stuck in the huge creature's throat and caused it to choke to death.

TEETH, MOUTHS, BEAKS

You can tell a lot about a plant-eater and what it ate by the type of teeth it had and the shape of its mouth or beak. All plant-eaters didn't eat the same things or eat in the same way. Some nipped and cut their food. Others grated and ground their food. Still others gulped their food down whole.

SNIP AND SWALLOW
Plateosaurus had small, weak teeth that worked like scissors, snipping off mouthfuls of soft leaves. *Plateosaurus* could not chew. It swallowed food whole.

PLUCK AND GRIND
Lambeosaurus plucked off leaves and fruit with its horny beak, ground them up, and then swallowed. Grinding wore its teeth down, but it had hundreds of replacements.

Word Builders

- *Don* is Latin for "tooth." It's a good word for cracking the code of dinosaur names.
- **Heterodontosaurus** means "lizard with different types of teeth," since the dinosaur had three types of teeth.
- **Iguanodon** means "iguana tooth." The man who discovered *Iguanodon* thought its teeth were like an iguana's.

That's Amazing!

Plant-eating dinosaurs ate cycads, horsetails, ginkgo leaves, conifer needles, ferns, and even flowers. But they couldn't have eaten grass—because there was none to eat! The first grasses didn't grow on Earth until the Eocene epoch, about 25 million years after the last dinosaur had died.

Pathfinder

- What did dinosaur plant food look like? Go to page 15.
- Do you want to see other plant-eaters in armor, like *Stegosaurus*? Go to pages 38–39.
- How long was the longest plant-eating dinosaur ever? How small was the smallest? Go to pages 40–41.

Hadrosaurs had batteries of hundreds of tiny teeth.

STONES IN THEIR STOMACHS

The long-necked sauropods couldn't break up their food with their teeth. So they swallowed stones, called gastroliths, which did the job in their stomachs. The gastroliths moved around, stirring the plants in a dinosaur's stomach, helping the mixture to brew.

NIP AND SLICE

Protoceratops had a parrotlike beak at the front of its mouth for nipping off leaves. Slicing teeth at the back of its mouth then sliced them into a paste.

CUT, STAB, AND CHOP

Heterodontosaurus had three kinds of teeth. It had small cutting teeth at the front of its mouth. Then it had two sets of stabbing, fanglike teeth, and chopping teeth in the back.

STRIP AND SWALLOW

Brachiosaurus had teeth that looked like chisels. It stripped the leaves from tall trees with these teeth but could not chew its food up before swallowing.

The Long Necks

THE LONG-NECKED SAUROPODS were the biggest, heaviest, and longest animals ever to walk Earth. The most massive of them, *Seismosaurus*, grew to 140 feet (42.7 m) long and weighed as much as 10 elephants. No wonder its name means "earthquake lizard."

All the sauropods had incredibly long necks with tiny heads on top. For defense they had long tails, which some could use like whips. In between, their thick, barrel-shaped bodies were held up by four powerful legs. Sauropods such as *Diplodocus* and *Barosaurus* had back legs that were longer than their front legs. They probably reared up onto their hind legs to reach the tasty leaves in the tallest trees, or maybe to scare off predators. *Brachiosaurus*'s front legs were longer than its back legs, helping to lift its long, straight neck even higher into the trees.

The long-necked dinosaurs were at their biggest and most diverse during the Jurassic period. The world was thick with conifer forests and lush ferns for them to eat. Many roamed in small herds to protect their babies and to look for fresh food. These dinosaurs had appetites as big as their bodies, and spent most of the day munching through the tons of food they needed to keep their stomachs full.

THE LONGEST NECK IN THE WORLD
This *Mamenchisaurus* skeleton was found in China and is on display in the capital, Beijing. Its neck was comparatively light because some parts of the bones were as thin as eggshells. This huge fossil needs a metal frame to hold everything in place.

LONG, LONGER, LONGEST
Mamenchisaurus wins the prize, with a 35-foot (10.6-m) long neck that was about half the length of its entire body. With a neck like that, you could easily peek through a fourth-story window. Compared with the sauropods, a giraffe's 7-foot (2-m) neck, with its seven vertebrae, looks a little puny. Sauropods had 12 to 19 neck vertebrae, plus extra pieces of bone for support.

Mamenchisaurus had the longest neck—35 feet (10.6 m)—of any animal we know about.

INSIDE STORY

Dinosaur National Monument

About 150 million years ago, the area was a sandbar. Bodies of dinosaurs washed downriver and stopped there. Now it's Dinosaur National Monument, a big dinosaur graveyard on the border between Utah and Colorado, U.S.A.

There you can see hundreds of bones that belonged to dozens of different dinosaurs, including long-necked sauropods such as *Camarasaurus, Barosaurus, Apatosaurus*, and *Diplodocus*. You can tour the workshops, watch paleontologists prepare fossils, and check out the skeletons and models on display. You can also explore the cliff face that is studded with hundreds of huge bones, and visit a dinosaur graveyard.

Strong, broad hips held the weight of the body.

Thick shoulder blades fixed the front legs to the body.

The barrel-shaped rib cage protected the internal organs.

A long, whiplike tail balanced the long neck, like a seesaw.

The legs were as straight and strong as columns.

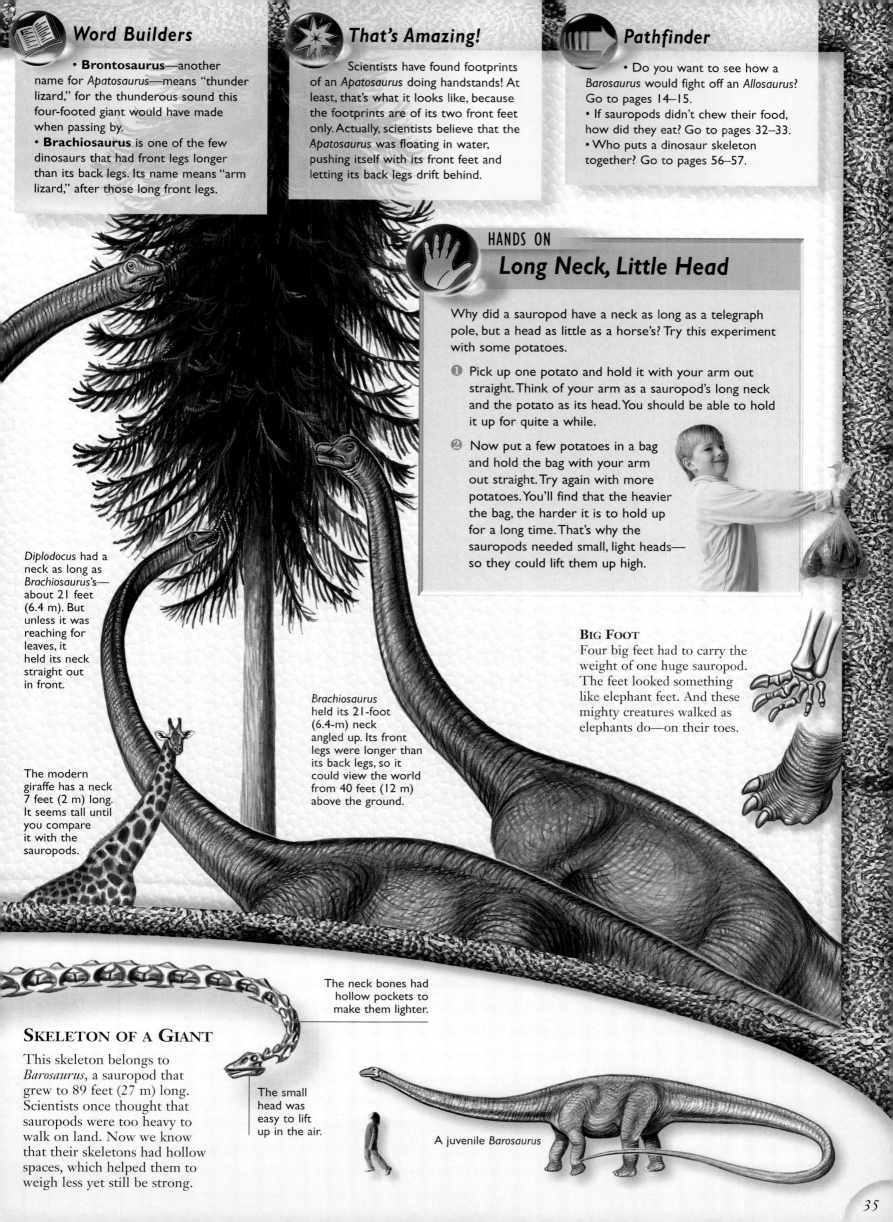

Word Builders

• **Brontosaurus**—another name for *Apatosaurus*—means "thunder lizard," for the thunderous sound this four-footed giant would have made when passing by.
• **Brachiosaurus** is one of the few dinosaurs that had front legs longer than its back legs. Its name means "arm lizard," after those long front legs.

That's Amazing!

Scientists have found footprints of an *Apatosaurus* doing handstands! At least, that's what it looks like, because the footprints are of its two front feet only. Actually, scientists believe that the *Apatosaurus* was floating in water, pushing itself with its front feet and letting its back legs drift behind.

Pathfinder

• Do you want to see how a *Barosaurus* would fight off an *Allosaurus*? Go to pages 14–15.
• If sauropods didn't chew their food, how did they eat? Go to pages 32–33.
• Who puts a dinosaur skeleton together? Go to pages 56–57.

HANDS ON
Long Neck, Little Head

Why did a sauropod have a neck as long as a telegraph pole, but a head as little as a horse's? Try this experiment with some potatoes.

1 Pick up one potato and hold it with your arm out straight. Think of your arm as a sauropod's long neck and the potato as its head. You should be able to hold it up for quite a while.

2 Now put a few potatoes in a bag and hold the bag with your arm out straight. Try again with more potatoes. You'll find that the heavier the bag, the harder it is to hold up for a long time. That's why the sauropods needed small, light heads— so they could lift them up high.

Diplodocus had a neck as long as *Brachiosaurus's*— about 21 feet (6.4 m). But unless it was reaching for leaves, it held its neck straight out in front.

The modern giraffe has a neck 7 feet (2 m) long. It seems tall until you compare it with the sauropods.

Brachiosaurus held its 21-foot (6.4-m) neck angled up. Its front legs were longer than its back legs, so it could view the world from 40 feet (12 m) above the ground.

BIG FOOT
Four big feet had to carry the weight of one huge sauropod. The feet looked something like elephant feet. And these mighty creatures walked as elephants do—on their toes.

The neck bones had hollow pockets to make them lighter.

SKELETON OF A GIANT

This skeleton belongs to *Barosaurus*, a sauropod that grew to 89 feet (27 m) long. Scientists once thought that sauropods were too heavy to walk on land. Now we know that their skeletons had hollow spaces, which helped them to weigh less yet still be strong.

The small head was easy to lift up in the air.

A juvenile *Barosaurus*

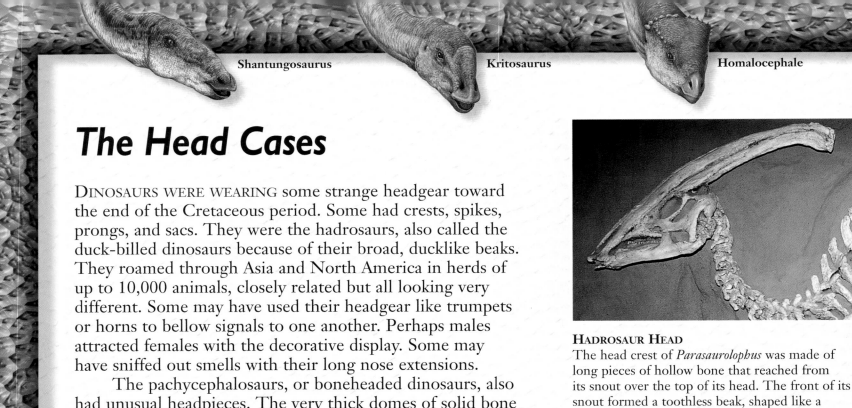

Shantungosaurus

Kritosaurus

Homalocephale

The Head Cases

DINOSAURS WERE WEARING some strange headgear toward the end of the Cretaceous period. Some had crests, spikes, prongs, and sacs. They were the hadrosaurs, also called the duck-billed dinosaurs because of their broad, ducklike beaks. They roamed through Asia and North America in herds of up to 10,000 animals, closely related but all looking very different. Some may have used their headgear like trumpets or horns to bellow signals to one another. Perhaps males attracted females with the decorative display. Some may have sniffed out smells with their long nose extensions.

The pachycephalosaurs, or boneheaded dinosaurs, also had unusual headpieces. The very thick domes of solid bone on their skulls were like crash helmets. One idea is that in a fight, a bonehead would charge at its rival and crash head-on. Its thick, bony helmet would protect its tiny brain from damage while it pounded the opponent.

The duckbills walked or ran on two legs but browsed for food on four. The boneheads traveled on two legs. Both duck-billed and boneheaded dinosaurs ate many types of plants, which helped some of the species survive right up to the end of the Age of Dinosaurs.

HADROSAUR HEAD
The head crest of *Parasaurolophus* was made of long pieces of hollow bone that reached from its snout over the top of its head. The front of its snout formed a toothless beak, shaped like a duck's bill, for pecking at leaves and fruit.

DOME OF BONE
This *Pachycephalosaurus* skull shows the thick dome of bone that sat like a helmet on the top of this dinosaur's head. Its brain was set deep inside the mass of bone, safe from damage during any clashes with other males. This skull also has some bony spikes down near the nose.

GETTING AHEAD IN THE LATE CRETACEOUS
Different head wear marks out two very different plant-eating dinosaurs. The male *Parasaurolophus* (near right) was a duck-billed dinosaur. Its long, curved head crest was hollow and could honk out a sound like a trombone, perhaps helping it to find a mate or alerting others in the herd to danger. The solid, bony dome of the *Pachycephalosaurus* (far right) may have been for fighting, a tough weapon for head-butting rivals.

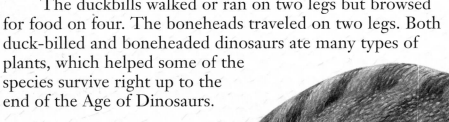

Maiasaura

Word Builders

• Dinosaurs get their names for all different reasons. Sometimes, it's because of a particular feature. **Saurolophus** means "lizard crest," for the bony crest on this dinosaur's skull.
• Sometimes, a dinosaur is named in honor of a person or a place. **Edmontosaurus** was named after the Edmonton Formation, a series of rocks near the city of Edmonton, in Canada.

That's Amazing!

How do you tell a male dinosaur from a female? Usually, it's impossible to spot the difference by just looking at their fossilized bones. Scientists need to study their internal organs. Skeletons may provide some clues, however. With *Parasaurolophus*, the female may have been smaller and had a smaller head crest than the male. A male *Tyrannosaurus* had longer bones at the base of its tail than a female.

Pathfinder

• Do you want to see a herd of hadrosaurs on the move? Who traveled with them? Go to pages 16–17.
• What colors were dinosaurs? Go to pages 22–23 and 58.
• How well could dinosaurs hear, see, and smell? Go to pages 44–45.

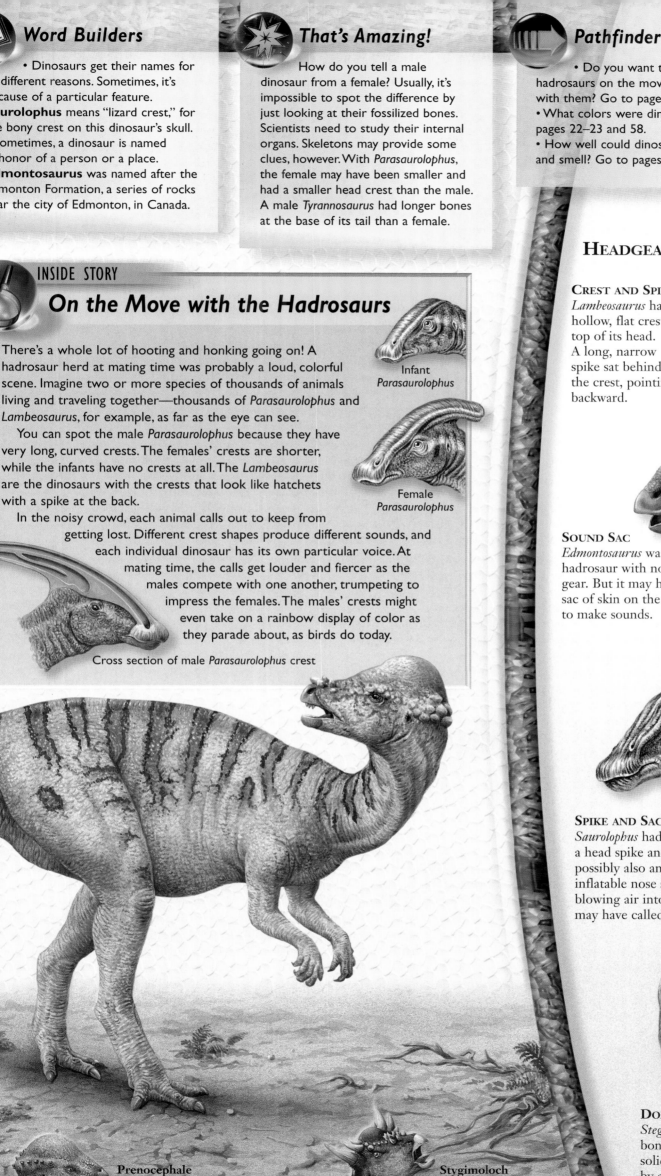

INSIDE STORY

On the Move with the Hadrosaurs

There's a whole lot of hooting and honking going on! A hadrosaur herd at mating time was probably a loud, colorful scene. Imagine two or more species of thousands of animals living and traveling together—thousands of *Parasaurolophus* and *Lambeosaurus*, for example, as far as the eye can see.

You can spot the male *Parasaurolophus* because they have very long, curved crests. The females' crests are shorter, while the infants have no crests at all. The *Lambeosaurus* are the dinosaurs with the crests that look like hatchets with a spike at the back.

In the noisy crowd, each animal calls out to keep from getting lost. Different crest shapes produce different sounds, and each individual dinosaur has its own particular voice. At mating time, the calls get louder and fiercer as the males compete with one another, trumpeting to impress the females. The males' crests might even take on a rainbow display of color as they parade about, as birds do today.

Infant
Parasaurolophus

Female
Parasaurolophus

Cross section of male *Parasaurolophus* crest

Prenocephale

Stygimoloch

HEADGEAR

CREST AND SPIKE
Lambeosaurus had a hollow, flat crest on top of its head. A long, narrow spike sat behind the crest, pointing backward.

SOUND SAC
Edmontosaurus was a flatheaded hadrosaur with no fancy headgear. But it may have inflated a sac of skin on the front of its face to make sounds.

SPIKE AND SAC
Saurolophus had a head spike and possibly also an inflatable nose sac. By blowing air into this sac, it may have called to others.

DOME AND STUDS
Stegoceras was a bonehead. Its dome of solid bone was circled by a frill of bony studs.

Polacanthus *skin*   Ankylosaurus *tail club*   Triceratops *horn*

The Armored Division

SOME PLANT-EATING DINOSAURS were built to stand and fight off an attacker. They were armed with spikes and horns, and protected by plates and shields. This array of weaponry helped them defend themselves, but the armor was heavy and prevented a quick getaway.

Stegosaurs had bony plates sticking out along their backs, and spikes at the end of their tails. The plates on *Stegosaurus* were like big triangles. The plates on *Kentrosaurus* were thinner, but it had spikes all along its tail. It may have had shoulder spikes, too. These slow-moving creatures were most common in the late Jurassic period.

Ankylosaurs appeared at the same time as stegosaurs and lived well into the Cretaceous period. With their coats of bony armor across their backs, they were like moving tanks. Spikes poked out along their shoulders and sides. Some, such as *Euoplocephalus*, also had heavy tail clubs.

The ceratopsians were the horned dinosaurs. Their heads were built for a frontal attack, with a variety of nose and brow horns, and collars of bone around the neck. The ceratopsians were late arrivals to the Cretaceous world, spreading in vast herds across North America and Asia. Some were around at the time of the dinosaur extinction.

FOSSIL FRILL
This fossil skeleton of *Triceratops* shows its frill of solid bone. The frill covered the soft neck of *Triceratops*, protecting it from attack. The two horns above its eyes could grow longer than 3 feet (1 m). The third horn on its nose was stumplike.

INSIDE STORY
The Big Dig

One of the biggest dinosaur digs took place in the rock beds near the village of Tendaguru in Tanzania, Africa. Dinosaur bones were first reported in the area by a German mining engineer in 1907. Soon afterward, the Natural History Museum in Berlin, Germany, organized an excavation that lasted for five years. At its peak, more than 500 people were digging for bones and carrying them through the jungle on the four-day march to the coast. More than 250 tons of rocks and fossils were dug up, carted away, and shipped to Germany. Among the bones were skeletons of the huge *Brachiosaurus*, the stegosaur *Kentrosaurus*, and the swift, plant-eating *Dryosaurus*.

CHARGE!
An angry *Triceratops* on the attack would have been an awesome sight. Think of a charging rhinoceros, double in size, and you'll begin to get the idea. Hungry meat-eaters weren't the only dinosaurs that had to beware those lethal horns. Damage found on the skulls of some *Triceratops* shows that they probably used their horns when battling for a mate.

SOME DINOSAUR HARDWARE

PLATES, SPIKES, CLUB
Euoplocephalus was 17 feet (5 m) long and covered in bony plates. Predators would have had a hard time biting through this armor—if they could get close enough. First they had to get past its shoulder spikes and tail club.

SCOOTING *SCUTELLOSAURUS*
Scutellosaurus was one of the earliest armored dinosaurs. The armor covering its body had rows of bony lumps called scutes. This dinosaur was light, so it could run from trouble on its two back legs.

Word Builders

- **Stegosaurus** means "roofed lizard." The scientists that found *Stegosaurus* thought at first that its plates lay flat along its back, like roof tiles, instead of standing upright.
- *Keratos* means "horn," and *ops* means "face" in ancient Greek. Join them together for **ceratopsian,** or "horned face." Add *tri*, which means "three," and you get **Triceratops,** the "three-horned-face" dinosaur.

That's Amazing!

- In Alberta, Canada, there is a mass grave of ceratopsians. Scientists think they tried to cross a river and drowned, just as buffaloes have sometimes done.
- In the Rockies, fossils of a herd of up to 10,000 *Maiasaura* have been found. They may have been wiped out by poisonous gas released from a volcano.

Pathfinder

- What happened to dinosaurs, such as *Triceratops*, during the mass extinction? Go to pages 60–61.
- How did *Stegosaurus* use its back plates to help it warm up or cool down? Go to page 21.
- Do you want to see a dinosaur with a tail club in action? Go to pages 22–23.

HANDS ON
Make a Dinosaur Mobile

1. Choose six big dinosaurs from this book. Trace or draw their outlines onto a sheet of cardboard.

2. Cut out each shape and color both sides. Punch a hole in the top center of each dinosaur.

3. Cut six different lengths of string. Thread a string through the hole in each dinosaur and tie it. With the other ends of the strings, tie three dinosaurs to one stick and the other three dinosaurs to a second stick.

4. Use two more strings to tie the two sticks to a third stick.

5. Hang up your mobile.

SPIKED *STEGOSAURUS*
Stegosaurus, which reached a length of 30 feet (9 m), used its tail spikes to swipe at and stab attackers. The plates of bone along its back were probably not for defense, but instead helped it to keep warm or cool.

SHIELDED *SAUROPELTA*
This was a 19-foot (5.8-m) nodosaur, a type of ankylosaur. Its bony back shield, lined with cones and studs, and its shoulder spikes gave it good protection, especially if it hunkered down to cover its soft underbelly.

39

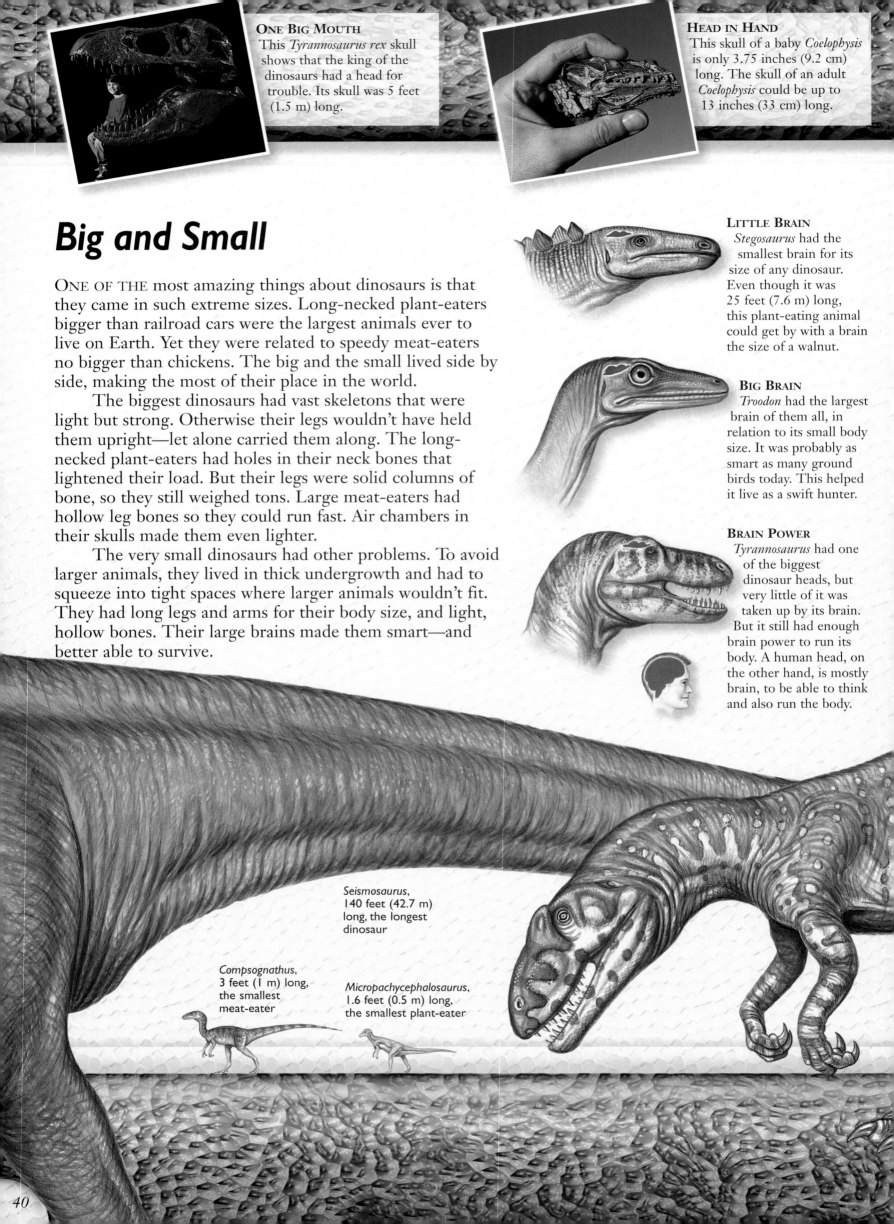

ONE BIG MOUTH
This *Tyrannosaurus rex* skull shows that the king of the dinosaurs had a head for trouble. Its skull was 5 feet (1.5 m) long.

HEAD IN HAND
This skull of a baby *Coelophysis* is only 3.75 inches (9.2 cm) long. The skull of an adult *Coelophysis* could be up to 13 inches (33 cm) long.

Big and Small

ONE OF THE most amazing things about dinosaurs is that they came in such extreme sizes. Long-necked plant-eaters bigger than railroad cars were the largest animals ever to live on Earth. Yet they were related to speedy meat-eaters no bigger than chickens. The big and the small lived side by side, making the most of their place in the world.

The biggest dinosaurs had vast skeletons that were light but strong. Otherwise their legs wouldn't have held them upright—let alone carried them along. The long-necked plant-eaters had holes in their neck bones that lightened their load. But their legs were solid columns of bone, so they still weighed tons. Large meat-eaters had hollow leg bones so they could run fast. Air chambers in their skulls made them even lighter.

The very small dinosaurs had other problems. To avoid larger animals, they lived in thick undergrowth and had to squeeze into tight spaces where larger animals wouldn't fit. They had long legs and arms for their body size, and light, hollow bones. Their large brains made them smart—and better able to survive.

LITTLE BRAIN
Stegosaurus had the smallest brain for its size of any dinosaur. Even though it was 25 feet (7.6 m) long, this plant-eating animal could get by with a brain the size of a walnut.

BIG BRAIN
Troodon had the largest brain of them all, in relation to its small body size. It was probably as smart as many ground birds today. This helped it live as a swift hunter.

BRAIN POWER
Tyrannosaurus had one of the biggest dinosaur heads, but very little of it was taken up by its brain. But it still had enough brain power to run its body. A human head, on the other hand, is mostly brain, to be able to think and also run the body.

Seismosaurus, 140 feet (42.7 m) long, the longest dinosaur

Compsognathus, 3 feet (1 m) long, the smallest meat-eater

Micropachycephalosaurus, 1.6 feet (0.5 m) long, the smallest plant-eater

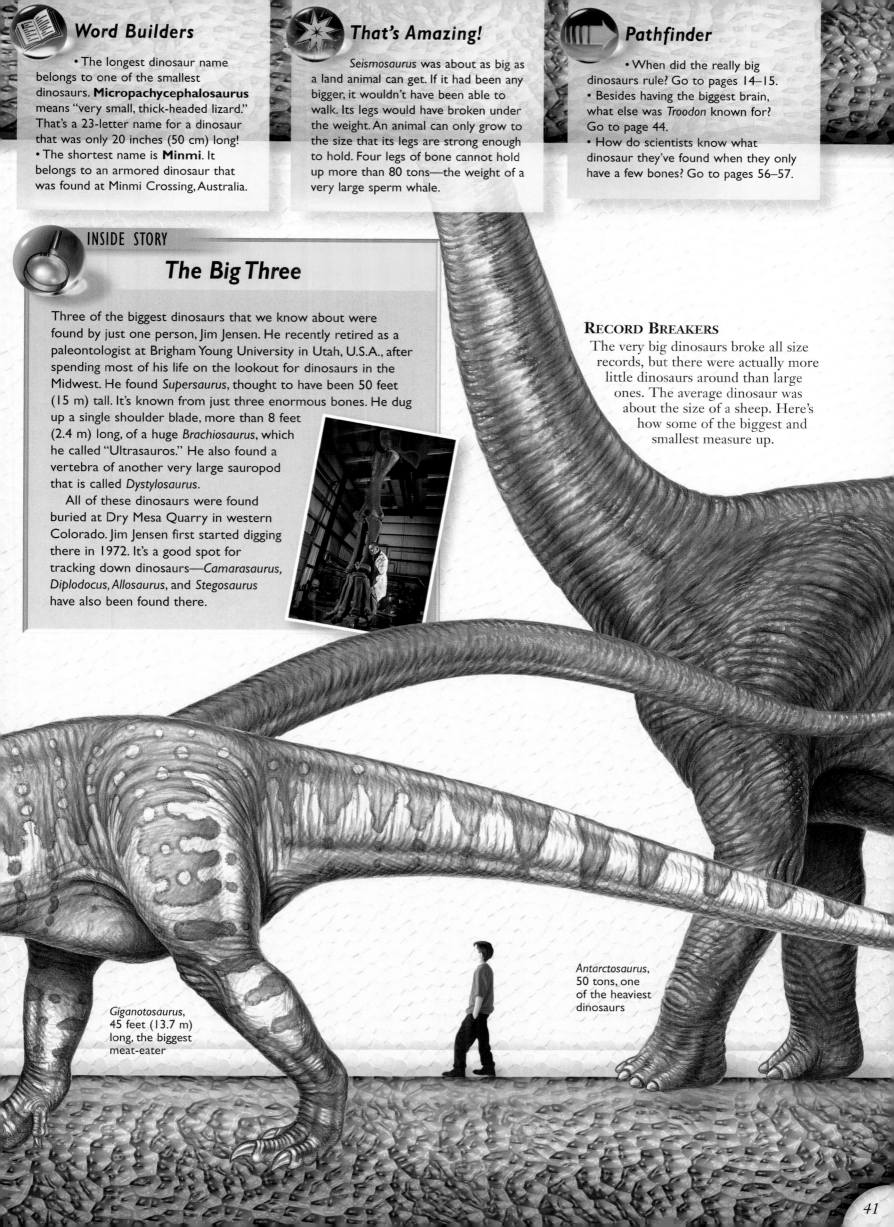

Word Builders

• The longest dinosaur name belongs to one of the smallest dinosaurs. **Micropachycephalosaurus** means "very small, thick-headed lizard." That's a 23-letter name for a dinosaur that was only 20 inches (50 cm) long!
• The shortest name is **Minmi**. It belongs to an armored dinosaur that was found at Minmi Crossing, Australia.

That's Amazing!

Seismosaurus was about as big as a land animal can get. If it had been any bigger, it wouldn't have been able to walk. Its legs would have broken under the weight. An animal can only grow to the size that its legs are strong enough to hold. Four legs of bone cannot hold up more than 80 tons—the weight of a very large sperm whale.

Pathfinder

• When did the really big dinosaurs rule? Go to pages 14–15.
• Besides having the biggest brain, what else was *Troodon* known for? Go to page 44.
• How do scientists know what dinosaur they've found when they only have a few bones? Go to pages 56–57.

INSIDE STORY

The Big Three

Three of the biggest dinosaurs that we know about were found by just one person, Jim Jensen. He recently retired as a paleontologist at Brigham Young University in Utah, U.S.A., after spending most of his life on the lookout for dinosaurs in the Midwest. He found *Supersaurus*, thought to have been 50 feet (15 m) tall. It's known from just three enormous bones. He dug up a single shoulder blade, more than 8 feet (2.4 m) long, of a huge *Brachiosaurus*, which he called "Ultrasauros." He also found a vertebra of another very large sauropod that is called *Dystylosaurus*.

All of these dinosaurs were found buried at Dry Mesa Quarry in western Colorado. Jim Jensen first started digging there in 1972. It's a good spot for tracking down dinosaurs—*Camarasaurus*, *Diplodocus*, *Allosaurus*, and *Stegosaurus* have also been found there.

RECORD BREAKERS

The very big dinosaurs broke all size records, but there were actually more little dinosaurs around than large ones. The average dinosaur was about the size of a sheep. Here's how some of the biggest and smallest measure up.

Giganotosaurus, 45 feet (13.7 m) long, the biggest meat-eater

Antarctosaurus, 50 tons, one of the heaviest dinosaurs

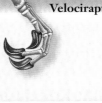

The Tough Guys

THE FIERCEST OF all the dinosaurs were the large, meat-eating theropods. They stood at the top of the food chain in the Mesozoic world, and they ate whatever came their way. They were huge in size. Some of them could grow to more than 30 feet (10 m) long—bigger than a dump truck. Their heads could be as long as a child's body, and each tooth could grow as big as a carving knife.

Big theropods first evolved during the Jurassic period. The carnivore that wore the "king of the dinosaurs" crown changed over time and from continent to continent. To start, *Allosaurus* ruled the late Jurassic world. But as the Cretaceous period dawned, *Carcharodontosaurus* took over in Africa, followed by *Spinosaurus*. North America was the domain of *Acrocanthosaurus* in the early Cretaceous period. Then *Albertosaurus* and *Tyrannosaurus* took the lead. South America saw the arrival of possibly the biggest meat-eater of all, *Giganotosaurus*, at the end of the Age of Dinosaurs.

Then there were the "princes of the dinosaurs," much smaller but equally fierce dromaeosaurs such as *Velociraptor*, *Deinonychus*, and *Dromaeosaurus*. Fast and smart, they probably hunted in packs, jumping on larger animals or terrorizing smaller ones. The sickle claws on their feet were the lethal weapons of these tough guys.

LARGE AND LIGHT
This *Allosaurus* skeleton is typical of the big theropods. Its skull was light but strong. Powerful legs held up its solid body. Some theropods had stubby arms that couldn't do much, but *Allosaurus* had arms that worked like grappling hooks.

 INSIDE STORY

A Dinosaur Called Sue

Sue is the most complete *Tyrannosaurus rex* skeleton in the world—and the most expensive. She was found in 1990 in South Dakota, U.S.A., but then a fight started over who actually owned her. Did she belong to the team of paleontologists who found her? Or to the farmer who managed the area where she was found? Or to the federal government, which owned the land? Different states and countries have different laws about who owns a fossil after it is found. In some places, fossils belong to the person who owns the land where the fossils were actually discovered. In other places, the fossils belong to the finder or to the government.

A court finally decided that Sue belonged to the farmer, and he sold her at an auction. She was bought by the Field Museum in Chicago for $8.3 million. There she will be looked after properly, where scientists can study her and the public can see her.

TERRIBLE CLAW
What *Deinonychus* lacked in its 10-foot (3-m) size, it made up for with a lethal killing claw, 5 inches (13 cm) long. The claw was attached to the second toe of each foot, where it swiveled up and down. When *Deinonychus* attacked an animal, it kicked its leg out. The claw would first stab through flesh and then swivel, slashing a long, fatal gash in its prey.

Word Builders

Tyrant is the name given to a harsh ruler, which is why **Tyrannosaurus** got the name meaning "tyrant lizard." Sometimes it is called **Tyrannosaurus rex**. Because *rex* is Latin for "king," this name means "king of the tyrant lizards." **Tyrannosaurus** is the name of the genus that this dinosaur belongs to, while **rex** is the name of its species. Every dinosaur has a genus name and a species name.

That's Amazing!

Did meat-eating predators attack one another? Scientists think that they probably didn't, having learned from experience that other meat-eaters were armed with sharp teeth and slicing claws. But they might have attacked a sick or weak meat-eater, or scavenged on one that was already dead.

Pathfinder

• What was it like during the Jurassic and the Cretaceous periods? Go to pages 14–17.
• What did meat-eaters' teeth look like? Go to page 30.
• How fast could big predators run? Go to page 45.

KILLER SKULLS

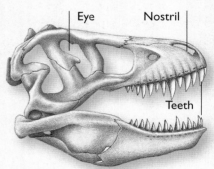

Eye   Nostril   Teeth

EXTRA WIDE

The skull of *Tyrannosaurus* had to be strong to crunch down on and kill its prey. Its heavy jaw had an extra joint in the middle, so the mouth could open wider to take extra-large bites. It had bony bits above and below its eyes to make sure they weren't poked out by struggling prey.

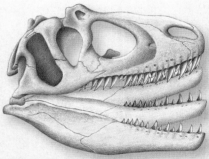

BITE ACTION

Allosaurus's skull was 3 feet (1 m) long. The powerful head was kept light by big holes at the front and back of the skull. Its jaw could open wide to bite and slide through flesh. Here, the jaw opens and closes to show its bite action.

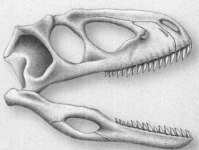

LIGHT BITE

Deinonychus was a smaller meat-eater, but it could still deliver a ferocious bite with its wide, gaping mouth. Dozens of small, curved teeth acted like a saw to cut through muscles and skin.

HEAD-ON

Tyrannosaurus weighed as much as a killer whale but was twice the size and built for head-on attack. *Tyrannosaurus* could see what was happening on all sides, even when it was looking straight ahead. *Tyrannosaurus* could see, in perfect three-dimensional vision, whatever lay directly in front of it. After powerful back legs pushed *Tyrannosaurus* forward, its huge mouth could gape wide to crunch down with more than 50 stabbing teeth.

The Fast Movers

THROUGH THE MESOZOIC landscape zipped some very sleek and speedy dinosaurs. Some were plant-eaters, in a hurry to get away from hungry predators. But certain types of meat-eaters were the really fast movers of the dinosaur world. These dino-speedsters developed during the Cretaceous period, racing around parts of North America, Africa, and Asia. They usually had small, streamlined bodies and long back legs—the perfect build for a sprinter.

The fastest dinosaurs of all were ornithomimids such as *Struthiomimus* and *Gallimimus*. They were about the size of humans and looked something like ostriches—with long, gangly arms and legs, and small, toothless heads. They probably fed on insects or small mammals and lizards. They ran at up to 40 miles (64 km) per hour to escape larger, more powerful predators.

The troodontids were fast—but not that fast. They were smaller, too, and not quite so birdlike. But they were some of the smartest dinosaurs. Their large eyes would spot small animals, and then they'd use speed and agility to dash after their dinner. They had many small teeth and a sickle claw, which probably worked like a stabbing weapon. They were the pursuit predators of the prehistoric world.

World's fastest human, 22.8 mph (36.5 km/h)

Dromiceiomimus, a very fast dinosaur, 30 mph (48 km/h)

Struthiomimus, world's fastest dinosaur, 40 mph (64 km/h)

Ostrich, world's fastest running bird, 50 mph (80 km/h)

THE WORLD RECORD HOLDERS
In a race, the ornithomimids would have left humans far behind. *Struthiomimus* could have topped 40 miles (64 km) per hour, almost twice as fast as the fastest human in the world. Only a few modern animals, such as the ostrich, could run faster than a speeding ornithomimid.

DINOSAUR SENSES

Cast of *Iguanodon* brain

TASTING AND SMELLING
The front part of *Iguanodon*'s brain—that part of the brain that did the tasting and smelling work—was well developed. This plant-eater had a good sense of smell and taste, so it might have sniffed out hidden predators or distant plants.

SEEING
It's not easy to find out from a pile of fossils what dinosaurs could see. But certain dinosaurs' skeletons give scientists some clues. For example, *Troodon* had large eye sockets for its big eyes, and a large part of its brain was devoted to seeing. So it probably had a good sense of sight, and may have seen in the dark.

Word Builders

- *Mimos* is the Greek word for mimic, which means "to look like or resemble." *Ornitho* means "bird," so the **ornithomimids** were "bird mimics."
- *Struthio* is the Latin name for "ostrich," which makes **Struthiomimus** an "ostrich mimic."
- *Gallus* is the Latin name for "chicken." **Gallimimus** is a "chicken mimic."

That's Amazing!

How fast could big predators run? Not very quickly, scientists think. The faster they ran, the more they could injure themselves. If a 6-ton *Tyrannosaurus* tripped while running more than 9–12 miles (15–20 km) per hour, it would have crushed its head and rib cage when it fell. So the big meat-eaters probably lumbered along at an earth-shuddering fast walk.

Pathfinder

- Why could dinosaurs move around better than most other animals that lived during the Mesozoic era? Go to pages 18–19.
- *Gallimimus* and *Albertosaurus* were both meat-eaters. What other meat-eaters were there? Go to pages 30–31.
- How does a footprint turn into a fossil in rock? Go to pages 50–51.

CAN'T CATCH *GALLIMIMUS*

When fleet-footed *Gallimimus* got going, there was no way a lumbering *Albertosaurus* could catch it. *Gallimimus* could tear along at speeds of up to 30 miles (48 km) per hour. It could also change direction suddenly, dodging and weaving out of *Albertosaurus*'s reach. At over 6 feet (2 m) tall and 17 feet (5 m) long, *Gallimimus* was the biggest ornithomimid. But its slender frame made it seem much smaller than it really was.

INSIDE STORY

Follow Those Feet

Fossilized footprints can reveal much about an extinct animal. As well as showing how big its feet were and how long its stride was, a set of footprints can tell you how fast the animal traveled. The faster it ran, the farther apart its footprints were.

A leading expert on dinosaur footprints, James Farlow is a paleontologist at Indiana–Purdue University, in the U.S.A. He has studied footprints of birds such as emus. From them, he's been able to estimate the speeds of several dinosaurs that left footprints in Texas. One Jurassic carnivore ran at 26.5 miles (42.8 km) per hour, while sauropods Farlow has studied ambled about at 1–2 miles (2–3 km) per hour.

HEARING

Most hadrosaurs, such as *Saurolophus*, had special headgear for making sounds. But sound would have been useful only if they also had a good sense of hearing so they could make out what other hadrosaurs in the herd were honking back at them.

TOUCHING

Touch is the toughest sense of all for scientists to understand about an extinct animal. But with its thick, scaly skin, a dinosaur's sense of touch must have been very different from ours.

The Dinosaur Puzzle

Dinosaurs are a big mystery because they've been dead for so long. Here is your chance to see how scientists have put together the puzzle of the dinosaurs by following the pieces back in time. The fossil evidence dinosaurs left behind is the place to start. Glimpse some famous fossil finds before visiting an excavation site. Then head to the laboratory to see a dinosaur being brought back to life. Your journey finishes with the big mystery of why all dinosaurs died—even though some of their relatives are still alive today.

page **48** How could an insect turn into a fossil?

Go to FOSSIL EVIDENCE.

page **50** What dinosaur made these tracks?

Go to FOLLOWING FOSSIL CLUES.

page **52** It's hot, dry, and a good place for finding dinosaur fossils. Where is it?

Go to FAMOUS FINDS.

page **54** How do you dig a dinosaur out of the ground?

Go to HUNTING FOR A DINOSAUR.

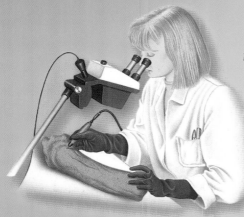

page **56**

What happens to dinosaur bones after they are taken to the laboratory?

Go to **RECONSTRUCTING A DINOSAUR**.

page **58**

This book is full of pictures of creatures that no one has ever seen. Who draws them, and how?

This dinosaur keeps changing the way it looks. Why?

Go to **BROUGHT BACK TO LIFE**.

page **60**

Dinosaurs died out 65 million years ago. Was it because of a huge volcanic eruption?

Go to **WHEN THE DINOSAURS DIED**.

page **62**

Is this a bird or a dinosaur? What do dinosaurs and birds have in common?

What animal does this dinosaur remind you of?

Go to **DINOSAUR RELATIVES TODAY**.

Snakefly fossil

Fish skeleton fossil

Fossil Evidence

EVERYTHING WE KNOW about dinosaurs has come from the study of their fossils. But not even one in every thousand dinosaurs that walked Earth left bits of fossil evidence behind. That's because conditions have to be just right for an animal to turn into a fossil. First, the animal has to die in the right place, by a river or a lake. Then a flood might hit, and its body might get washed into the water, to be buried by mud and sand, and eventually preserved as a fossil.

Usually the hard parts—the bones and teeth—are preserved. The soft bits, like the flesh and guts, tend to rot or get eaten by scavengers. So most fossils are bones and teeth. Sometimes paleontologists turn up some footprints, eggs, and dung. Occasionally, a dinosaur was mummified by fine grit, so the fossil has impressions of dinosaur skin.

Fossils are found in sandstone, mudstone, shale, and limestone—rocks that started out as sediment in rivers and lakes. There are some places on Earth where these types of rocks are packed full of dinosaur fossils. Dinosaur bones from throughout the Mesozoic era have been found since the 1870s in the midwestern United States and Canada. Parts of China, Mongolia, Africa, and South America are also good hunting grounds for dinosaur evidence.

INSIDE STORY
A Dinosaur Bone Park

Dinosaur Provincial Park is a slice of the dinosaur world preserved in fossil form. It is located in the badlands of Alberta, in Canada, on the Red Deer River. This river has cut deep ravines into the Canadian prairie and the surrounding rock to expose the final resting place of countless Cretaceous dinosaurs.

If you visit the park, you can walk along trails that pass right through these erosion gullies and see dinosaur fossils still stuck in the rock. The landscape has been weathered into mysterious formations, called hoodoos, which look like soldiers standing guard. You can also visit the Royal Tyrrell Museum Field Station at the site. It has displays that recreate the late Cretaceous world and show some of the spectacular skeleton fossils that have been excavated in the park.

HOW A DINOSAUR FOSSIL IS FORMED

BODY OUT OF REACH
After a dinosaur died, its carcass was washed into a river. Its flesh rotted or was eaten, and only the skeleton remained.

SKELETON COVER-UP
The skeleton was buried under layers of sand or mud. This protected it from further decay or from being washed away.

Word Builders

- The word **fossil** comes from the Latin *fossilis*, meaning "dug up."
- A word for stone is *lithos*. So **gastroliths** are "stomach stones," while the "study of stones" is known as **lithology**. *Ology* means "study of."
- *Geo* means "Earth." So **geology** is the word for the "study of Earth."

That's Amazing!

Scientists estimate that for every 100 different living things that have ever existed on Earth, 95 of them are now extinct. Of all the animals and plants that are extinct, only a small proportion have been preserved as fossils. So we will never know anything at all about most of the plants and animals that have lived on Earth.

Pathfinder

- Is a pliosaur a type of dinosaur? Go to pages 26–27.
- What dinosaurs used to live in the area that is now the Gobi Desert? Go to pages 17 and 52.
- How do paleontologists remove dinosaur fossils from the ground? Go to pages 54–55.

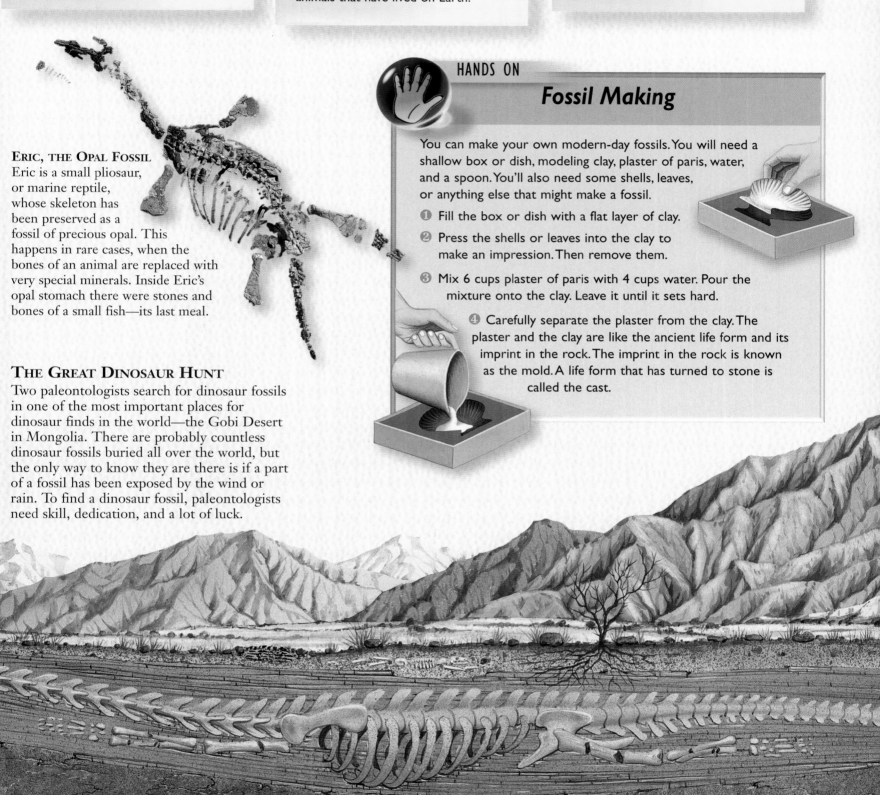

ERIC, THE OPAL FOSSIL

Eric is a small pliosaur, or marine reptile, whose skeleton has been preserved as a fossil of precious opal. This happens in rare cases, when the bones of an animal are replaced with very special minerals. Inside Eric's opal stomach there were stones and bones of a small fish—its last meal.

THE GREAT DINOSAUR HUNT

Two paleontologists search for dinosaur fossils in one of the most important places for dinosaur finds in the world—the Gobi Desert in Mongolia. There are probably countless dinosaur fossils buried all over the world, but the only way to know they are there is if a part of a fossil has been exposed by the wind or rain. To find a dinosaur fossil, paleontologists need skill, dedication, and a lot of luck.

HANDS ON

Fossil Making

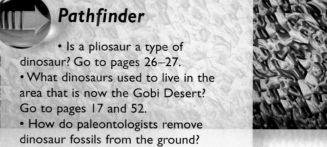

You can make your own modern-day fossils. You will need a shallow box or dish, modeling clay, plaster of paris, water, and a spoon. You'll also need some shells, leaves, or anything else that might make a fossil.

1. Fill the box or dish with a flat layer of clay.
2. Press the shells or leaves into the clay to make an impression. Then remove them.
3. Mix 6 cups plaster of paris with 4 cups water. Pour the mixture onto the clay. Leave it until it sets hard.
4. Carefully separate the plaster from the clay. The plaster and the clay are like the ancient life form and its imprint in the rock. The imprint in the rock is known as the mold. A life form that has turned to stone is called the cast.

BONES INTO FOSSILS

The river sediments turned to rock over time. The bones were replaced by minerals to form fossils, hard like rock.

FOSSILS BACK ON TOP

Movements inside Earth lifted up the rock and brought the fossil close to Earth's surface. Erosion exposed the fossil.

Following Fossil Clues

FOSSIL TEETH AND bones do more than give us clues about what dinosaurs looked like. These fossils also tell us about how dinosaurs lived. Dinosaur bones that fractured and healed again, and bones with arthritis and tumors, show some injuries and illnesses that dinosaurs suffered. Bones with gnaw marks or bite marks can reveal what creature killed a dinosaur or scavenged on its carcass. We can find out even more about the killer from the teeth that are often scattered around fossil skeletons, because predators' teeth fell out as they chomped and chewed on their prey.

But dinosaurs left behind other fossil clues, too. Fossilized dung reveals what dinosaurs ate as well as how they ate it—whether they chewed prey or plants into pieces or swallowed them whole. Dinosaur footprints in rocks show how fast or slowly they moved. From their tracks, we also know that some traveled in vast herds, while others lived alone. Their skin impressions show that they were protected by a tough outer layer. And from their nests and eggs, we know how dinosaurs took care of their babies, living together to bring up the next generation. With these clues, we can create a picture of dinosaurs and their world.

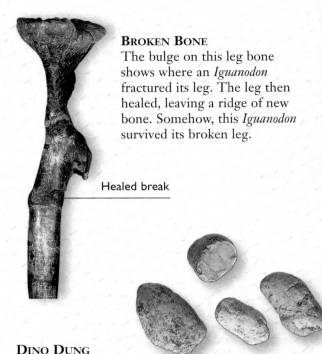

BROKEN BONE
The bulge on this leg bone shows where an *Iguanodon* fractured its leg. The leg then healed, leaving a ridge of new bone. Somehow, this *Iguanodon* survived its broken leg.

Healed break

DINO DUNG
Sometimes, dinosaur droppings turned into fossils as hard as rock, called coprolites. Coprolites come in all shapes and sizes and can contain bits and pieces of seeds, pinecones, plant stems, and even crushed bones. Scientists study dino dung to learn what dinosaurs ate and how they ate it.

INSIDE STORY

Stampede

At Lark Quarry in Australia, there are hundreds of dinosaur footprints, fossilized in a minute of action. Paleontologists have studied the footprints and have a good idea of what happened there millions of years ago. Dozens of small meat-eaters and plant-eaters were gathered around the edge of a water hole, taking a drink or feeding. Suddenly, a large meat-eater appeared out of nowhere, so the smaller dinosaurs made a quick getaway, leaving prints in the mud as they ran, all heading in the same direction. The predator's footprints go right through the middle of these small footprints, and indicate that it wasn't moving very fast. Maybe it just wanted to drink at the water hole and wasn't even interested in hunting the smaller dinosaurs. But its presence was enough to scare them away, just as in the scene on this page.

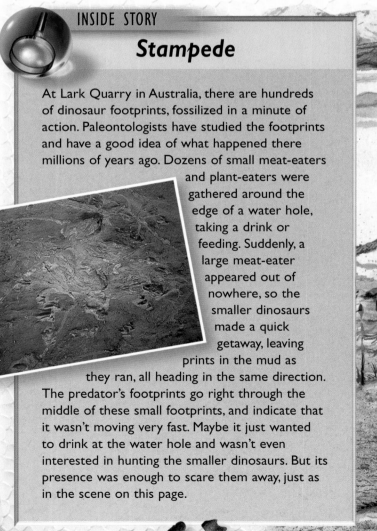

STUCK IN THE MUD
A few minutes ago, these small plant-eaters and meat-eaters were minding their own business, having a drink in the river. But the minute they sense a meat-eating predator, they make a run for it, leaving their footprints behind in the soft mud. The riverbank is soon covered in a mess of muddy prints. It is the perfect place for prints to be preserved as fossils.

Ankylosaur prints

Prosauropod prints

Word Builders

• Lite comes from *lithos*, which means "stone." *Copro* means "dung," so **coprolite** means "dung stone."
• *Ichnos* means "footprint," and an **ichnite** is the technical name for a "footprint fossil."
• Fossil eggs are called **oolites**, because *oo* means "egg."

That's Amazing!

The largest known dinosaur doesn't have a name. We know about it only because it left some footprints near Broome, in Australia, where there are many dinosaur footprints. Some of them, over 3 feet (1 m) round, may have belonged to a sauropod that was even bigger than *Seismosaurus* or "Ultrasauros."

Pathfinder

• Why did some dinosaurs live in groups and herds, while others lived by themselves? Go to pages 22–23.
• How did dinosaurs build nests? Go to pages 24–25.
• What does dinosaur skin look like? Go to page 45.

HANDS ON
Make Tyrannosaurus Feet Move

❶ Trace the *Tyrannosaurus* footprint opposite onto a piece of paper. Ask an adult to help you enlarge this so the footprint is 3 feet (1 m) long. Now trace the enlarged footprint twice, onto two pieces of cardboard. Cut out the two footprints.

❷ Take your footprints outside for some *Tyrannosaurus* traveling. Lay the two footprints 20 feet (6 m) apart, one in front of the other. That would be the distance between the footprints if *Tyrannosaurus* were walking through your yard. Have the dinosaur run by laying the footprints 40 feet (12 m) apart. How many steps do you need to take to match a *Tyrannosaurus* when it's walking? Running?

3 feet (1 m)

MAKING TRACKS

COELUROSAUR PRINTS
Most small meat-eaters left footprints that looked a lot like birds' footprints with slender toe marks. They were much smaller than the large meat-eaters' footprints.

CARNOSAUR PRINTS
Large meat-eaters walked on their two back feet, each of which had three large toes. Some of their footprints even show the clear imprint of the claw on the end of each toe.

SAUROPOD PRINTS
The big sauropods walked around on four feet. Their back feet made huge footprints that were almost circular. Their front feet made smaller, U-shaped prints.

CERATOPSIAN PRINTS
The ceratopsians traveled on all fours. Their smaller front prints were farther out than their larger, four-toed back prints because they walked with their front legs a little farther apart.

Hadrosaur prints

Foot bones

Hand bones

Famous Finds

FOR THOUSANDS OF years, people dug up oversized bones, but they couldn't work out what they were. No one could imagine creatures being so huge and so different from all the animals they knew. Then, in the 1820s, Gideon Mantell realized that the big fossil teeth and bones he had collected came from a gigantic creature that no longer existed. He thought it had been a reptile, and called it *Iguanodon*.

From then on, people became more and more fascinated with dinosaurs. New discoveries of large bones caused a big stir, even though it wasn't until 1858 that the first almost-complete dinosaur skeleton was found—a *Hadrosaurus*, near Haddonfield, New Jersey, U.S.A. In 1878, the skeletons of 24 *Iguanodons* were found by coal miners near the town of Bernissart, in Belgium. This was the first opportunity to study many complete dinosaurs.

With more dinosaur discoveries, knowledge about them kept on growing. There was even a dinosaur rush at the end of the 19th century, when new American sites like Bone Cabin and Como Bluff revealed many huge dinosaurs, such as *Apatosaurus*, *Diplodocus*, and *Barosaurus*. Expeditions to Africa and Asia in the first half of the 20th century uncovered more fabulous treasure troves of fossils. The quest for dinosaurs continues today, on all continents.

CALL THEM DINOSAURS
Sir Richard Owen was a great English paleontologist and is called the father of the dinosaurs. In 1842, he realized that several large fossilized reptiles all belonged to the same extinct group of animals. He called them Dinosauria. He also described many new dinosaurs, including the sauropod *Cetiosaurus* and the armored *Scelidosaurus*.

DOWN IN THE SWAMP
A swamp becomes the final resting place for dozens of *Iguanodons*—perhaps an *Iguanodon* graveyard, like elephant graveyards in Africa today. The swamp gradually turned into a coal bed, and the *Iguanodon* skeletons became fossils. Millions of years later, 24 of them were dug out of a coal mine in Belgium. A Belgian scientist, Louis Dollo, studied them and the surrounding fossils to learn more about *Iguanodon* and its environment.

INSIDE STORY

Back to the Gobi

Scientists have known about the good dinosaur hunting grounds in the Gobi Desert, in Mongolia and China, since the first dinosaur expeditions in the 1920s. More dinosaur expeditions went to the Gobi during the 1980s. These were led by the paleontologists Philip Currie and Dale Russell from Canada, and Dong Zhiming from China.

Battling heat and ferocious desert sandstorms, the teams made some fantastic finds. They discovered the largest dinosaur that has ever been found in Asia, a sauropod called *Mamenchisaurus*. They dug up five different

types of dinosaur eggs. And at one site, they found the skeletons of seven young armored dinosaurs called *Pinacosaurus*. These dinosaurs had huddled together in a sandstorm and been buried alive— 80 million years ago.

Head and neck bones

Tooth fossil

Word Builders

• *Paleo* means "ancient" or "from the distant past," while *ology* is "study of." So **paleontology** is "the study of the past."
• Botany is the study of plants. **Paleobotany** means "the study of ancient plants," using plant fossils.
• Another word for studying dinosaurs is paleozoology. Zoology is the study of animals, so **paleozoology** is "the study of ancient animals"—such as dinosaurs.

That's Amazing!

Dinosaur fossils were considered many things before they were finally recognized as dinosaur bones. In the 1600s, an English scientist thought that one particular dinosaur bone belonged to a giant human. In the early 1800s, some American scientists believed that trails of dinosaur footprints belonged to flocks of giant birds.

Pathfinder

• Where are the best places to find dinosaurs? Go to page 10.
• What did the first expeditions to the Gobi Desert find? Go to page 17.
• How have scientists changed their minds about what *Iguanodon* looked like? Go to pages 58–59.

HANDY *IGUANODON*

Scientists took a long time to figure out that *Iguanodon*'s large fossil spike belonged on its thumb, to be used like a dagger in defense. This was just one feature of *Iguanodon*'s amazing hands. Its three middle fingers had hooflike claws, to take its weight when walking. Its fifth finger could bend and grasp plants and other objects.

SOLVING A MYSTERY

GIDEON MANTELL

This English country doctor was an amateur paleontologist. He spent much of his life studying dinosaurs. His special discovery was *Iguanodon*, which he described in detail.

THE MYSTERY TEETH

Gideon's wife found some fossils in rocks in England. Gideon concluded they were teeth. In 1825, he decided they looked like the teeth of a modern iguana, except they were bigger. Gideon named his first dinosaur *Iguanodon*.

THE SLAB OF BONES

In 1834, some of Gideon's friends bought him the large slab of rock shown here. After studying the huge fossil bones it contained, Gideon realized that they were from the same animal as the fossil teeth he already had.

THE FIRST *IGUANODON*

Gideon studied the bones and teeth that he had and then drew this sketch. This is what he imagined *Iguanodon* would have looked like.

Tailbones

Hunting for a Dinosaur

WHEN YOU GO out hunting for a dinosaur, you must know where to look. Paleontologists usually start in places where fossils have already been found. The badlands of Wyoming, Montana, and South Dakota, U.S.A., have been searched again and again, because ongoing erosion can reveal new skeletons. At other times, paleontologists go to places where no one has looked before, but where the rocks are the right age and type to contain dinosaur fossils.

The paleontologists spend long hours walking through the area, their eyes fixed on the ground, looking for any sign that dinosaur bones are lurking below. Small bone chips are one sign. The chips can be scattered over a wide area. By following the trail of bone chips back to their origin, the paleontologists find the right spot to dig. Occasionally, they are really lucky and stumble on a whole skull or bones poking out of the ground, ready to collect.

Dinosaur fossils are very heavy but very fragile. Paleontologists spend long hours patiently digging with shovels, picks, brushes, and trowels to expose the fossils. Then the fossils are hardened with special chemicals and wrapped in plaster and burlap. Finally, they can be put onto waiting trucks for the journey to their new home.

DOWN IN THE BADLANDS
These badlands in North America are a hive of activity as a team of paleontologists excavates a Cretaceous bone bed. Some paleontologists carefully expose the remains of an almost complete hadrosaur in the foreground, while others map the skeleton before wrapping the individual bones in plaster and carrying them to a waiting truck. Another group is at work in the background, excavating a ceratopsian skeleton.

INSIDE STORY
The American Dinosaur Race

In the late 1800s, there was a dinosaur-bone race in the Wild West. Two of North America's greatest paleontologists, Othniel Charles Marsh (pictured in the middle of the back row) and Edward Drinker Cope, were in a rush to find the most dinosaur fossils.

They and their workers explored the Midwest in the U.S.A. for almost 30 years, digging up bigger and better fossils. They started out as friends but ended up as fierce rivals. They would even turn up at each other's excavations and pay off the workers to get hold of their rival's fossils. Between them, Marsh and Cope described and named 130 new dinosaur species, as well as many other fossil animals. Cope named more dinosaurs, but Marsh's discoveries were more accurate.

FROM SITE TO MUSEUM

DIG IT
First, paleontologists chip away any dirt or rock covering the top of the fossil. Then they free it from the rock by cutting a deep trench in the rock all the way around the fossil. The rock can be so hard that paleontologists may have to use a drill to break it up.

MAP IT
Before any bones are moved, the paleontologists draw a detailed map of the site. This map shows exactly where each fossil bone and fragment was found, plus any other interesting details. This is an important guide for the paleontologists back at the laboratory.

Word Builders

Taphonomy is the study of what happens to an animal from the time it dies to the time it is dug up again as a fossil. The word comes from two Greek words—*taphe*, meaning "grave," and *nemo*, meaning "arrangement." A taphonomist studies the animal's fossilized bones and the surrounding rocks, which reveal a lot about the animal and its environment.

That's Amazing!

An animal often weighs more when it is dead and fossilized than it did when it was alive. That's because the minerals that replace the animal's bones and turn them into fossils are usually very heavy. Some fossilized skeletons can weigh many tons.

Pathfinder

• What huge dinosaur hunt had more than 500 people working at the site? Go to page 38.
• What did a hadrosaur look like? And a ceratopsian? Go to pages 36–39.
• How do dinosaur fossils form? Go to pages 48–49.

HANDS ON

Finding Fossils

Finding a fossil can be an adventure. First you need to find out where to look for fossils. Local and state museums will direct you to the nearest fossil sites. You will need a geologist's hammer, chisels, old newspaper in which to wrap your finds, and goggles to protect your eyes.

At the site, work carefully to break open rocks with your hammer and chisels. Fossils are usually found between flat planes of rock. Use trial and error to find the best way to open a particular rock to reveal any fossils. Chip away as much rock from around the fossil as you can without damaging it. Then take the fossil home, wrapped in newspaper.

You will likely find very common fossils, such as shellfish. But if you do find a bone or other rare fossil, notify your local museum and leave the rest of the excavation to the experts.

WRAP IT
A fossil may be harder than rock, but because it is very old, it can be easily damaged. So paleontologists put a layer of tinfoil or wet newspaper around the fossil. Then they cover it with plaster of paris and burlap to protect it during the move to the laboratory.

MOVE IT
At last, the paleontologists dig holes under the fossil to loosen it. The bundle of fossil and rock in its plaster covering is lifted out of the ground and onto a waiting truck. When the bone is big, this can be a team effort, involving many people, levers, hoists, and chains. Once in place, the fossil can be driven away.

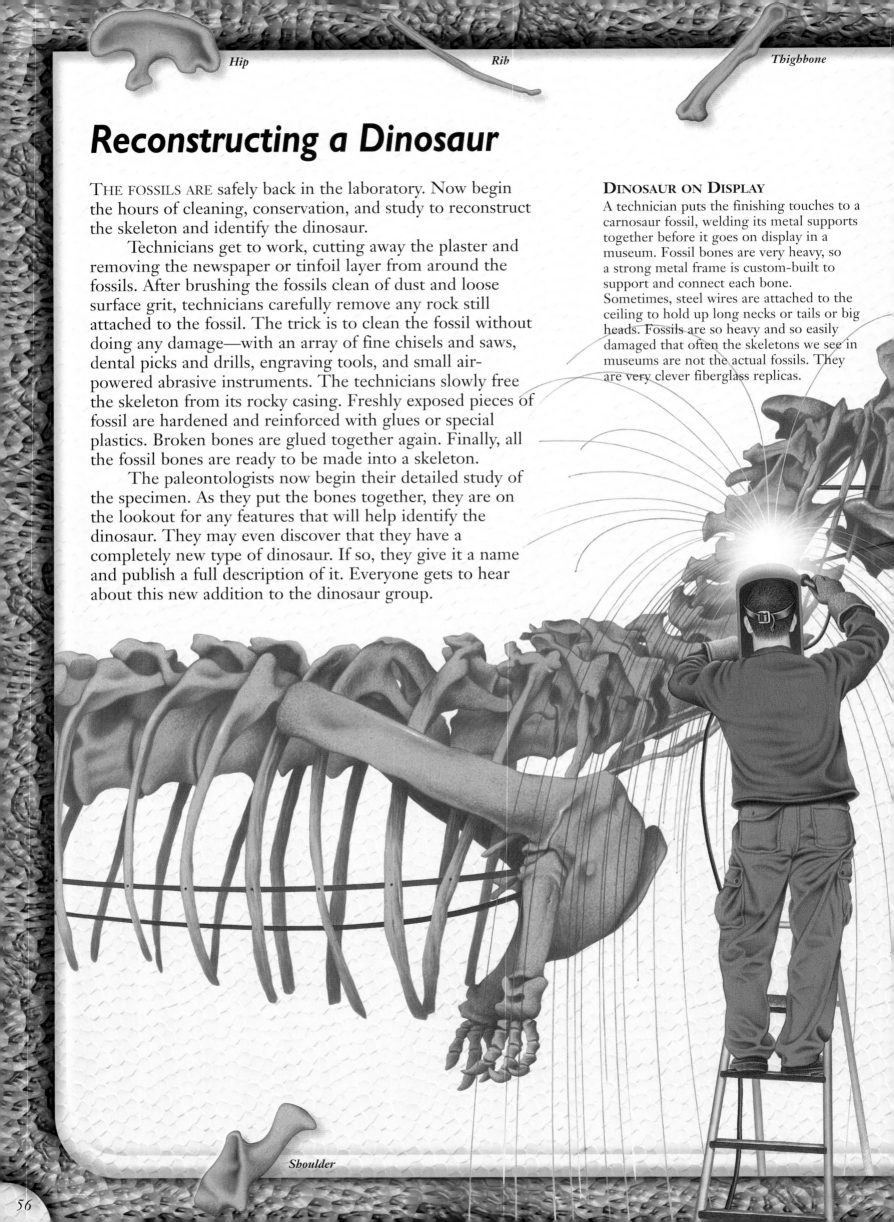

Reconstructing a Dinosaur

THE FOSSILS ARE safely back in the laboratory. Now begin the hours of cleaning, conservation, and study to reconstruct the skeleton and identify the dinosaur.

Technicians get to work, cutting away the plaster and removing the newspaper or tinfoil layer from around the fossils. After brushing the fossils clean of dust and loose surface grit, technicians carefully remove any rock still attached to the fossil. The trick is to clean the fossil without doing any damage—with an array of fine chisels and saws, dental picks and drills, engraving tools, and small air-powered abrasive instruments. The technicians slowly free the skeleton from its rocky casing. Freshly exposed pieces of fossil are hardened and reinforced with glues or special plastics. Broken bones are glued together again. Finally, all the fossil bones are ready to be made into a skeleton.

The paleontologists now begin their detailed study of the specimen. As they put the bones together, they are on the lookout for any features that will help identify the dinosaur. They may even discover that they have a completely new type of dinosaur. If so, they give it a name and publish a full description of it. Everyone gets to hear about this new addition to the dinosaur group.

DINOSAUR ON DISPLAY

A technician puts the finishing touches to a carnosaur fossil, welding its metal supports together before it goes on display in a museum. Fossil bones are very heavy, so a strong metal frame is custom-built to support and connect each bone. Sometimes, steel wires are attached to the ceiling to hold up long necks or tails or big heads. Fossils are so heavy and so easily damaged that often the skeletons we see in museums are not the actual fossils. They are very clever fiberglass replicas.

Word Builders

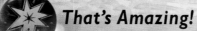

Dinosaur technicians can specialize in different parts of the job of preparing fossils.
• Technicians that clean and restore fossils are called **preparators**.
• Those that harden fossils and prevent their decay are called **conservators**. Often, one technician can be both a preparator and a conservator. But big museums usually have both types of specialists in the different techniques.

That's Amazing!

Paleontologists learn a lot about extinct animals by looking at living ones. For example, the legs of an ostrich are not very different from a meat-eating dinosaur's. So by watching ostriches walk, paleontologists can get a good idea of how meat-eaters moved. Paleontologists also observe the breeding grounds and nesting behavior of living birds to imagine how dinosaurs cared for their young.

Pathfinder

• Why is it unusual to find a complete dinosaur skeleton? Go to pages 48–49.
• What did one of the earliest dinosaur reconstructions look like? Go to page 53.
• Where can you go to see dinosaur bone beds and watch technicians preparing fossils? Go to page 34.

CLEANING FOSSILS

A PUZZLE

Each fossil bone is a piece in the puzzle of a dinosaur. Long hours of patient study can solve the puzzle. Paleontologists often have only a few fragments of bone, so they must work out the shapes of all the missing bones and fit them together by looking at other dinosaur fossils.

SAW AND CHISEL AWAY

Technicians can spend months patiently freeing a fossil from its casing of rock, called the matrix. They start by removing as much of the rock as possible with hammers and fine chisels or pneumatic saws.

BLAST AWAY

If the fossil bone is harder than sand, technicians can use a small shotblaster. Blasts of tiny sand particles erode the rock away. Or the technician may dip the fossil in an acid bath to free it from the rock.

INSIDE STORY

Dinosaurs at the Smithsonian

You can visit one of the world's best collections of dinosaurs at the Smithsonian's National Museum of Natural History in Washington, D.C., U.S.A. As you walk through the series of galleries, you can explore the fossil exhibits of early plants and mammals. Then you enter the Hall of Dinosaurs.

The centerpiece of the hall is a huge skeleton of *Diplodocus*, more than 85 feet (26 m) long. Stalking beside it is a skeleton of meat-eating *Allosaurus*. The gallery is filled with other dinosaurs, including *Tyrannosaurus*, *Edmontosaurus*, and *Triceratops*. You can climb up to a balcony and look down on all the dinosaurs below. From here, you also get a good view of the skeletons mounted high on the opposite wall. Scenes recreate life in the Jurassic and Cretaceous periods, and show what the world would have looked like just before the dinosaurs disappeared.

STUCK HARD

The fossil needs to be hardened so it will be preserved forever. Technicians apply special glues and plastics to the fossil to make sure it won't fall apart.

FINE FINISH

To remove the last bits of rock or to work on a fine fossil, technicians need a microscope. They may use an air-powered engraver, a scalpel, a dentist's drill—even a pin held in a hand vice—to finish the job.

Neck vertebra

Einiosaurus

Mononykus

Brought Back to Life

TO RE-CREATE A dinosaur, paleontologists carefully study the complete fossil skeleton to make sure the bones are put together the right way. They look at the joint surfaces between the bones to work out how the dinosaur moved.

Now the paleontologists put some internal organs inside those bones—a brain, heart, stomach, lungs, and so on. But most dinosaur organs rotted before they could become fossils, so we don't really know what they were like. Paleontologists look at living dinosaur relatives such as crocodiles and birds for some clues. They do this again when they clothe the skeleton in muscles, adding many layers of muscles to give the dinosaur its body shape.

Then it's time for the finishing touch—the skin. Because there are some fossil impressions of dinosaur skin, paleontologists have a good idea of its texture. But they have to guess its color, because colors do not fossilize.

Paleontologists can know only some details about a dinosaur from its fossils. They can work out more details by comparing it with other dinosaur skeletons as well as certain animals alive today. They add a bit of guesswork and a good imagination. And that's how they bring a dinosaur that has been dead for millions of years back to life.

INSIDE STORY
Drawing Dinosaurs

Illustrations are an important part of re-creating a dinosaur. A dinosaur illustrator is a specialist who draws all the fossil bones of a new dinosaur skeleton. These drawings help tell the world about the new dinosaur.

The dinosaur illustrator also works with a paleontologist to create an image of what the newly discovered dinosaur looked like. They discuss the fossils and everything that is known about the dinosaur and its environment. The

illustrator then makes sketches of the dinosaur. After more discussions with the paleontologist, the illustrator uses color to bring the dinosaur to life.

THE BONES
The complete skeleton is constructed. Broken bones are glued together. Fiberglass replacements are made for missing bones. *Giganotosaurus* was missing some tail bones, but the paleontologists could model new ones by looking at a close relative such as *Allosaurus*.

A MODEL DINOSAUR
Thanks to modern robotics, we can build realistic, life-sized models of dinosaurs that move just like the real thing. These dino-robots even roar and grunt. We don't know what sounds dinosaurs really made, but we can always guess.

CHANGING *IGUANODON*

LIKE AN IGUANA
A dinosaur's appearance changes as new studies and theories appear. When this sculpture was made in 1853, scientists thought *Iguanodon* was like a giant iguana, with a spike on its nose.

LIKE A DRAGON
When complete skeletons of *Iguanodon* were dug up in the late 1800s, scientists learned it could walk on two legs and that the spike was a daggerlike thumb claw. But they imagined that such a big animal would be like a dragon.

Word Builders

The scientific name for an animal can be used only once. Occasionally, a name is given to two different animals, so one has to have a name change. **Mononychus** means "one claw." It was the name given to a small theropod that had a single claw on each small arm. But a beetle already had that name, so the theropod got a new name, **Mononykus,** which also means "one claw."

That's Amazing!

Sometimes the bones of two different dinosaurs get mixed up. This happened to "Brontosaurus," which had the skeleton of an *Apatosaurus* with the head from another dinosaur. Nobody realized the mistake for decades, and "Brontosaurus" became famous. But in the early 1990s, the correct head was put on the specimen in the American Museum of Natural History, and "Brontosaurus" was no more.

Pathfinder

• When was *Giganotosaurus* the king of the dinosaurs? Go to page 42.
• How did the man who discovered *Iguanodon* imagine it looked, when he only had some teeth and a few bones? Go to page 53.
• Are birds close relatives of the dinosaurs? Go to pages 62–63.

THE SKIN

No *Giganotosaurus* skin has ever been found, but rare fossils of other dinosaurs' skin do exist. Paleontologists create its skin by looking at these fossils and at living reptiles such as crocodiles and lizards. To get the color, they guess, based on animals that live in similar environments today.

THE ORGANS

Dinosaurs' internal organs turn into fossils only in the most exceptional circumstances. Usually, they are too soft to be preserved. So scientists mostly have to guess about the position and size of *Giganotosaurus*'s heart, lungs, intestines, and other organs. Their guesses are helped by studying living relatives such as crocodiles and birds.

THE MUSCLES

Millions of years ago, the muscles of *Giganotosaurus* left scars where they connected to its bones. By reading the scars on the bones, scientists can work out how big the muscles were and how they were positioned. To get *Giganotosaurus*'s body shape, scientists add layers of muscles.

Giganotosaurus

CREATIVE COLOR

We don't know what colors dinosaurs were. But illustrators can try out ideas. Maybe the frill of a horned dinosaur had circles like a bull's eye, to look bigger and more scary. Or maybe it was really colorful to attract mates. Perhaps it was drab, for good camouflage.

LIKE A REPTILE

In later re-creations of *Iguanodon*, it started looking less like a dragon and more like a gigantic reptile. But it was seen as sluggish and so big and heavy that it needed to rest on its tail.

LIKE AN *IGUANODON*

The modern reconstruction of this dinosaur is very different from when it was first found. We now think that *Iguanodon* was very active. It usually walked on all fours, carrying its tail up in the air.

59

When the Dinosaurs Died

AFTER RULING EARTH for 160 million years, the dinosaurs suddenly vanished 65 million years ago. This was one of the most mysterious disappearances in the Earth's history. But dinosaurs were not the only ones to die out at the end of the Cretaceous period. Thousands of other animals became extinct. In the oceans, some fish survived, but all the marine reptiles died except the turtles. In the air, the pterosaurs didn't make it, while the birds and insects did. On land, the dinosaurs vanished, but the other reptile groups—the crocodiles, lizards, snakes, and tortoises—continued, along with the amphibians and the mammals. Almost half the plants that thrived during the Cretaceous period were no longer growing in the Tertiary period.

The catastrophic event that caused this mass extinction had to be powerful enough to decimate 75 percent of all the animals and plants but still leave some things alive. It was so long ago that it's hard to prove what happened. Scientists have a number of theories. Some believe there were major changes in the weather or a volcanic disaster. The main theory is that a huge meteorite collided with Earth, causing environmental chaos around the world. The dinosaurs, along with many other animals and plants, were wiped out.

A SURVIVOR
Mammals such as this *Purgatorius* were some of the animals that survived the mass extinction. Cretaceous mammals were small, so maybe they burrowed and hid away from the worst effects. They soon evolved into thousands of new species and replaced the dinosaurs as the ruling animals of Earth. Birds, insects, fish, crocodiles, amphibians, turtles, tortoises, snakes, and lizards also survived.

INSIDE STORY

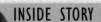

If a Meteorite Hit

A rock bigger than Mount Everest and spinning through outer space at 30,000 miles (50,000 km) per hour slammed into Earth at the end of the Cretaceous period. It left a massive crater, like the one pictured below, but much bigger. The Earth's atmosphere ignited, half the world was ablaze, and the air filled with thick smoke and dust. Acid rain started pouring down, dissolving everything that it touched. The sun was completely blocked out, so plants stopped growing. Many animals that survived the blast, the fires, and the acid rain soon died from starvation because there was nothing for them to eat.

This is what many paleontologists think is the best explanation for what caused the mass extinction that brought the Cretaceous period and the Age of Dinosaurs to an end.

METEORITE STRIKE
The sky is set alight when a massive meteorite crashes into Earth. Fire burns everything for thousands of miles, including this *Triceratops*. *Triceratops* was one of the types of dinosaurs that lived right up until the end of the Cretaceous period. *Tyrannosaurus*, *Edmontosaurus*, and *Pachycephalosaurus* also survived until the mass extinction.

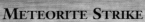

Word Builders

Decimate means to kill or destroy most of a population. It comes from the Latin word *decimus*, meaning "tenth." Decimation was an ancient Roman practice of punishing soldiers who had not fought well. One in every 10 soldiers was picked out and killed as an example to the others.

That's Amazing!

There are hundreds—maybe even thousands—of asteroids in the solar system that are as big as the meteorite that may have caused the Cretaceous extinction. Luckily, most of these asteroids are safely locked in orbits that will never come near Earth. But some do get close. There is a chance that one of these asteroids might collide with Earth a long time in the future.

Pathfinder

• What were the marine reptiles and pterosaurs? Go to pages 26–27.
• How did dinosaurs control their body temperature? Go to pages 20–21.
• What was the world like in the Cretaceous period, before the mass extinction? Go to pages 16–17.

FUNNY THEORIES
One of the silliest theories for why dinosaurs disappeared is that aliens from outer space kidnapped them. Other theories claim the dinosaurs died of boredom, or they drowned in their dung, or they were just too dumb to survive. We know this wasn't so.

Turtle

MORE EXTINCTION THEORIES

HOT CLIMATE CHANGE
Maybe the world's climate heated up. Food became more scarce in the harsh conditions. Larger animals such as dinosaurs had trouble keeping cool, and they died of excess heat.

COOL CLIMATE CHANGE
Maybe the climate got too cold. Dinosaurs couldn't keep warm or get enough to eat because many plants could not grow. Freezing and starving, the dinosaurs eventually died out.

VOLCANIC ERUPTIONS
Maybe a series of massive volcanic eruptions poisoned the atmosphere and clouded the skies. With no sunlight getting through the clouds, plants couldn't grow. Plant-eaters starved, leaving meat-eaters to starve and die out, too.

Alligator

 Hoatzin

Dinosaur Relatives Today

DINOSAURS ARE DEAD, but some of their relatives—birds and crocodiles—are alive today. Scientists believe the first bird was *Archaeopteryx*, and it appeared during the Jurassic period. It was an evolutionary offshoot from a group of small, meat-eating dinosaurs. Some of these dinosaurs, such as *Caudipteryx* and *Sinosauropteryx*, even had feathers, but not for flying. The fossils of these feathered meat-eaters clearly show the link between dinosaurs and birds.

Birds today don't look much like their dinosaur ancestors, but they still share certain features. The most obvious is their feet. Birds have three toes pointing forward and a fourth toe pointing backward. The feet of meat-eating dinosaurs were the same. Look at a chicken and you will see that its feet are similar in shape to those of *Tyrannosaurus*. Some scientists even say that dinosaurs are still alive because birds are really dinosaurs and they are still living.

The other dinosaur relatives alive today, the crocodiles, have very similar skulls to dinosaurs. Both share early archosaur ancestors. Unlike the dinosaurs, however, crocodiles did not die out 65 million years ago. They have hardly changed since then, and can teach us many things about their extinct relatives.

DISTANT COUSINS
With its long, wavy smile and big, snaggly teeth, the meat-eating dinosaur *Baryonyx* had a head very similar to a crocodile's. *Baryonyx* and crocodiles were very distant cousins. Their jaws look alike because they probably did the same job—catch fish.

FOSSIL WITH FEATHERS
Caudipteryx was a feathered dinosaur. Its fossil, including the faint marks of its feathers, was recently discovered in China. The long feathers on its hands and tail were not for flying. They were probably used for display, or perhaps to trap and catch insects.

 Emu

Crocodile

Word Builders

Pteryx is Greek for "wing" or "feather." The word can be found in some dinosaur and bird names.
• *Archaeo* means "ancient," so **Archaeopteryx** means "ancient wing."
• *Caudal* means "tail," so **Caudipteryx** means "tail feather."
• *Sino* means "Chinese." **Sinosauropteryx** means "Chinese lizard with feathers." This dinosaur with feathers was found in China.

That's Amazing!

The first person to recognize the relationship between dinosaurs and birds was the British paleontologist Thomas Huxley. As Huxley ate partridge one night, he thought about a dinosaur ankle bone that had been puzzling him for some time. Looking at the ankle of the bird he was eating, he realized that it was exactly the same bone. This led him to theorize that dinosaurs and birds were relatives.

Pathfinder

• Why did birds evolve from the dinosaurs with lizardlike hips and not from the dinosaurs with birdlike hips? Go to page 19.
• What creatures flew before birds? Go to pages 26–27.
• What dinosaurs looked like ostriches and could run almost as fast? Go to pages 44–45.

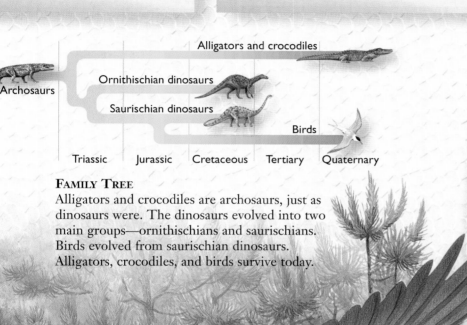

Alligators and crocodiles
Ornithischian dinosaurs
Saurischian dinosaurs
Archosaurs
Birds
Triassic Jurassic Cretaceous Tertiary Quaternary

FAMILY TREE
Alligators and crocodiles are archosaurs, just as dinosaurs were. The dinosaurs evolved into two main groups—ornithischians and saurischians. Birds evolved from saurischian dinosaurs. Alligators, crocodiles, and birds survive today.

FROM DINOSAUR TO BIRD

Small meat-eating dinosaurs such as *Compsognathus* ran around on their two back legs, leaving their arms free to catch prey. The first bird, *Archaeopteryx*, turned this grasping movement into a flapping movement by using its early wings. Modern birds have lost the claws on the wings, the long bony tail, and the teeth of this ancient bird. Flapping has become soaring flight.

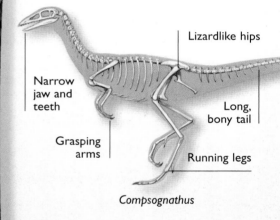

Lizardlike hips
Narrow jaw and teeth
Long, bony tail
Grasping arms
Running legs

Compsognathus

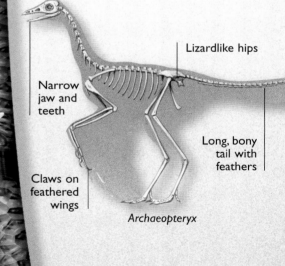

Lizardlike hips
Narrow jaw and teeth
Long, bony tail with feathers
Claws on feathered wings

Archaeopteryx

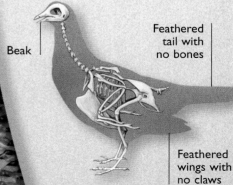

Feathered tail with no bones
Beak
Feathered wings with no claws

Modern Bird

RUN, FLAP, LEAP, FLY
Archaeopteryx runs along the ground, flapping its feathered wings to get a little extra lift as it chases an insect. *Archaeopteryx* is thought to have been the first bird. Dinosaurs probably had feathers to help keep them warm. Later, when *Archaeopteryx* evolved from the dinosaurs, its feathers grew longer so it could fly after prey.

Secretary bird

Glossary

ankylosaurs A group of armored plant-eating dinosaurs that lived in North America, Asia, Europe, and Australia by the late Cretaceous period. Their barrel-shaped bodies were protected by thick plates of bone and rows of spikes.

archosaurs A major group of reptiles. It includes the crocodiles and alligators, archosaurs that are still alive. It also includes the extinct dinosaurs and pterosaurs.

badlands The landscape where many dinosaur fossils are found. Badlands are often remote and barren areas where rivers and wind have eroded layers of rock to reveal fossils. There are badlands in Montana, Utah, Wyoming, Colorado, and New Mexico in the United States; in Alberta in Canada; in Patagonia in South America; and in the Gobi Desert in China and Mongolia.

bipedal Traveling on two legs.

bone bed A layer of rock full of fossil bones. You can see a bone bed at Dinosaur Provincial Park in Canada. Thousands of ceratopsians drowned there crossing a river in the Cretaceous period. Their bodies turned into a bed of fossilized bones.

camouflage A way of disguising something so that it blends with or remains hidden in its environment. Some dinosaurs' skin may have been the same color as their environment, to camouflage them from their prey or other predators.

carnivore An animal or a plant that eats meat.

carnosaurs A group of massive, powerful, meat-eating theropods, like *Allosaurus* and *Giganotosaurus*. Some could grow bigger than a dump truck. They were active hunters that probably scavenged when they could. Because of their size and weight, they couldn't run very fast or far.

ceratopsians A group of four-legged plant-eaters such as *Triceratops*. Their large heads had horns and bony neck frills. They were one of the last groups of dinosaurs to evolve, spreading in huge herds throughout North America and Asia, browsing and traveling over the plains.

coelurosaurs The most famous of the meat-eating dinosaurs. They ranged in size from 10-foot (3-m) *Coelophysis* to 40-foot (12-m) *Tyrannosaurus*. They were most common in the Cretaceous period, and birds evolved from them.

cold-blooded Animals such as snakes and lizards are called "cold-blooded." They get their body heat from the outside environment, by sitting in the sun. On a cold day they are less active.

coprolite A dinosaur dropping that has become a fossil.

Cretaceous period The third and last geological period of the Mesozoic era. It lasted from 144 to 65 million years ago, when a great variety of dinosaurs evolved and then became extinct.

erosion The wearing away of the Earth's surface by rivers, rain, waves, glaciers, or winds.

evolution The changing of plants and animals over millions of years. Dinosaurs evolved from their ancestors and then evolved into different species during the 183 million years of the Mesozoic era.

excavation Uncovering something and then digging it out of the ground. Any kind of fossil has to be excavated very carefully.

extinction The dying-out of a species. Dinosaurs became extinct at the end of the Cretaceous period. Their close relatives, the birds, did not.

fossil Any evidence of pre-existing life. It may be the remains of a plant or animal that have turned to stone or have left their impression on rock.

gastroliths Stomach stones. The sauropods swallowed these stones to help digest food in their stomachs.

hadrosaurs A group of duck-billed, plant-eating dinosaurs such as *Parasaurolophus* and *Edmontosaurus*. They had broad, ducklike beaks and batteries of grinding teeth. Many had bony head crests with unusual shapes. They first evolved in Asia during the early Cretaceous period, and became the most common and the most varied ornithopods of that period.

herbivore An animal that eats only plants.

ichthyosaurs One of the groups of marine reptiles living at the same time as the dinosaurs. They had dolphin-shaped bodies, and gave birth to live young in the sea.

iguanodonts Large, plant-eating dinosaurs such as *Iguanodon* that mostly walked on four feet. They first appeared during the Jurassic period and became widespread during the early Cretaceous period.

Jurassic period The middle geological period of the Mesozoic era. It lasted from 208 to 144 million years ago. The conditions on Earth were just right for new types of dinosaurs to flourish, particularly the huge, long-necked sauropods.

mammals A group of backboned animals that have hair or fur and feed their young on milk. Humans are mammals. So are dogs, cats, and bats.

matrix The rock still attached to a fossil after it has been dug out of the ground. The matrix is carefully removed from around the fossil by skilled technicians in the laboratory.

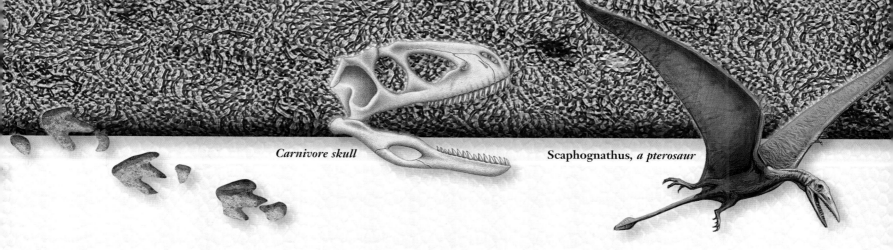

Mesozoic era The Age of Dinosaurs. It began 245 million years ago, before dinosaurs had evolved, and ended 65 million years ago with a mass extinction of plants and animals. It spanned the Triassic, Jurassic, and Cretaceous periods.

meteorite A mass of rock or metal that has fallen to Earth. It comes from an asteroid in outer space.

migration A number of animals moving from one region to another, perhaps to breed or to find food during winter or summer. Hadrosaurs and ceratopsians migrated across North America in vast herds.

mosasaurs Marine lizards also known as sea dragons. They lived in inshore waters during the late Cretaceous period. They had thick, eel-shaped bodies with four flippers.

mummified Dried out by heat or wind. Some dinosaurs were preserved in this way, after being buried in a sandstorm or volcanic ash. Even their skin and organs may have been fossilized.

ornithischians The bird-hipped dinosaurs. They had a hip structure where the pubis bone pointed backward, parallel to the ischium. All ornithischians were plant-eaters.

ornithopods The bird-footed, bird-hipped dinosaurs. These plant-eaters included some of the oldest and most successful dinosaur families, like the iguanodonts and hadrosaurs.

pachycephalosaurs The boneheads, a group of plant-eating dinosaurs with skulls thickened into domes of bone. They included *Pachycephalosaurus* and *Prenocephale*. Most lived during the late Cretaceous period in North America and Asia.

paleontologist A scientist who learns about ancient life forms by studying fossils of plants and animals.

plesiosaurs Large marine reptiles that flourished during the Jurassic and Cretaceous periods. Their long necks could rise above the sea's surface. They swam through the water using their four paddlelike flippers.

pliosaurs Marine reptiles that had large heads with strong teeth, short necks, and sturdy, streamlined bodies. They were the killers of the Mesozoic seas.

predator An animal that hunts or preys on other animals for its food.

prosauropods One of the earliest groups of dinosaurs. These saurischian plant-eaters, such as *Plateosaurus*, lived during the late Triassic and early Jurassic periods.

pterosaurs Flying reptiles such as *Scaphognathus* that first appeared during the late Triassic period.

quadrupedal Traveling on four legs.

reptiles A group of backboned animals. They have scaly skin, and their young hatch out of eggs. Snakes and lizards are modern-day reptiles.

saurischians The lizard-hipped dinosaurs. They had a hip structure where the pubis bone pointed forward. All meat-eaters were saurischians. The plant-eating prosauropods and sauropods were also saurischians.

sauropods The quadrupedal dinosaurs such as *Diplodocus* and *Brachiosaurus* with very long necks and tails. They were one of the two types of plant-eaters with lizardlike hips— most plant-eaters had birdlike hips. Evolving in the late Triassic period, they included the largest animals ever to walk Earth.

scavenger A meat-eating animal that feeds on dead animals. It either waits until the hunter has eaten its fill, or it steals the dead animal from the hunter.

species A group of animals or plants that have common features. A group of similar species forms a genus. *Tyrannosaurus rex* was a species of the *Tyrannosaurus* genus of dinosaurs.

stegosaurs Four-legged, plant-eating dinosaurs with bony plates along their backs, and pairs of long, sharp spikes on the end of their strong tails. From the late Jurassic period, they roamed North America, Europe, Asia, and Africa, and included *Stegosaurus* and *Kentrosaurus*.

synapsids A group of animals that appeared with reptiles. They lived before the dinosaurs, and mammals evolved from them.

therizinosaurs A group of exotic dinosaurs that were theropods but had some features similar to prosauropods. They included *Segnosaurus* and *Erlikosaurus*, and lived during the Cretaceous period.

theropods All the meat-eating dinosaurs. They were lizard-hipped and walked on their back legs.

trackways A series of footprints left by an animal walking or running over soft ground. Some dinosaur trackways became fossilized.

Triassic period The first geological period in the Mesozoic era, from 248 to 208 million years ago. Dinosaurs first appeared about halfway through this period, around 228 million years ago.

vertebrae The bones along the spine, from the base of the skull to the tail. They protect the spinal column.

warm-blooded Animals such as mammals and birds are called "warm-blooded." Their body temperature stays about the same, because they generate heat inside their bodies from the food they eat. They can be active all the time.

Index

A

Acrocanthosaurus, 42
age, of dinosaurs, 23
Albertosaurus, 42, 45
alligators, 63
Allosaurus, 14–15, 41–43, 57
Alphadon, 27
ankylosaurs, 16, 38, 50
Ankylosaurus, 22–23, 38
Antarctosaurus, 41
Apatosaurus, 18, 34–35, 52, 59
Archaeopteryx, 62–63
Archelon, 27
archosaurs, 63
arms, 22, 31
asteroids, 61

B

badlands, 10, 54
Barosaurus, 14–15, 22, 34–35, 52
Baryonyx, 22, 31, 62
Bernissartia, 26
birds, 62–63
body armor, 38–39
body color and markings, 22–23, 59
body size, 40–41
body temperature, 20–21
boneheaded dinosaurs, 36
bones, 20–21, 38–39, 56–57
Brachiosaurus, 14, 33–35, 38, 41
brains, 40
Brontosaurus, 35, 59

C

Camarasaurus, 41
Carcharodontosaurus, 42
carnosaurs, 30, 51, 56
Carnotaurus, 31
carnivores, 31
Caudipteryx, 62–63
ceratopsians, 16, 32, 38–39, 51
Ceratosaurus, 31
Cetiosaurus, 52
Chasmosaurus, 16–17
climate change, 60–61
Coelophysis, 12–13, 22, 40
coelurosaurs, 31, 51
cold-blooded dinosaurs, 20–21
Compsognathus, 31, 40, 63
conservators, 57
coprolites, 50–51
Corythosaurus, 16–17, 32
Cretaceous period, 10–11, 16–17, 36, 38, 44, 60

crocodiles, 62–63
Cryptoclidus, 27

D

Daspletosaurus, 30
decimation, of dinosaurs, 60–61
Deinonychus, 20, 30, 42–43
Dilophosaurus, 10–11
Dimorphodon, 26
Dinosaur National Monument, 34
Dinosaur Provincial Park, 48
dinosaur, meaning of, 11
Diplodocus, 20, 22–23, 32, 34–35, 41, 52, 57
disappearance, of dinosaurs, 60–61
drawing, of dinosaurs, 58
Dromaeosaurus, 23, 30, 42
Dromiceiomimus, 30, 44
Dryosaurus, 23, 38
duck-billed dinosaurs, 36
dung, 50
Dystylosaurus, 41

E

eating habits, 32–33
ectotherms, 21
Edmontosaurus, 23, 37, 57, 60
Einiosaurus, 58
eggs, 24–25
Elasmosaurus, 26
elephant birds, 25
endotherms, 21
Eoraptor, 13
Eric (fossil), 49
Erlikosaurus, 19
Eudimorphodon, 13
Euoplocephalus, 38
extinction, of dinosaurs, 60–61

F

feathers, 21, 62–63
feet, 22, 35, 52
flying reptiles, 9, 13, 27
food, for dinosaurs, 15, 17
footprints, 50–51
fossils, 38–39, 48–59

G

Gallimimus, 31, 44–45
geology, 49
Giganotosaurus, 40–42, 58–59
Gobi Desert, Mongolia, 17, 48–49, 52
Gondwana, 14, 15, 16

H

hadrosaurs, 16, 25, 32–33, 36–37, 51
Hadrosaurus, 52
hands, 52–53
heads, 35–37
hearing, sense of, 45
herbivores, 31
Heterodontosaurus, 32–33
hips, 18–19
hoatzin, 62
horns, 38–39
humans, and dinosaurs, 26
hunting, by dinosaurs, 31
hunting, for dinosaur fossils, 54–55
Hypsilophodon, 19, 22, 32

I

ichnites, 51
ichthyosaurs, 26
Ichthyosaurus, 26
Iguanodon, 32–33, 44, 50, 52–53, 58–59
insects, 27

J

Jurassic Park (film), 14
Jurassic period, 10, 11, 14, 15, 17, 34, 38, 42, 62

K

Kannemeyeria, 13
Kentrosaurus, 14, 38
Komodo dragons, 10
Kronosaurus, 26

L

Lambeosaurus, 18–19, 23, 32, 37
Lark Quarry, Australia, 50
Laurasia, 14–16
Leaellynasaura, 20, 25
Liopleurodon, 26
lithology, 49
lizards, 27

M

Maiasaura, 24–25, 36, 39
Mamenchisaurus, 34–35, 52
mammals, 27
Massospondylus, 12
meat-eating dinosaurs, 18, 22, 24, 30–31, 40, 42–43
Mesozoic era, 10, 26, 42, 44, 48
meteors, 60
Micropachycephalosaurus, 40–41
Mononychus, 59
Mononykus, 58–59

mouths, 32–33
muscles, 59

N

necks, 34–35
nodosaurs, 39
Nothosaurus, 13

O

omnivores, 31
oolites, 51
organs, 59
ornithischians, 18–19, 63
Ornitholestes, 30
ornithomimids, 44–45
ornithopods, 14
Orodromeus, 24
Oviraptor, 18, 24

P

pachycephalosaurs, 22, 36
Pachycephalosaurus, 17, 23, 36, 60
Pachyrhachis, 27
paleobotany, 53
paleontologists, 11, 52–59
paleontology, 53
paleozoology, 53
Pangaea, 12–14
Parasaurolophus, 36, 37
Pholidophorus, 27
Pinacosaurus, 31, 52
plant fossils, 32
plant-eating dinosaurs, 18, 22, 25, 32–33, 38, 40
plants, 15
Platecarpus, 27
Plateosaurus, 12, 32
plesiosaurs, 26–27
pliosaurs, 26, 49
Polacanthus, 38
predators, 42–43
Prenocephale, 37
preparators, 57
Prosauropods, 50
Protoceratops, 22, 33
Pterodaustro, 26
pterosaurs, 11, 13, 26, 27
Purgatorius, 60

Q

Quetzalcoatlus, 27

R

reproduction, 24–25
Rhamphorhynchus, 27

S

saurischians, 18–19, 63
Saurolophus, 37
Sauropelta, 39
sauropods, 14, 16, 22, 24,

32, 34–35, 51
Scaphognathus, 27
Scutellosaurus, 38
scutes, 38
Seelidosaurus, 52
Segnosaurus, 19
Seismosaurus, 32, 34, 40–41
senses, 44–45
sight, sense of, 44
Sinosauropteryx, 62–63
skeletons, assembling, 18, 56–59
skulls, 43
smell, sense of, 44
Smithsonian National Museum of Natural History, 57
snakes, 27
speed, of dinosaurs, 44–45
Spinosaurus, 20, 42
Stegoceras, 37
stegosaurs, 16, 38
Stegosaurus, 14, 21, 32–33, 38–41
stones, in dinosaurs' stomachs, 33
Struthiomimus, 44–45
Stygimoloch, 37
Supersaurus, 41
survival tactics, 22–23
synapsids, 11

T

taphonomy, 55
Tarbosaurus, 30
teeth, 30–33, 53
therizinozaurs, 19
theropods, 16, 22, 31, 42
time periods, 10–11
touch, sense of, 45
Triassic period, 10–11, 12–13
Triceratops, 22, 32, 38–39, 57, 60–61
Troodon, 24, 30, 40, 44
troodontids, 44
Tuojiangosaurus, 23
Tyrannosaurus, 16, 22–23, 31, 37, 40, 42–43, 45, 57, 60
Tyrannosaurus rex, 42–43

V

Velociraptor, 16, 22, 24, 31, 42

W

warm-blooded dinosaurs, 20–21
Wuerhosaurus, 18

Earthquakes and Volcanoes

Contents

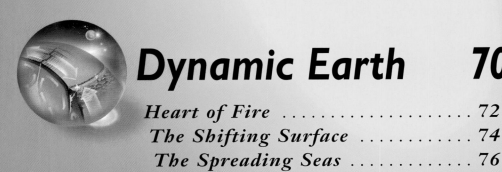

Dynamic Earth   70

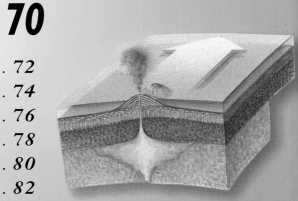

Heart of Fire 72
The Shifting Surface 74
The Spreading Seas 76
Collisions 78
Fault Lines 80
Hot Spots 82

Earthquakes   84

On Shaky Ground 86
After the Quake 88
Monitoring Earthquakes 90
Preparing for Earthquakes 92
Major Earthquakes 94
California 96
Japan 98

Volcanoes   100

Under the Volcano 102
Lava Flows 104
Ash and Gas 106
Aftereffects 108
Geysers and Hot Springs 110
Volcanic Landscapes 112
Volcanology 114
Major Eruptions 116
The Mediterranean 118
Iceland 120
Western North America 122
Extraterrestrial Volcanoes 124

Glossary 126
Index 128

Pick Your Path!

Earthquakes and Volcanoes is different from any other information book you've ever read. Start at the beginning and learn about Earth's fiery interior, then read through to the end and find out about volcanoes on other planets. Or, if you have a special interest in earthquakes, jump right into "On Shaky Ground" and move through the book from there.

You'll find plenty of other discovery paths to choose from in the special features sections. Read eyewitness accounts of volcanoes and earthquakes in "Inside Story," or get creative with "Hands On" activities. Delve into words with "Word Builders," or amaze your friends with fascinating facts from "That's Amazing!" You can choose a new path with every reading—Reader's Digest Pathfinders will take you wherever *you* want to go.

INSIDE STORY
Where the Action Is

Fly over Mount St. Helens as it erupts with geologists Keith and Dorothy Stoffel. Read photographer Carl Mydans' account of a major Japanese earthquake. Learn how postmaster Masao Mimatsu watched a volcano grow before his eyes. Study the shape of the seafloor with oceanographer Harry Hess. Read about great scientists, terrifying tremors, and spectacular eruptions in INSIDE STORY. Imagine you are there, and you will understand how it feels to experience earth-shattering events or discover something that changes our view of the world.

Word Builders

What a strange word! What does it mean? Where did it come from? Find out by reading *Word Builders*.

HANDS ON
Shake and Bake

Create a volcanic eruption in your kitchen. Learn about earthquake-proof buildings by making a shake table. Bake a volcano cake that oozes chocolate lava. Construct your own seismometer and use it to record tremors. Use binoculars to study ancient lava flows on the surface of the Moon. HANDS ON features experiments, projects, and activities—each one related to that page's main subject.

That's Amazing!

Awesome facts, amazing records, fascinating figures— you'll find them all in *That's Amazing!*

Pathfinder

Use the *Pathfinder* section to find your way from one subject to another. It's all up to you.

Ready! Set!
Start exploring!

Dynamic Earth

TREMORS AND EXPLOSIONS constantly rock our planet. Most of these earthly hiccups are caused by the shifting of rocks in the ground. These movements, in turn, are powered by heat from Earth's core. The heat causes some of the rock between the core and the surface to rise and sink like currents in hot water. This circulation constantly tugs at the crust and, over millions of years, has broken it into pieces, or plates. The plates slowly pull apart, collide, and grind past each other. When a plate shifts suddenly, we feel the movement as an earthquake. If the rock below a plate melts, the liquid rock may spurt out of the ground, forming a volcano.

page **72**

Do you know how the planets in our solar system formed?

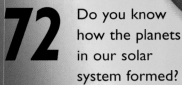

Earth is made up of several layers. What are they called?

Go to HEART OF FIRE.

page **74**

How do some collisions between plates form volcanoes?

Currents inside Earth cause the crust to move. What are these currents called?

Go to THE SHIFTING SURFACE.

page **76**

Can a continent really split in half? What happens when it does?

Did you know that the longest mountain range in the world lies under the sea?

Go to THE SPREADING SEAS.

page **78** What happens when sections of the crust collide?

A collision between which two continents created the largest mountain range on Earth?

Go to **COLLISIONS**.

page **80** When rock layers move in different directions, faults form. What type of fault is this?

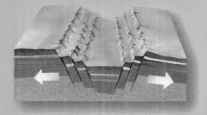

Some types of faults create distinctive landforms. What's this landform called?

Go to **FAULT LINES**.

page **82** Did you realize that this island is the top of a volcano?

How can you make your own chain of volcanoes?

Go to **HOT SPOTS**.

EARTH'S LAYERS
Earth is a bit like a boiled egg. The crust is the shell, the mantle is the stiff white, and the core is the yolk.

Crust
3–43 miles
(5–70 km) thick

Mantle
1,800 miles
(2,900 km) thick

Outer core
1,400 miles
(2,250 km) thick

Inner core
750 miles
(1,200 km) thick

Heart of Fire

LOOK DOWN at the ground. Have you ever wondered what lies beneath your feet? Did you know that you live on a huge ball of rock? No one can travel to the center of this giant rock because the heat and pressure inside our planet are so great that even the toughest drills would melt just 8 miles (13 km) below the surface. But if you could go on such a trip, this is what you would find.

First, you would pass through a layer of rocks called the crust. The crust is thicker under land than it is under the ocean. At its thinnest, the crust is only 3 miles (5 km) deep. You could walk that far in an hour. However, the thickest part of the crust is 43 miles (70 km) deep, a distance that would take you at least two days to walk. Beyond the crust, you would enter the mantle. The upper part of the mantle is solid, but the deeper part is soft. The mantle is more than 40 times wider than the thickest part of the crust.

If you could descend through the mantle, you would arrive at the core. The outer part of the core is made of molten iron, but near the center it is solid iron. Earth's center lies about 4,000 miles (6,370 km) below you—a distance that would take about eight hours to travel by plane. Here, in our planet's fiery heart, the temperature is 50 times hotter than that of boiling water, and the pressure is 5 million times greater than the pressure of the air on our bodies at Earth's surface.

IN THE UNDERWORLD
For centuries, people have wondered what lies inside Earth. In the 17th century, a German religion professor named Alhanasius Kircher climbed into a volcano to learn more about the planet's interior. His studies led him to suggest that volcanoes were linked by rivers of lava that sprang from fires within the Earth.

A GROWING PLANET

IN THE BEGINNING
Our solar system emerged from a giant cloud of dust and gas. About 4.6 billion years ago, this cloud started spinning rapidly, pulling hot gases toward its center. These gases formed the Sun. Farther out, pieces of dust and rock collided and bonded to form planets. Earth, the third planet from the Sun, was born about 4.5 billion years ago. The remaining gases and dust were blown out of the solar sytem by a blast of radiation from the Sun.

HEATING UP
While meteorites continuously bombarded Earth, radioactive materials inside the planet began to decay and heat up. Rocks started to melt, and heavy metal materials sank to the center, leaving lighter minerals in the outer part. Shortly after Earth formed, a small planet slammed into it, spraying debris into space. Some of this material spun into a ball, forming the Moon.

Word Builders

- The word **mantle** comes from the Latin word *mantellum,* meaning "cloak" or "cover." The mantle cloaks, or covers, the core.
- As a rock hurtles through space, it is called a **meteoroid**. If it passes through Earth's atmosphere, it is known as a **meteor**. If it reaches the ground, it is called a **meteorite**. All three words come from the Greek *meteoron,* meaning "something high in the sky."

That's Amazing!

- The energy released when Earth formed was so great that it still powers volcanic eruptions after more than 4 billion years of cooling.
- Volcanoes can bring up rocks and minerals from as deep as 375 miles (600 km) below Earth's surface. These materials can include diamonds.
- We know more about distant stars than about the workings of Earth's core.

Pathfinder

- Earth's crust is solid, but it is broken into pieces that constantly move around. Learn more on pages 74–75.
- Movement of Earth's crust is one cause of earthquakes. Read about the biggest quakes in history on pages 94–95.
- Earth isn't the only planet that has earthquakes and volcanoes. Find out more on pages 124–25.

SPACE ROCKS

Meteorites are rocks that crash onto Earth from space. Most come from the asteroid belt, a band of rocky lumps that orbit between Mars and Jupiter. Many are made of iron, much like the rocks at the center of our planet. Scientists study asteroids to learn more about Earth's core.

FROM THE HEART

In many parts of the world, red-hot streams of soft, hot rock called magma rise through the crust and emerge on Earth's surface as lava. Scientists study the rock and minerals in lava to learn about our planet's hot interior.

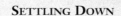

INSIDE STORY

Watching the Waves

Scientists study Earth's interior by monitoring the shock waves created by big earthquakes. The speed and direction of the waves tell them what kinds of rocks make up Earth's layers. In the 1930s, scientists knew only that Earth had a crust, mantle, and core. Then a Danish scientist named Inge Lehmann began to study earthquakes. A nephew, Niels Groes, recalls that his aunt kept records of the speed of shock waves on cards that she filed in oatmeal boxes. These records showed that some waves changed direction as they passed through the core. Using this information, Lehmann published a paper in 1936 that proposed a possible solid inner core within Earth's outer core.

COOLING OFF

The constant bombardment by meteorites left giant scars and huge oceans of lava on the surfaces of Earth and the Moon. As the lava cooled, it created a hard outer crust on both bodies. Inside Earth, a metallic core formed. By about 3 billion years ago, the Moon was almost completely solid.

SETTLING DOWN

Gradually, the rocks and minerals inside Earth separated into three main layers—the core, mantle, and crust. Volcanoes and meteorites added gases and water to the atmosphere. Oceans began to form, and eventually plants and animals emerged.

Villarrica, a volcano in Chile

Torres del Paine, eroded volcanic peaks in Chile

Cotopaxi, a volcano in Ecuador

The Shifting Surface

BETWEEN 50 AND 150 MILES (80 and 240 km) below Earth's surface, something strange happens to the rocks of the mantle. They soften, and in places start to melt, forming pockets of molten rock. This creates a weak zone called the asthenosphere. Above the asthenosphere, the solid top of the mantle and crust form a hard shell known as the lithosphere. This shell floats on top of the squishy asthenosphere and slowly moves around.

Because the asthenosphere is soft, its hotter parts rise and begin to cool. Once they have cooled sufficiently, they start to sink again. This rising and sinking creates a kind of circulation called a convection current. These currents constantly push and tug at the lithosphere, breaking Earth's outer shell into pieces called tectonic plates.

Where currents push upward, they force tectonic plates apart. As the plates move, they carry land with them. Over millions of years, moving plates split, forcing continents to collide, and opening and closing oceans. Slowly but surely, this process continues to transform the surface of our planet.

RISING AND FALLING

The East Pacific Rise in the Pacific Ocean is a divergent margin. Here, rising magma pushes the Pacific and Nazca plates outward. Parts of the plates move at different rates, creating cracks called transform faults. The Nazca Plate collides with the South American Plate, forming a convergent margin. Here, the thin ocean plate slides under the continental plate and melts in the mantle.

PUSH AND PULL

The lithosphere is divided into pieces called tectonic plates. These plates have three kinds of margins, or edges. A divergent margin occurs where plates move apart. A convergent margin forms where plates collide. Plates moving past each other create transform fault margins.

Nansen Ridge

EURASIAN PLATE

Reykjanes Ridge

Anatolian Fault

ARABIAN PLATE

AFRICAN PLATE

Mid-Atlantic Ridge

Great Rift Valley

Java Trench

INDO-AUSTRALIAN PLATE

Southwest Indian Ocean Ridge

Southeast Indian Ocean Ridge

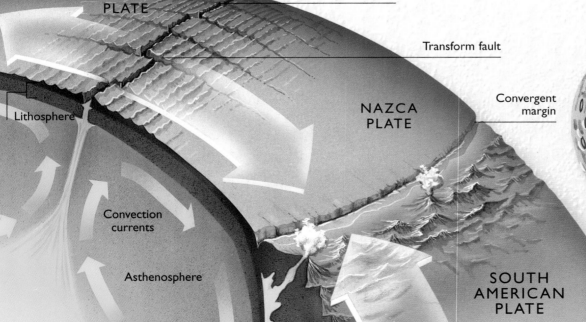

PACIFIC PLATE

Divergent margin

Transform fault

Convergent margin

NAZCA PLATE

Lithosphere

Convection currents

Asthenosphere

SOUTH AMERICAN PLATE

EYE IN THE SKY

By constantly measuring the distance between a satellite, such as the one pictured here, and a receiving station on Earth, scientists can detect the movement of tectonic plates.

Word Builders

• **Lithosphere** comes from the Greek words *lithos,* for "stone," and *sphaira,* for "sphere." The soft **asthenosphere** takes its name from *sphaira* and another Greek word *asthenes,* meaning "weak."
• Buildings and other constructions were called *tektonikos* by the ancient Greeks. In geology, **tectonics** refers to the structures that make up Earth's surface.

That's Amazing!

• Rocks that now lie 6,000 miles (9,660 km) apart, in South America and South Africa, once lay beside each other. They slowly spread apart as a result of the movement of the seafloor.
• The Pacific and Nazca plates are moving apart at the rate of more than 7 inches (18 cm) each year.

Pathfinder

• Diverging plates can create new oceans. To learn how this happens, turn to pages 76–77.
• Plates converge, or collide, in different ways. Turn to pages 78–79.
• Scientists use satellite measurements to predict earthquakes. Find out more on pages 90–91.

KEY TO SYMBOLS

Direction of movement	
Divergent margin	
Convergent margin	
Major transform fault	
Minor transform faults	

NORTH AMERICAN PLATE

Aleutian Trench

Kuril Trench

JUAN DE FUCA PLATE
GORDA PLATE

San Andreas Fault

Mariana Trench

PHILIPPINE PLATE

CARIBBEAN PLATE

COCOS PLATE

CAROLINE PLATE

PACIFIC PLATE

FIJI PLATE

Tonga Trench

SOUTH AMERICAN PLATE

NAZCA PLATE

East Pacific Rise

Peru-Chile Trench

Alpine Fault

SCOTIA PLATE

ANTARCTIC PLATE

PIECES OF A PUZZLE

In 1910, a German scientist, Alfred Wegener (above), noticed that the continents looked like puzzle pieces. He suggested that they had once formed a single continent, which he called Pangaea. Recent studies have proved his theory. In these maps, the changing positions of the continents are shown over the present positions.

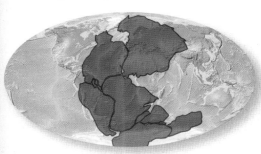

Earth's landmasses formed one huge continent about 200 million years ago. Soon after, spreading in the seafloor began to split this continent into smaller landmasses.

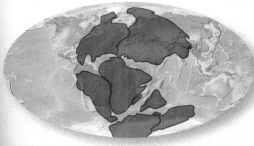

Spreading in what is now the Atlantic Ocean split North America from Africa 120 million years ago. The widening Indian Ocean pushed India northward.

The Atlantic was already a broad ocean 65 million years ago, and India was on a collision course with the Eurasian Plate.

HANDS ON

Convection Currents

You can see for yourself how convection currents form.

❶ Take a large glass container and fill it with cold water. Fill a smaller jar with hot water and add a few drops of red food coloring.

❷ Cover the top of the small jar with your hand while placing the jar on the bottom of the big container. Take your hand away and watch what happens.

The red water rises toward the top of the cold water and spreads outward. This happens because the red water is hotter than the clear water. As the red water cools, it sinks. This creates a convection current. The same thing happens in Earth's mantle. Hot rock rises toward the lithosphere, then it cools and sinks. As the rock moves, it shifts Earth's tectonic plates.

The Spreading Seas

DEEP BENEATH THE SEAS, massive ridges wend their way along the ocean floors, forming the longest mountain range on Earth. If you could see these ridges from space, they would look like the seams on a giant baseball. Inside the ridges lie huge cracks in the crust. Convection currents in the mantle push magma up through these cracks. Some lava spills out onto the ocean floor and some hardens inside the cracks. As the lava in the cracks cools, it pushes the seafloor outward. Slowly, the plates on either side of the cracks spread, like two conveyor belts moving in opposite directions.

New ocean crust builds up in two layers. Lava that reaches the seafloor cools quickly in the water and forms mounds called pillow lava. Lava that solidifies in the cracks creates vertical sheets called dikes. Beneath the dikes, the mantle forms massive blocks of coarse-grained rock.

It is pitch dark on the ridges, but scientists use various methods to reveal the secrets of this murky world. Ships and satellites bounce laser beams, radar signals, and sonar (sound) waves off the ocean floor to discover its shape. Dredges and drills recover samples of seafloor rocks. And brave explorers descend in submersibles to witness and photograph seafloor spreading in action.

EXPLORING OCEAN RIDGES

Explorers find an eerie world inside ocean ridges. Volcanoes erupt, but the pressure of the seawater keeps these explosions from being felt at the surface. The seafloor bristles with chimneys called black smokers. Mineral-rich water pours out of the chimneys, attracting strange creatures including fish and sea worms.

INSIDE STORY
Spreading the Word

American geologist Harry Hess was the first scientist to explain seafloor spreading. During World War II, he served in submarines, and between battles he studied mountain ranges on the ocean floor. Later, in the 1960s, other scientists revealed that the ocean floor was very thin. Hess realized that molten rock must be constantly oozing up through the thin seafloor to form new crust and mountains. He also suggested that as the seafloor spread outward, it collided with continents and sank back into the mantle. Hess had no way of proving his theory, but scientists have since shown that he was correct.

MAPPING THE SEAFLOOR
Scientists use information from satellites, and from surveys carried out using radar and sonar devices, to create maps of the ocean floor. Here, the ocean ridges are highlighted in pale blue.

PARTING THE LANDSCAPE

Many oceans began life as rift valleys. Rift valleys form where convection currents rise upward, stretching and splitting the crust. As a rift valley widens, water may flood in from a nearby ocean. This creates a new sea that will continue to grow.

RIFTING
When convection currents split the land, faults form. The land tilts and drops, forming a wide valley. Lava may seep through the valley floor.

FLOODING
The hot asthenosphere bulges upward into the fault zone. As the land drops farther, water pours in. Seafloor forms and pushes the landmasses apart.

Word Builders

• By bouncing **radar** and **sonar** signals off the ocean floor, scientists can build up a picture of its shape. The word radar is short for "RAdio Detection And Reading." Sonar is an abbreviation of "SOund NAvigation Ranging."
• **Rift** comes from the Danish word *rift* which means "cleft" or "split."

That's Amazing!

• The Mid-ocean Ridge stretches 48,000 miles (75,000 km) from the Arctic through the Atlantic Ocean, around Africa and Australia, and across the Pacific Ocean to North America.
• In the 1980s, two new species of sea worms, the red-plume worm and the Pompeii worm, were found near black smokers in the Pacific Ocean. The worms live in water that can be three times as hot as boiling water and feed on bacteria.

Pathfinder

• Ocean ridges form where convection currents force magma upward. Learn how to make your own convection currents on page 75.
• Rift valleys are a kind of fault. Discover more about faults on pages 80–81.
• Seafloor spreading is tearing apart the island of Iceland. Turn to pages 120–21.

Black smokers

Pillow lava

Dike

BIRTH OF A SEA
The Red Sea in North Africa started to form 20 million years ago. The process began on land, when rifting created a valley. As the valley widened and deepened, seawater flooded in. Today the Red Sea continues to grow, pushing apart Africa and the Arabian peninsula.

Mid-ocean ridge

SPREADING
As spreading continues, the ocean grows wider. As the seafloor moves outward, it settles and sinks, leaving a high ridge on either side of the rift.

MAGNETIC STRIPES
Like trees, seafloors contain growth bands. As molten rock cools, particles of iron minerals within it line up with Earth's magnetic field like the needle of a compass. Over millions of years, the magnetic field has reversed many times. This has created bands of rock that have either normal magnetism to the north or reverse magnetism to the south. These bands help scientists to date the seafloor and measure its rate of spreading.

▲ Normal magnetism
▼ Reverse magnetism

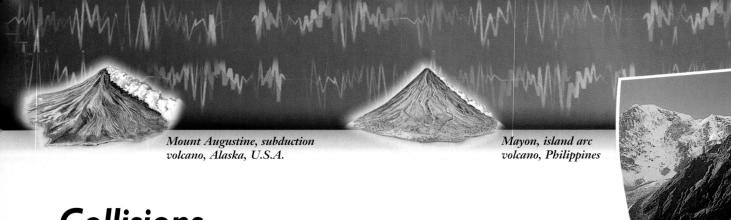

Mount Augustine, subduction volcano, Alaska, U.S.A.

Mayon, island arc volcano, Philippines

Collisions

TECTONIC PLATES are on collision courses. When they meet, moving plates smash into each other with enormous force. The effects of these collisions depend on the types and thicknesses of the plates involved. When two plates carrying continental crust collide straight on, the land buckles to form large mountain ranges. Plates colliding at a small angle may grind past each other, forming a fault line. In most collisions, however, the duel between the plates is like an arm wrestle, with the thicker, stronger plate forcing the thinner, weaker plate downward. This is called subduction.

Subduction usually occurs when a thin ocean plate meets a thicker ocean plate or continental plate. During subduction, the thicker plate crumples and buckles along the impact zone. This, along with the downward movement of the thinner plate, can trigger earthquakes. As the thinner plate sinks, the mantle heats up and begins to melt. Heat and pressure force the molten rock to the surface where it erupts, forming volcanoes. On land, this usually creates a line of volcanic mountains. When two ocean plates are involved, a chain of volcanic islands called an island arc is formed.

HIGH RISE
The highest mountain range on Earth, the Himalayas in Asia, formed when India collided with Eurasia 60 million years ago. Buckling of the land has made the continental crust here up to 43 miles (70 km) thick.

KINDS OF COLLISION
This cross section shows the three main kinds of plate collisions. On the left, oceanic crust crashes into continental crust, forming subduction volcanoes. In the center, two continents collide, creating a mountain range. On the right, two oceanic plates meet, forming an island arc.

The folding of the continental crust creates a high mountain range.

The process of subduction can form an ocean trench.

Magma rises to the surface and erupts, forming volcanoes.

Subduction zone

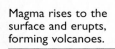

WHEN CONTINENTS MEET
After the breakup of Pangaea, India was part of a large southern continent called Gondwana. About 145 million years ago, India broke away and began to drift northward.

About 60 million years ago, India and Eurasia approached each other. India's seafloor began to subduct under Eurasia's, pushing the crust upward and forming a line of volcanoes.

Word Builders

• The word **subduction** comes from two Latin words, *sub,* meaning "under," and *duco,* for "lead." Subduction leads one plate under another.
• The name of the **Himalaya** mountain range comes from the Sanskrit words *hima,* meaning "snow," and *alaya,* meaning "home." For local people, the Himalayas are the home of the snow.

That's Amazing!

• The deepest ocean trench, the Mariana Trench in the Pacific Ocean, is 36,198 feet (11,033 m) deep. That means it could swallow the world's tallest mountain on land, Mount Everest.
• Parts of the Oman Mountains in Arabia were originally seafloor. They formed hundreds of miles away under the Indian Ocean 100 million years ago, but were forced up onto land by plate movements.

Pathfinder

• Collisions occur as oceanic plates spread outward. Learn about seafloor spreading on pages 76–77.
• Plate collisions create shock waves, which in turn cause earthquakes. That's why most quakes occur along plate edges. See pages 94–95.
• Subduction forces magma upward through the crust, where it erupts as lava. Learn about different kinds of volcanic eruptions on pages 102–03.

HANDS ON
Fold Your Own Crust

You can observe how Earth's crust folds and buckles.

❶ Take several pieces of different-colored modeling clay. Roll the pieces into thin strips and layer the strips on top of each other. Imagine that the pile is part of Earth's crust.

❷ Place the clay on a smooth surface. Slowly push the ends of the clay inward using your hands or two wooden blocks. Watch what happens.

The clay folds and rises upward in the middle. This is similar to what happens when two continents collide. The crust buckles and folds, rising slowly upward to form mountains.

ON THE ARC
Mount Tavurvur, near Rabaul in Papua New Guinea, is an island arc volcano. It lies on a convergent margin between the Pacific and Indo-Australian plates. In 1994, Mount Tavurvur and neighboring Mount Vulcan both erupted violently.

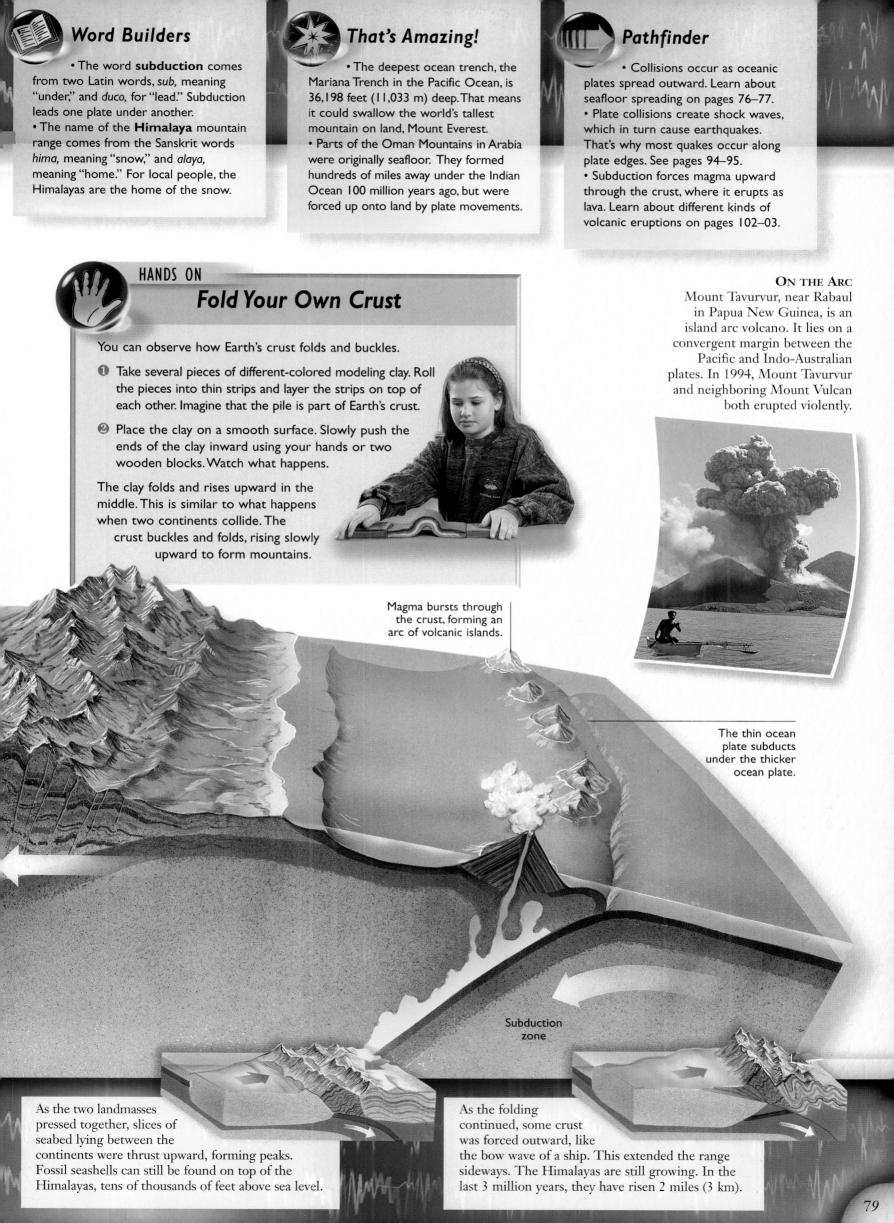

Magma bursts through the crust, forming an arc of volcanic islands.

The thin ocean plate subducts under the thicker ocean plate.

Subduction zone

As the two landmasses pressed together, slices of seabed lying between the continents were thrust upward, forming peaks. Fossil seashells can still be found on top of the Himalayas, tens of thousands of feet above sea level.

As the folding continued, some crust was forced outward, like the bow wave of a ship. This extended the range sideways. The Himalayas are still growing. In the last 3 million years, they have risen 2 miles (3 km).

Reverse fault

Normal fault

Fault Lines

THE IMMENSE PRESSURES of plate movements snap even the toughest rocks. Cracks between shifting rock layers are called faults. You can see small faults in rock faces, riverbanks, and road cuts. Large faults may extend for hundreds of miles.

Small or large, the type of fault that forms depends on the way the rocks move. When rocks pull apart, one side slips downward. This is called a normal fault. When rocks push together, one side usually rides up over the other, creating a reverse fault. Sometimes rocks slide past each other in opposite directions or at different speeds. This creates a fault called a lateral, or transform, fault. All three kinds of movement may occur along a major fault line.

Large faults shape the landscape in particular ways. Normal faults create long cliffs. A sunken block of land called a rift valley may form between two normal faults. Reverse faults create mountains with a stacked-up or notched look. Low-angle reverse faults, called thrust faults, form wide, low ranges of hills or peaks. Lateral faults may bring different types of rock alongside each other, creating an obvious line in exposed ground. The movement of plates along large faults causes many earthquakes. As the plates press in opposite directions, there may be a sudden release of tension. This jolts the ground, setting off shock waves.

TAKE THE FAULT TEST
Small faults show up best in layered rocks. In this picture, can you tell which side dropped down, by how much, and on what sort of fault? If you said the left side dropped by about an arm's length, and that it's a normal fault, then you're getting the hang of this!

PASSING PLATES
The San Andreas Fault stretches 650 miles (1,046 km) through California in the United States. From an airplane, the fault is clearly visible for most of its length. On the western side, the Pacific Plate grinds slowly northwest. On the eastern side, the North American Plate slides southeast. In the last 150 million years, the plates have moved 350 miles (563 km) in opposite directions.

LARGE-SCALE FAULTS

LATERAL FAULTS
Giant lateral faults can create long grooves in the landscape by placing different types of rock alongside each other. Sometimes folding along the fault forms low mountains. Major lateral faults include the San Andreas (U.S.A.), Atacama (Chile), and Philippine faults.

Lateral fault

Reverse faults

REVERSE FAULTS
On a large scale, reverse faulting can create mountain ranges. As one plate pushes against the other, parts of the crust crack and tilt. As they compress, the blocks of land rise upward. The resulting mountains have a steep face on one side and a shallower incline on the other.

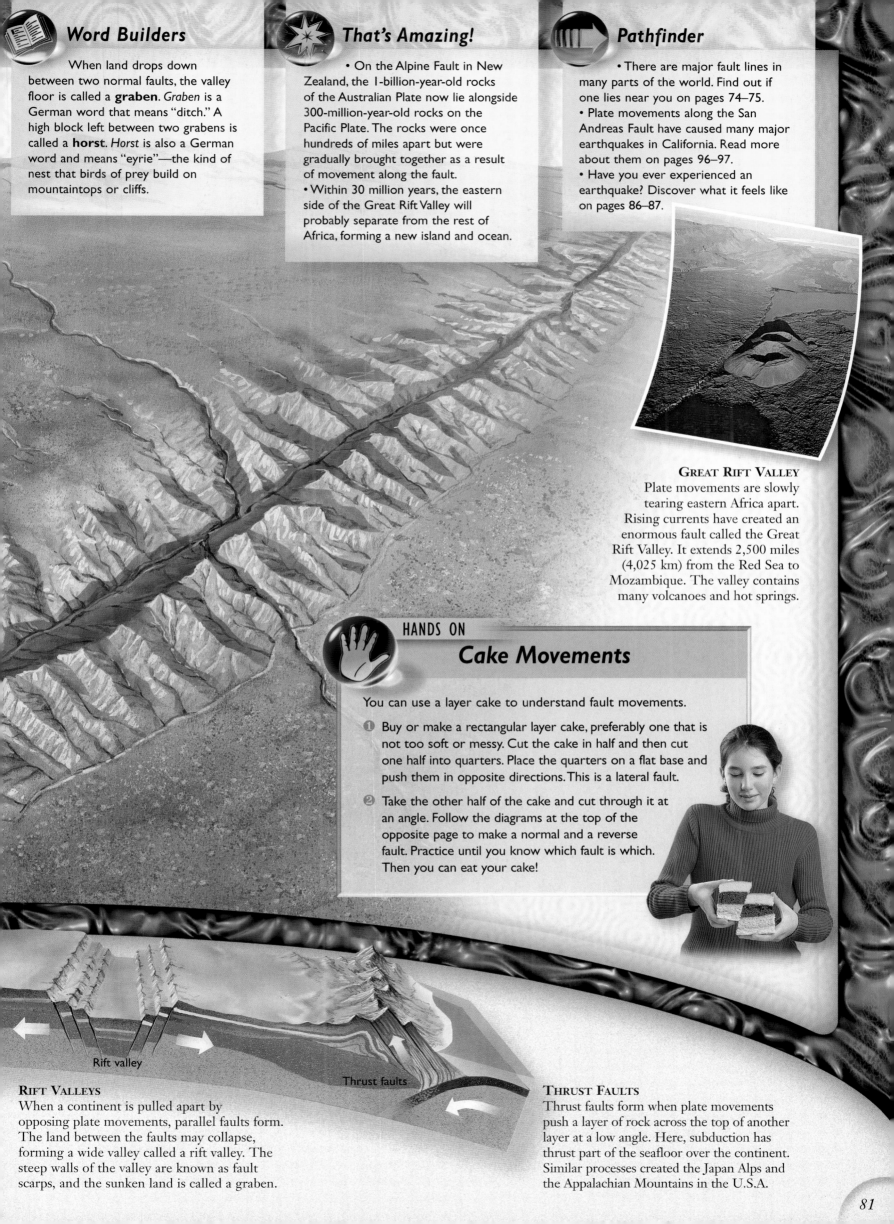

Word Builders

When land drops down between two normal faults, the valley floor is called a **graben**. *Graben* is a German word that means "ditch." A high block left between two grabens is called a **horst**. *Horst* is also a German word and means "eyrie"—the kind of nest that birds of prey build on mountaintops or cliffs.

That's Amazing!

• On the Alpine Fault in New Zealand, the 1-billion-year-old rocks of the Australian Plate now lie alongside 300-million-year-old rocks on the Pacific Plate. The rocks were once hundreds of miles apart but were gradually brought together as a result of movement along the fault.
• Within 30 million years, the eastern side of the Great Rift Valley will probably separate from the rest of Africa, forming a new island and ocean.

Pathfinder

• There are major fault lines in many parts of the world. Find out if one lies near you on pages 74–75.
• Plate movements along the San Andreas Fault have caused many major earthquakes in California. Read more about them on pages 96–97.
• Have you ever experienced an earthquake? Discover what it feels like on pages 86–87.

GREAT RIFT VALLEY
Plate movements are slowly tearing eastern Africa apart. Rising currents have created an enormous fault called the Great Rift Valley. It extends 2,500 miles (4,025 km) from the Red Sea to Mozambique. The valley contains many volcanoes and hot springs.

HANDS ON
Cake Movements

You can use a layer cake to understand fault movements.

❶ Buy or make a rectangular layer cake, preferably one that is not too soft or messy. Cut the cake in half and then cut one half into quarters. Place the quarters on a flat base and push them in opposite directions. This is a lateral fault.

❷ Take the other half of the cake and cut through it at an angle. Follow the diagrams at the top of the opposite page to make a normal and a reverse fault. Practice until you know which fault is which. Then you can eat your cake!

Rift valley

Thrust faults

RIFT VALLEYS
When a continent is pulled apart by opposing plate movements, parallel faults form. The land between the faults may collapse, forming a wide valley called a rift valley. The steep walls of the valley are known as fault scarps, and the sunken land is called a graben.

THRUST FAULTS
Thrust faults form when plate movements push a layer of rock across the top of another layer at a low angle. Here, subduction has thrust part of the seafloor over the continent. Similar processes created the Japan Alps and the Appalachian Mountains in the U.S.A.

Bora-Bora, French Polynesia
(10 million years old)

Lord Howe Island, Australia
(7 million years old)

Molokini, Hawaii,
U.S.A. (4,000 years old)

Hot Spots

AT MANY PLACES and times in Earth's history, a region of hotter rock, called a hot spot, has formed deep in the mantle. This hot rock rises, forming a column called a thermal plume. The plume material melts to form magma, which moves up through the lithosphere like a blowtorch, forcing lava onto the surface and forming a volcano.

Because plates are always on the move, hot spots usually create chains of volcanoes. As the first volcano grows, it is carried away from the hot spot, and another volcano grows in its place. This process may continue for tens or even hundreds of millions of years, creating lines of volcanoes linked like the posts in a fence. Eventually, the plate may carry the hot-spot volcanoes to a subduction zone, where they are pulled back into the mantle and destroyed. Sometimes a hot spot beneath an ocean ridge can create a concentration of volcanoes in a rift valley. That was how Iceland was formed in the North Atlantic.

Hot spots can occur almost anywhere. They can create undersea mountain ranges, oceanic islands, or continental volcanoes, and the resulting volcanic chains may cross sea or land. In addition to Iceland, hot spots formed the Hawaiian and Galápagos islands in the Pacific Ocean, Réunion Island in the Indian Ocean, and the Yellowstone plateau in the United States.

HOT-SPOT REMNANTS

The spectacular Glasshouse Mountains in Queensland, Australia, are the remains of an old continental hot-spot chain. Twenty-five million years of wear and tear have eroded the softer rock, leaving only the hard cores of lava that filled the volcanoes' vents.

Coral atolls

Eroded, extinct volcanoes

Active "shield" volcano above hot spot

New volcano forming

Magma chamber

Feeder channel

Mantle melting in thermal plume

Word Builders

• Hot spots usually form low, wide volcanoes. These are known as **shield volcanoes** because, especially from above, they look like the shields that warriors once used in battle.
• An **atoll** is a coral island that encircles a lagoon. "Atoll" comes from *atolou,* a word used for this type of island in the Maldives in the Indian Ocean.

That's Amazing!

• Measured from seafloor to peak, hot-spot volcano Mauna Loa on Hawaii is the world's tallest mountain. It is nearly 6 miles (over 9 km) high— far taller than Mount Everest, the tallest mountain on land.
• A hot spot now under Marion Island in the southern Indian Ocean has been erupting for almost 185 million years.

Pathfinder

• Scientists now think that hot patches on the outside of Earth's core may be the source of hot spots. Learn about the core on pages 72–73.
• Vast hot-spot lava flows, called flood basalts, cover huge areas of the globe. Find out more on pages 112–13.

THE HOT-SPOT CYCLE

This diagram illustrates the birth, life, and death of hot-spot volcanoes. At the front, active volcanoes are erupting above the hot spot. Behind lie older volcanoes that have been worn down by erosion. Those whose rims are fringed with coral are called atolls. Those that lie underwater are called seamounts. The oldest seamounts are sliding into a subduction trench, slowly returning to Earth's fiery interior.

Seamount

Continental plate

Subduction zone

Direction of plate movement

Oceanic plate

THE LINKS IN THE CHAIN

When magma first bursts through a plate, so much lava floods out that, within a million years, it may be deeper than the Grand Canyon and wider than Greenland. But then the flow eases and smaller volcanoes form.

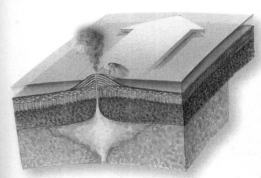

First, a single volcano forms above the hot spot, growing in size as the lava builds up. However, as the plate moves, it carries the volcano away from the hot spot.

After millions of years, the volcano separates from the hot spot, its lava supply is cut off, and it becomes extinct. A new active volcano then forms above the hot spot.

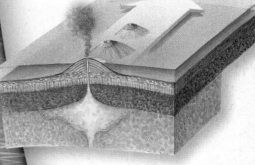

In this way, the chain of volcanoes continues to grow in the direction of the plate movement. But if the hot spot fades, the chain of volcanoes stops growing.

HANDS ON
Homemade Hot Spot

❶ Take a large sheet of cardboard and punch a line of four or five holes in it.

❷ Ask a friend to hold a tube of toothpaste under the first hole and squeeze gently. As your friend squeezes the tube, slowly move the cardboard so that the other holes pass over the tube. Watch what happens.

As you move the holes over the tube, a line of blobs appears on the card. These are your hot-spot volcanoes. The toothpaste seeps through the cardboard in the same way that magma bursts through a plate to form hot-spot volcanoes.

Earthquakes

AS PLATES MOVE, some rocks are pulled apart and others are pushed together. Strain builds up in the rocks until they suddenly crack and shift. This sudden movement creates vibrations that travel through the ground. We call these vibrations earthquakes. Earthquakes shake the ground up and down and from side to side. Large quakes can cause severe damage and claim many lives. Because of this, scientists called seismologists study earthquakes to try to understand their causes. From these studies, seismologists have learned a great deal about Earth's crust and its interior. But so far, they are unable to predict when an earthquake will occur.

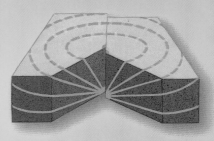

page **86** Where do earthquakes begin?

Do you know how to create shock waves?

Go to ON SHAKY GROUND.

page **88** Earthquakes under the sea can create huge waves. What are they called?

How can dogs help after a major earthquake?

Go to AFTER THE QUAKE.

page **90** What kind of seismic wave moves the land from side to side?

Scientists use machines called seismometers to measure earthquakes. How would you make your own seismometer?

Go to MONITORING EARTHQUAKES.

page **92** What kinds of buildings resist earthquakes best?

If you live in an earthquake zone, you should learn how to protect yourself. What should you have ready for emergencies?

Go to **PREPARING FOR EARTHQUAKES.**

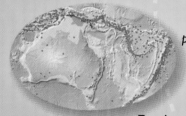

page **94** Most earthquakes occur at the edges of tectonic plates. Is there an earthquake zone near you?

Earthquakes are measured using the Richter Scale. How does this scale work?

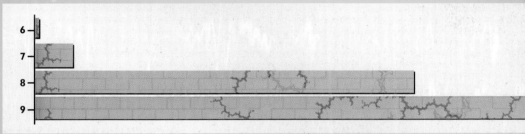

Go to **MAJOR EARTHQUAKES.**

page **96** Why do earthquakes occur regularly along the west coast of the United States?

What happened to this freeway near Los Angeles?

Go to **CALIFORNIA.**

page **98** The highest mountain in Japan is also a volcano. What is it called?

Japan has many volcanoes, and experiences regular earthquakes and occasional tsunamis. Do you know why?

Go to **JAPAN.**

Epicenter

Hypocenter

On Shaky Ground

YOU ARE AT HOME, sitting on the sofa, watching TV. Suddenly, you feel the sofa move. You notice the lights swinging and the windows rattling. Objects fall off shelves. You feel like you are on a boat at sea. Fortunately, the movement ceases after a few minutes, and calm returns.

You have just experienced an earthquake. Hundreds of tremors like this shake different parts of the world every day, and many people have experienced them. Fewer, less fortunate people have found themselves at the center of a major quake. This can be a terrifying experience. Inside buildings, ceilings collapse, furniture is tossed around, and windows shatter. Outside, the ground heaves violently. Trees and telephone poles fall. Pipes, drains, and electrical wiring are torn apart.

Just how badly a quake hits depends on its magnitude, how deep it is, and its distance from you. The hypocenter is where the quake begins, usually when rocks suddenly shift along a fault line. The epicenter is the point on Earth's surface directly above the hypocenter. As shock waves spread out from here, they decrease in strength. So, the farther you are from the epicenter, the better. The effects of the quake also depend on the type of ground it hits. Strong bedrock resists shaking, but soft, loose ground shakes violently and may even turn into a muddy liquid, a process called liquefaction.

OFF TRACK

The sideways movement of earthquake waves often shows up in railroad tracks. These tracks in Kobe, Japan, were buckled by snaking surface waves after the main shock waves passed through during a major earthquake in 1995.

THE MERCALLI SCALE

In 1883, Italian scientist Giuseppe Mercalli created a 12-point scale for measuring earthquakes. It is based on the observed effects of a tremor on buildings and people.

LEVELS 1-3

At level 1, the lowest level, tremors go unnoticed. At level 2, people sleeping on upper stories feel movement. At level 3, hanging objects start to swing.

LEVELS 4-5

At level 4, objects rattle and standing cars rock. At level 5, everyone feels the movement, liquids slosh, pictures move, and doors swing.

Word Builders

• **Hypocenter,** which is where a quake begins beneath Earth's surface, comes from the Greek *kentres,* meaning "center or location," and the prefix *hypo,* meaning "under." **Epicenter,** which is the point on Earth's surface directly above the hypocenter, comes from *kentres* and the prefix *epi,* meaning "over."
• **Tremor** is from the Latin *tremoris,* meaning "a trembling or quaking."

That's Amazing!

The biggest earthquakes of all were caused by giant meteorites that struck our planet. One collision 65 million years ago in the Yucatán Peninsula may have caused the extinction of dinosaurs. This bang was so big that a giant shock wave rippled right through Earth.

Pathfinder

• The trouble isn't over when the shaking stops. Find out about the aftereffects of quakes on pages 88–89.
• No one can say for certain when a quake is going to occur. But by studying ground movements, scientists can warn if one is likely. Go to pages 90–91.
• Major quakes have devastated many parts of the globe. Find out where and when the biggest tremors have occurred on pages 94–95.

QUAKE!

Major earthquakes are most destructive when they occur near densely populated cities. Most of the danger comes from falling buildings. But bridges and freeways can also collapse, killing drivers and passengers. Broken gas pipes and electrical wires can set off dangerous fires. Outside of cities, quakes can also trigger large landslides.

HANDS ON

Shock Tactics

You can simulate seismic waves by using a small table, a hammer, and sand.

❶ Sprinkle a handful of sand on one side of the table. Strike the table about 3–4 inches (7.5–10 cm) away from the sand with the hammer. Watch the sand jump as the shock waves hit it.

❷ Now hit the table about 8 inches (20 cm) away from the sand. The sand will jump, but not so high.

In the same way, the farther away a place is from the epicenter of an earthquake, the less the ground is affected by seismic waves.

LEVELS 6-7
At level 6, walking is difficult, windows break, pictures fall, and plaster cracks. At level 7, people fall over and chimneys crack.

LEVELS 8-9
At level 8, cars are hard to control, walls crumble, and chimneys fall. At level 9, some buildings collapse, the ground cracks, and pipes split.

LEVELS 10-12
Buildings are reduced to rubble, and landslides occur on hills. Rail tracks bend, and pipes are destroyed. At level 12, destruction is total.

Paramedics

Sniffer dog

Infrared camera

After the Quake

MAJOR EARTHQUAKES are followed by chaos, particularly when they strike cities. Emergency sirens wail, buildings crumble, and trapped and injured people call for help. Rescue teams rush to aid the injured. They use cranes to shift debris and sniffer dogs to locate trapped survivors.

Rescuers and survivors often have to cope with aftershocks. These are the additional tremors that follow a major quake. They are caused by the release of pressure still present in the crust after the first jolt. Usually, aftershocks are weaker than the main quake, but occasionally they are even stronger, and they may continue for a long time. For example, the aftershocks that followed a major earthquake at New Madrid, Missouri, U.S.A., in 1811 lasted for more than a year. Some were just as severe as the main quake, and many people had to move out of the area altogether.

In mountainous areas, quakes may be followed by landslides and avalanches, which may cause further damage to buildings and cut road and rail connections. Earthquakes that occur near the coast can trigger tsunamis. These are waves that spread across the ocean at the speed of a jet plane, growing in size as they approach shallower water close to the shore.

OUT OF CONTROL

After a large earthquake, ruptured gas mains often catch fire. Here, firefighters struggle to contain a blaze following the 1994 Northridge quake near Los Angeles, California, U.S.A. If fires like this are not brought under control quickly, they can be devastating.

WAVES OF TERROR

A towering tsunami is a terrifying sight. As the wave reaches land, it collapses, smashing coastal buildings and hurling boats onto land. Often, tsunamis are far more destructive than the earthquakes that caused them.

INSIDE STORY
A Land Transformed

The prolonged aftershocks that followed the 1811 New Madrid earthquake in Missouri, U.S.A., completely transformed the local landscape. Fissures opened up, coal dust and sulfurous fumes from coal mines filled the air, and whole fields and forests disappeared under water. Rivers changed course, forming new swamps and lakes, among them Reelfoot Lake in Tennessee. One of the aftershocks rumbled all the way to such distant places as Washington, D.C., and Boston, Massachusetts. Nearby, in Kentucky, naturalist John Audubon observed that "the ground rose and fell in successive furrows like the ruffled waters of a lake. The earth waved like a field of corn before a breeze." Although there was tremendous damage to land, there were few casualties because the area was not heavily populated.

Word Builders

• **Tsunami** comes from a Japanese word that translates as "great harbor wave." The name relates to the fact that these waves cause little disturbance until they reach shallow areas of water such as harbors. Tsunamis are different from tidal waves, which are caused by powerful tides and hurricanes.

That's Amazing!

• On July 9, 1958, an avalanche that landed in Lituya Bay, Alaska, U.S.A., created the largest recorded tsunami. It was 1,720 feet (524 m) high—bigger than the tallest building on Earth.
• A tsunami as high as a six-story building hit the port of Arica, Chile, on August 13, 1868. It carried a navy ship, the U.S.S. *Wateree*, 2 miles (3 km) inland, leaving it and its crew unharmed but high and dry. The ship never sailed again.

Pathfinder

• After a major quake in 1906, the city of San Francisco in the U.S.A. was almost totally destroyed by fire. Learn more on pages 96–97.
• The New Madrid quake was unusual because it occurred in the middle of a plate. Find out why most quakes occur at plate edges on pages 74–75.
• Japan has suffered numerous quakes and tsunamis. Turn to pages 98–99.

CATCHING THE WAVES

Most tsunamis form when an earthquake occurs offshore, disturbing the seafloor. The resulting waves spread outward at up to 500 miles (800 km) an hour and rise to great heights when they reach shallow water. The Hawaiian Islands in the Pacific Ocean have been hit several times by tsunamis.

In 1946, an earthquake in the Aleutians created a tsunami that destroyed a lighthouse on Unimak Island. The tsunami swept across the Pacific Ocean, arriving five hours later in Hawaii, where waves up to 30 feet (9 m) high killed 159 people, 96 of them in the city of Hilo.

Hilo was devastated again in 1960 by a tsunami caused by an earthquake in Chile. The wave killed 60 people in Hawaii and 120 in the Philippines and Japan. Afterward, buildings in Hilo were moved away from the shore, and work began on the development of a tsunami warning system.

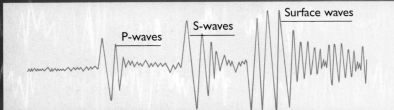

SEISMOLOGICAL RECORD

A seismogram is a visual record of an earthquake. On the one shown at left, the P-waves arrive as close-spaced vibrations. Some time later, the larger S-wave tremors occur. Finally, broad surface waves arrive. These cause the most damage on Earth's surface.

Monitoring Earthquakes

BECAUSE BIG EARTHQUAKES can be so destructive, people have been trying for centuries to find ways of predicting them. The study of earthquakes is known as seismology, and people who study quakes are called seismologists.

In 1876, two Italian seismologists, Luigi Palmeri and Filippo Cecchi, invented the seismometer. This machine contained a pendulum attached to a pillar. If the pillar shook, a pen at the end of the pendulum recorded the tremors on paper. Today, scientists install modern seismometers and other instruments in areas that are prone to earthquakes. They collect and study the information recorded by the instruments at observatories. By exchanging information with scientists at other observatories, they can compare the travel times of seismic waves and their strengths at different points. This helps them to locate an earthquake's epicenter and hypocenter.

By studying these records, scientists learn to recognize patterns that may indicate a buildup to a big tremor. But many factors influence the timing and strength of an earthquake, and even with today's sophisticated equipment, seismologists can only state that a big one will probably, but not certainly, occur.

MONITORING SYSTEMS

In earthquake zones, seismologists position a variety of instruments along the fault line to measure ground movements or other changes that may indicate that a quake is about to take place. Most of the instruments operate automatically and send digital data to observatories via phone lines.

HANDS ON
Tracing the Tremors

You can make your own seismometer and use it to record tremors.

1. Fill a large jar with water and replace the lid. Place the jar on a roll of paper on a table. Attach a pen to the side of the jar with tape, so that the point just touches the paper. Slowly pull the paper out from under the jar. The pen should make a straight line on the paper.

2. Keep pulling the paper out, but ask a friend to shake the table gently from side to side. The line will form squiggles like P-waves. Shaking the table a little harder will create larger squiggles, just like S-waves. If your friend then jolts the table from side to side, even bigger, longer squiggles will appear on the paper. These are like surface waves. Now you have your own seismogram!

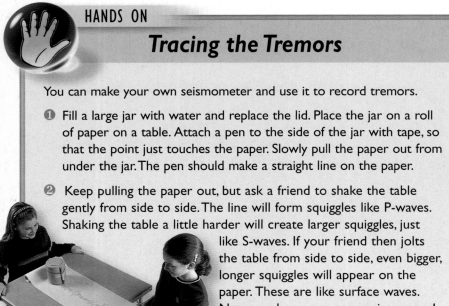

KEY TO SYMBOLS

GPS

Seismometer

Creepmeter

Magnetometer

P-WAVES

The first waves to arrive during an earthquake are called P-waves, or primary waves. P-waves compress (push together) and dilate (pull apart) the rocks in the ground.

S-WAVES

S-waves, or secondary waves, move more slowly than P-waves. As they pass through the ground, they move rock layers up and down and from side to side.

Word Builders

• **Seismology** comes from the Greek word *seismos,* for "earthquake," and the Greek word *logos,* meaning "branch of knowledge." **Seismometer** comes from *seismos* and another Greek word, *metron,* meaning "measurement." **Seismogram** includes yet another Greek word, *grammon,* meaning a "shake" or "line."

That's Amazing!

In some cases, animals have detected earthquakes before they happen. In 1975, in Lianong Province in China, seismologists noticed mice and rabbits leaving their holes and snakes emerging from hibernation. They took this as an indication of an imminent earthquake and asked thousands of people to leave their homes. The next day, a large tremor destroyed most of the province's buildings.

Pathfinder

• Because scientists cannot predict the exact time and place an earthquake will occur, we must take other precautions to protect ourselves. Learn more on pages 92–93.
• Scientists who study volcanoes are known as volcanologists. Find out more about what they do on pages 114–15.

GPS

Global Positioning Systems receive signals from satellites, which are then transmitted to an observatory. The signals record the exact location of the GPS. A change in its position indicates that the crust has shifted.

KEEPING WATCH

At a seismic observatory, seismologists gather information from the instruments in the field and monitor it for any significant changes. If anything suggests that an earthquake is about to occur, they warn emergency services.

SEISMOMETER

Seismometers record vibrations in the ground. Today's seismometers are incredibly sensitive and can pick up even the tiniest tremors. Many, like the ones pictured here, are powered by solar energy.

CREEPMETER

A creepmeter measures ground movement, or creep. It consists of a wire stretched between two rods on either side of a fault. A weight at one end of the wire lines up with a scale. If the fault moves, the measurement changes.

MAGNETOMETER

Earth's magnetic field changes as the strain in rocks varies, so a change in magnetism may warn that plates are on the move. Magnetism is measured using a magnetometer. It can distinguish between general changes and those caused by plate movements.

LOVE WAVES

P- and S-waves are followed by surface waves, which only affect Earth's surface. One type, called Love waves, makes the surface move from side to side like a snake.

RAYLEIGH WAVES

The second type of surface waves, known as Rayleigh waves, cause the ground to rise and fall like the surface of the ocean when a large wave passes through.

Helmet and
sturdy boots

First-aid
kit

Water, canned food,
and can opener

Preparing for Earthquakes

BECAUSE NO FOOLPROOF method for predicting plate
movements exists, people living in earthquake-prone
areas must always be ready to deal with disaster. Do you
live in an earthquake danger zone? If so, you should
know how to prepare for a quake, and what to do when
the ground starts shaking.

You and your family can make your house a safer place
by securing bookshelves to walls and placing heavy objects
on or near the floor. You can also learn and practice drills and
safety techniques that might save your life during a big
tremor. Lifesaving methods include first-aid, mouth-to-mouth
resuscitation, and fire extinguishing. Breathing from special
bags that are filled with oxygen can help you avoid smoke
inhalation. For people living in earthquake zones, these drills
are as important as learning to swim or cross the road safely.

Governments in places that are prone to earthquakes
can help protect their citizens. They can plan new building
and road developments carefully, making sure that schools,
hospitals, and emergency centers are built on stable land.
They can also make sure that new buildings include features
that make them resistant to earthquakes. These include
strong but flexible steel frames and deep, solid foundations.
Such features can save many lives if a disaster occurs.

Flexible upper
stories

Fire-resistant
materials used
throughout

All equipment
bolted to walls and
designed to resist
upward and
sideways movement

Pyramid shape
has low center
of gravity, which
resists shaking

HANDS ON

Make and Shake

Scientists and architects can see how well new buildings will resist
tremors by building a scale model and placing it on a shake table.
This machine shakes the model just as an earthquake would. You
can build your own simple shake table.

❶ Use a card table, nine medium-size balloons, books, and toy
bricks. Inflate the balloons, but don't blow them up all the way.
Place the table upside down on top of the balloons.

❷ Use the books and blocks
to build different kinds of
structures on the underside
of the table, as shown.

❸ Shake the table legs
gently. What happens? Now
shake the table harder.
Which structures collapse
first? Do some shapes resist
falling better than others?

Flashlight
and whistle

Radio and
batteries

Word Builders

- Preparing for **disasters** is essential in earthquake zones. You can't count on a lucky star to protect you. The word "disaster" actually comes from the Italian word *disastro*, which means "without (*dis-*) a lucky star (*astro*)."
- **Building** comes from the Indo-European word *bheue*, meaning "to be, exist, or grow." The Old English verb form *byldan* meant "to construct a house," but eventually the meaning grew to include any structure.

That's Amazing!

- Two similar-size quakes hit Armenia in 1988 and San Francisco, U.S.A., in 1989. The Armenian quake killed 25,000 people. In California, only 62 people died, mainly because of safer building practices.
- Ever since the Great Kanto quake in 1923, everyone in Tokyo, Japan, takes part in an annual earthquake drill. It occurs on September 1, the anniversary of the quake, which caused 140,000 deaths.

Pathfinder

- Scientists still can't predict earthquakes, but they can detect warning signs. Find out more on pages 90–91.
- San Francisco suffers frequent quakes because it lies on the San Andreas Fault. Learn about this fault on pages 80–81.
- The 1989 Loma Prieta quake was the largest in California in recent years. Read all about it on pages 96–97.
- Japan is one of the world's most quake-prone regions. Go to pages 98–99.

QUAKE-PROOF

Earthquakes occur regularly in San Francisco, U.S.A., so many of the city's buildings have been built to withstand large tremors. The Transamerica Pyramid was completed in 1972 and includes many features that help it absorb or resist shaking. During the 1989 Loma Prieta earthquake, the Pyramid shook for more than a minute and swayed one foot (0.3 m), but remained undamaged.

Emergency stairways built on western wing, eastern wing holds the elevators

White quartz covering reinforced with steel rods, designed to allow sideways movement

Rigid lower floors

20 four-legged support pyramids between second and fifth floors

Deep foundations firmly attached to solid rock move with tremors

BUILT TO LAST

Pagodas are pyramid-shaped temples found in many parts of Asia, with some dating back nearly a thousand years. Their form and structure make them resistant to earthquakes. Normally, the roofs are attached to a rigid central column. This column may sway during a tremor, but it is unlikely to fall down. Furthermore, the roofs can flex up and down without collapsing.

LIFESAVING LESSONS

Japan has regular tremors that are a serious threat to its large population. From a young age, children learn what to do during a quake. In particularly dangerous areas, they routinely practice drills and carry safety gear such as helmets. These children are learning to "duck and cover."

GETTING READY

If you live in an earthquake zone, you should know what to do before, during, and after a tremor.

Make your home a safer place by fastening furniture and appliances to the floor or walls. Keep an earthquake kit handy. It should contain the items shown at the top and bottom of the opposite page.

When a quake occurs, move away from windows and doors. If possible, you should "duck and cover." Duck under a sturdy desk, table, or bed. Hold on tight with one arm and cover your face with the other.

As you move around after a quake, watch out for broken glass, crumbling masonry, and exposed pipes or wires. If you smell gas, quickly ask an adult to turn off the main supply at once.

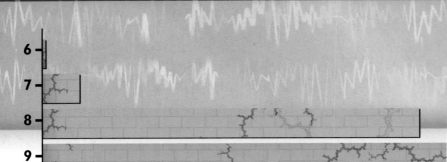

6 –	
7 –	
8 –	
9 –	

GIANT STEPS
Each step on the Richter Scale represents a tenfold increase in severity. That means that magnitude 7 is 10 times stronger than magnitude 6, magnitude 8 is 100 times stronger than magnitude 6, and magnitude 9 is 1,000 times stronger than magnitude 6.

Major Earthquakes

IN MANY AREAS where people live, an earthquake could strike at any moment. But you're much more likely to feel the Earth move in some places than in others. The shakiest parts of our planet lie at the boundaries of tectonic plates. Along these collision zones, quakes occur regularly as plates squeeze together, scrape edges, and dive beneath each other.

But earthquakes can also occur in the middle of plates, where you would least expect it. Rocks lying along an ancient fault line may suddenly shift. Shock waves from a plate that is subducting at a shallow angle may rise to the surface far inland. Events like this have caused huge tremors in places far from collision zones, such as Charleston in South Carolina, U.S.A., and Tennant Creek in central Australia.

Scientists compare the magnitude, or strength, of earthquakes using the Richter Scale. This was devised in the 1930s by an American seismologist named Charles Richter. The scale has no maximum, but with each step the severity of a quake increases 10 times, and the amount of energy released is at least 30 times greater. Fortunately, quakes of magnitude 8 or more rarely happen. About 1,200 magnitude 5 quakes occur each year. But in the same period, only 115 magnitude 6, 11 magnitude 7, and 1 or 2 magnitude 8 quakes will also happen.

7.4 IZMIT, TURKEY, 1999
On August 17, a sudden movement along the Anatolian Fault caused one of the century's biggest quakes. It reduced thousands of buildings to rubble and left at least 17,000 people dead.

EUROPE

Bucharest, 1977 **7.2**
Izmit, 1999 **7.4**

Northwest **7.7**
Iran, 1990 **7.7**

Al Asnam, 1980 **7.3**

Tabas, 1972

AFRICA

INSIDE STORY
Rising from the Ruins

One of the worst earthquakes in history occurred in Lisbon, Portugal, on November 1, 1755. Estimated at more than 8.7 on the Richter Scale, it hit the country's capital and main port at 9:40 AM. Englishman Thomas Chase described the quake vividly in letters to his mother. He climbed on top of his house to find out what was happening and saw "…shocks of the earthquake, which were attended with a tumbling sort of motion, like the waves of the sea." As he watched, the house collapsed beneath him. Amazingly, Chase survived, crawled from the rubble, and was rescued by friends. He was one of the lucky ones. More than 60,000 lives were lost, and a splendid European city was reduced to rubble.

THE BIG ONES
This map pinpoints some of the largest recorded quakes. Note how many have occurred along plate edges. The main danger zones lie around the Pacific Plate, where it collides with the American and Asian plates, and in southern Europe and central Asia, where the African, Arabian, and Indian plates collide with the Eurasian and Anatolian plates.

Word Builders

• **Magnitude** is a term for the measured size of an earthquake. It comes from the Latin word *magnitudo*, meaning "size" or "greatness."
• Earthquakes often create large cracks in the ground called **fissures**. The word "fissure" comes from the Latin word *fissus*, meaning "split."

That's Amazing!

• A few earthquakes are so severe that needles shoot off the seismographs that are recording them. One such earthquake occurred in Assam, India, in 1950. It had a magnitude of about 9 on the Richter Scale.
• The 1964 Alaska quake released about 200,000 megatons of energy—400 times the total energy of all the nuclear bombs ever exploded.

Pathfinder

• Discover what it feels like to experience a major earthquake on pages 86–87.
• The tsunami created by the quake in Chile in 1960 killed 61 people in Hawaii. Find out more on page 89.
• Most volcanic eruptions also occur along plate edges. Go to pages 116–17.

8.2 TANGSHAN, CHINA, 1976
A series of horrific quakes measuring between 7.1 and 8.2 stunned the residents of Tangshan in China on July 28–29, 1976. There were no warning shocks from the earthquake focus, which lay 7 miles (11 km) below the ground. About 242,000 people died.

8.4 ALASKA, U.S.A., 1964
A quake measuring 8.4 hit the city of Anchorage and Kodiak Island on March 27. Tsunamis swamped the harbors, fissures appeared in the land, buildings collapsed, and oil storage tanks caught fire. Miraculously, only 131 people died.

8.1 MEXICO CITY, MEXICO, 1985
On September 19, a quake measuring 8.1 rocked this city of 18 million people. Two days later, an aftershock of 7.6 struck. More than 10,000 people died.

Alaska, 1964 **8.4**

San Francisco, 1989 **7.1**

NORTH AMERICA

ASIA

8.2 Tangshan, 1976
7.5 Niigata, 1964
7.2 Kobe, 1995

7.7 Yunnan, 1970
7.6 Taiwan, 1999

7.8 Mindanao, 1976

Mexico City, 1985 **8.1**
Guatemala City, 1976 **7.5**

Northern Peru, 1970 **7.8**

SOUTH AMERICA

AUSTRALIA

7.1 Inangahua, 1968

Valdivia, 1960 **8.3**

KEY TO SYMBOLS

· Earthquake

7.0 Major earthquakes since 1960 with a magnitude of 7 or more (on the Richter Scale)

8.3 VALDIVIA, CHILE, 1960
One of the most powerful series of quakes ever recorded shook southern Chile between May 21 and May 30, 1960. It caused the deaths of 5,000 people, and created an enormous tsunami that swept across the Pacific Ocean.

Fence posts shifted by quake at Tomales Bay, 1906

Freeway destroyed by quake at Northridge near Los Angeles, 1994

California

IN CALIFORNIA, U.S.A., there are tiny tremors every day. Destructive earthquakes rock the state, on average, once a year. Most California quakes are caused by movement along the San Andreas Fault. To the east of the fault lies the North American Plate. To the west lies the Pacific Plate. The Pacific Plate moves slowly northwest as the North American Plate slides southeast. As the plates grind against each other, sudden releases of tension create shock waves.

Since record-keeping began, three massive quakes, or "Big Ones," have hit California—Tejon Pass in 1857 (magnitude 7.9), Owens Valley in 1872 (7.8), and Tomales Bay in 1906 (8.3). The most devastating was the 1906 quake, which destroyed much of San Francisco. More recent shockers include Whittier Narrows in 1987 (6.1), Loma Prieta in 1989 (7.1), and Northridge in 1994 (6.8).

Further major quakes are a certainty. Seismologists estimate that over the next 30 years people in California have a two-in-three chance of experiencing a magnitude 7 or greater earthquake. The state's citizens are therefore working hard to improve their fault monitoring, construct more earthquake-resistant buildings, and expand earthquake education programs. Come the next Big One, Californians will be better prepared than ever.

PORTRAIT OF A QUAKE
In June 1992, a satellite used radar to record a magnitude 7.5 quake centered on the Landers Fault in eastern California. In this image, the black line is the fault. The colored wavy lines show vertical ground movement. The closer the lines are to each other, the greater the movement.

Thirty seconds after the quake started, the shock waves hit San Francisco. A section of the upper deck of the Bay Bridge, which links San Francisco and Oakland, collapsed onto the lower deck, killing one person.

In San Francisco's Marina District, houses built on soft, sandy land shook for 15 seconds. Then several collapsed. The sandy soil bubbled like boiling porridge, water pipes cracked, and gas mains caught fire.

ACTION REPLAY
Just after 5 PM on October 17, 1989, a powerful quake jolted northern California. From the epicenter at Loma Prieta, in the Santa Cruz Mountains, shock waves tore north through San Francisco, east to the Sierra Nevada mountains, and south through Monterey. The quake caused $6 billion of damage and killed 62 people.

Oakland

San Francisco

SCENES FROM A SHATTERED CITY

The most devastating California quake occurred on the morning of April 18, 1906, when a 250-mile (400-km) section of the San Andreas Fault, between Point Arena in the north and San Juan Bautista in the south, suddenly shifted. The epicenter lay 40 miles (64 km) north of San Francisco, at Tomales Bay. In San Francisco, as many as 3,000 people died. About 20 percent of the city's buildings collapsed and almost 80 percent of the city was affected by the fires that followed.

The brick walls of San Francisco's city hall collapsed, and the building was gutted by fire. Only its metal frame remained. A new hall was completed in 1915.

Word Builders

- **Loma Prieta** is a Spanish term that means "Dark Hill." After the 1989 earthquake, the hill was frequently referred to as the "Dark Rolling Mountain."
- In North America, an earthquake is sometimes called a **temblor**. This word comes from the Spanish *temblar,* meaning "to tremble."

That's Amazing!

- Tens of thousands of quakes occur in California each year, but only one in every 10,000 does any damage.
- During the Owens Valley earthquake in 1872, the land along the fault shifted 20 feet (6 m) sideways and rose 23 feet (7 m).

Pathfinder

- In parts of California, the San Andreas Fault appears as a giant scar in the landscape. Go to pages 80–81.
- Find out how scientists monitor earth tremors on pages 90–91.
- Most new buildings in San Francisco are built to withstand large earthquakes. See pages 92–93.

INSIDE STORY

Strike One!

October 17, 1989, was a crucial day for sports fans in San Francisco. A World Series baseball game between the San Francisco Giants and the Oakland A's was due to take place at the city's Candlestick Park. Just before 5 PM, an eager crowd of 60,000 people took their seats in the stadium. At 5:04 PM, the fans suddenly felt their seats shake and saw the floodlights sway. Earthquake! People screamed as chunks of concrete and steel began to fall. But the stadium resisted the shaking. Amazingly, no one was injured. The game, however, was abandoned. Result: earthquake 1, baseball 0.

At the Pacific Garden Shopping Mall in Santa Cruz, shops built on soft river muds swayed wildly and knocked each other down. An old hotel in the mall crashed down onto a department store below.

At the Loma Prieta epicenter, huge cracks appeared in roads, trees swayed violently, and several houses collapsed.

As the seismic waves spread out from the epicenter, the magnitude of the quake gradually decreased.

At Big Sur, entire hillsides collapsed, sending tons of rocks crashing onto the road below.

5

6

San Jose

SAN ANDREAS FAULT

Loma Prieta

7

Santa Cruz

Monterey

Hypocenter

Big Sur

Huge tremors reduced much of the city to rubble. Wooden buildings, which are flexible, resisted the shaking better than stone structures.

After the quake, survivors faced another danger— fire. Toppled stoves and broken gas mains started blazes all over the city. They burned for four days, forcing thousands to flee their homes.
When the water mains broke, firefighters had to bring the blazes under control using seawater.

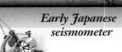

Mount Fuji volcano

Early Japanese seismometer

Japan

UNDER THE ISLANDS of Japan, three of Earth's plates jostle for position. To the southeast, the Philippine Plate slides beneath the Eurasian Plate. To the east, the Pacific Plate dives under the Eurasian Plate and the Philippine Plate as well. As a result of all of this shoving, diving, and sliding, Japan's 125 million inhabitants experience regular earthquakes, volcanic eruptions, and tsunamis.

Most of the country's quakes are caused by movement along faults that spread outward from the subduction zones. Others are due to volcanic activity. The largest quakes (magnitude 8 to 8.5) occur offshore and in central southern Japan. The far north is the country's safest region, as earthquakes here rarely reach magnitudes of 6.5 to 7.

The Japanese have kept records of earthquakes for about 2,000 years. Ancient Japanese legends suggested that Earth's tremors were caused by the thrashing of a giant catfish (the *namazu*) that lived underground. Today, Japanese seismologists use the latest technology to monitor plate movements and computer models to predict quakes. They also operate highly effective public education programs and one of the world's best earthquake observation networks.

THAT SINKING FEELING
Many of Kobe's modern buildings were built to withstand earthquakes. But some built on unstable ground collapsed as tremors caused the water-logged soil to liquefy.

INSIDE STORY
As It Happened

In June 1948, American photographer Carl Mydans was working in Fukui, Japan. Shortly after he arrived in the city, a magnitude 7.3 quake struck while he was eating dinner. "The concrete floor just exploded. Tables and dishes flew into our faces and we were all hurled into a mad dance, bouncing about like popping corn." Mydans rushed outside with his camera. He photographed buildings as they collapsed, and survivors "pinned in their homes." Shocked by the disaster, which killed 3,500 people, he campaigned for the Japanese government to supply every household with an earthquake kit, containing an ax, a crowbar, and a pair of wirecutters.

A RUDE AWAKENING
At 5:46 AM on January 17, 1995, the citizens of Kobe were shaken from their beds by a magnitude 7.2 earthquake. The tremors destroyed 150,000 buildings and left more than 5,000 people dead. A long section of the Hanshin Expressway toppled over as concrete supports gave way.

IN THE HOT SEAT
Japan sits on the edge of the Pacific Plate. As this plate moves northwest, it crashes into several other plates, forming a chain of volcanoes and earthquake-prone lands called the Ring of Fire, shown here in red. The Ring includes more than half the world's volcanoes and causes more than half the world's earthquakes.

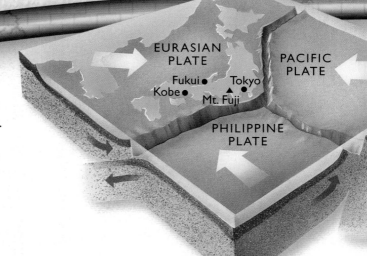

EURASIAN PLATE

PACIFIC PLATE

Fukui
Kobe
Mt. Fuji
Tokyo

PHILIPPINE PLATE

Word Builders

In Japanese legend, as long as the god Kashima keeps the **namazu**, or giant catfish, pinned down with a large stone, Japan is safe. But if Kashima allows the catfish to escape, it thrashes around and the ground trembles. Throughout history, artists have painted images of the catfish. These pictures, called **namazu-e**, are meant to bring good luck. They often have text that is supposed to cheer up earthquake survivors.

That's Amazing!

• Japan has 1,500 active faults. These have caused more than 400 major quakes in the last 1,000 years.
• On June 15, 1896, a tsunami struck southern Japan, demolishing coastal towns and killing 27,000 people. The wave passed undetected under a fleet of fishing boats out at sea. The fishermen returned to find their homes destroyed.

Pathfinder

• Subduction occurs as a thick plate forces a thinner plate down into the mantle. Learn more on pages 78–79.
• From an early age, Japanese children are shown how to protect themselves during earthquakes. Find out what they learn on page 93.
• To learn about major eruptions of some of Japan's active volcanoes, turn to pages 116–17.

FUELING THE FLAMES
Many of Kobe's traditional wooden houses caught fire, and more than 500 blazes flared up across the city.

DOUBLE TROUBLE
Both the Pacific Plate and the Philippine Plate subduct under Japan. The Pacific Plate moves at a rate of 4 inches (10 cm) per year and has dragged the ocean crust 325 miles (523 km) under the land. The Philippine Plate moves at half that speed and has sunk the seafloor 90 miles (145 km) below Japan. This double subduction front gives rise to many of Japan's earthquakes and volcanoes.

ON GUARD
Japan has many monitoring stations like this one. As soon as they detect a quake or eruption, they alert emergency services and disaster control centers.

Volcanoes

WHEN HEAT WITHIN Earth melts rocks, a hot, gooey liquid called magma forms. This liquid rises to the surface and bursts through weak zones in the crust, creating volcanoes. Every day, at every moment, a volcano is erupting somewhere in the world. Large or unexpected eruptions can be extremely dangerous and cause widespread destruction and loss of life. The main threats come from red-hot lava, poisonous gases, and clouds of ash. But eruptions can also trigger mudflows, avalanches, and floods. Because volcanoes are so destructive, volcanologists—the scientists who study volcanoes—try to determine when and how they might erupt.

page **102** What kind of eruption is this?

Go to UNDER THE VOLCANO.

page **104** Did you know that volcanoes make bombs?

Go to LAVA FLOWS.

page **106** Why would you need a gas mask near a volcano?

Go to ASH AND GAS.

page **108** Which volcano spread ash around the globe in 1991?

Go to AFTEREFFECTS.

page **110** Why do parts of Earth spout like a boiling kettle?

Go to GEYSERS AND HOT SPRINGS.

page **112** Would you recognize an ancient volcano if you saw one?

Go to VOLCANIC LANDSCAPES.

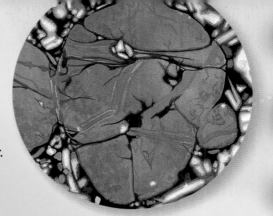

page **114** By studying lava under a microscope, scientists can learn about Earth's interior.

Go to VOLCANOLOGY.

page **116** On which Pacific island did the longest flank eruption in history occur?

Go to MAJOR ERUPTIONS.

page **118** How have volcanoes helped us to learn about ancient civilizations?

Go to THE MEDITERRANEAN.

page **120** Did you know that spreading along the Mid-Atlantic Ridge is tearing an island apart?

Go to ICELAND.

page **122** On May 18, 1980, one of the century's largest eruptions occurred in the U.S.A. What was the name of the volcano?

Go to WESTERN NORTH AMERICA.

page **124** Did you know that you can see traces of volcanic activity on the face of the Moon?

Go to EXTRATERRESTRIAL VOLCANOES.

Mount Etna,
Italy

Anak Krakatau,
Indonesia

Under the Volcano

FROM AFAR, a volcanic eruption may look exciting, even beautiful. But close up it is terrifying. You wouldn't want to be nearby when one occurs. So what are the signs that warn of an eruption? Often the ground rumbles, swells, and cracks. Gas seeps out of holes, and the stench of sulfur fills the air. Showers of rock spray out of pits in the ground, and lava oozes out of cracks. Hot springs bubble furiously. Animals become agitated—when they start leaving, so should you.

A small eruption may consist of little more than a belch of gas. But sometimes the gas throws up molten rock, creating a spray of lava like a fireworks display. As the pressure eases, the spray may dwindle to a steady stream of lava. Occasionally, if lava blocks the vent and a great deal of gas has built up beneath it, the eruption may hurl huge lumps of rock, giant blobs of lava, and vast amounts of dust and ash into the air.

Some eruptions are over in hours. Others continue for tens of years. Many are devastating. Torrents of lava or surges of pulverized rocks destroy everything in their path. Flying rocks can kill, and even gently falling ash and cinders can quickly bury plants, people, and buildings. Within hours, a volcano can transform a lush and lively landscape into a barren desert.

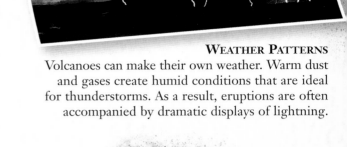

WEATHER PATTERNS
Volcanoes can make their own weather. Warm dust and gases create humid conditions that are ideal for thunderstorms. As a result, eruptions are often accompanied by dramatic displays of lightning.

INSIDE STORY
Diary of a Volcano

In late 1943, Masao Mimatsu, a postmaster at Subetsu in southern Hokkaido, Japan, felt tremors coming from a nearby volcano called Usu. Soon after, he noticed a new dome on the side of Usu. Intrigued, he began to make daily sketches of the new hill, which was called Showa-Shinzan. By the time the volcano stopped growing in September 1945, Mimatsu had a thick wad of sketches that provided one of the most complete records of an eruption ever made. The sketches have now been published in a book. If you flip its pages, Showa-Shinzan rises before your eyes.

Sept. 10, 1945

June 5, 1944

Fissure

Dike: a vertical channel of magma

Lava flow from side vent

Laccolith: a mass of magma that pushes rock layers upward

Sill: a sheet of magma that forms between layers of rock

CURTAINS OF FIRE
Long, vertical cracks in the crust are called fissures. When lava erupts through a fissure, it may form a spectacular red curtain. Fissures can stretch up to 17 miles (27 km) and eject enormous amounts of lava.

Word Builders

• When a volcano is erupting, it is said to be **active**. If it hasn't erupted for a long time but still shows signs of activity, it is said to be **dormant**. If no activity has occurred for thousands of years, the volcano is defined as **extinct**.
• The word **volcano** comes from the name of the Roman god of fire, Vulcan. He was said to live inside a crater on the island of Vulcano in Italy.

That's Amazing!

In February 1943, Dionisio Pulido, a farmer living at Paricutín in Mexico, heard strange rumblings in one of his fields. A few weeks later, he noticed smoke emerging from a hole. Next day, an ash cone 25 times his height covered the hole. A week later, a volcano as tall as a 40-story building covered the entire field. By September 1944, lava from the volcano had buried Dionisio's village.

Pathfinder

• Many volcanoes form above subduction zones. Turn to pages 78–79.
• Vulcanian, Plinian, and Peléean eruptions can all produce avalanches of rocks and ash called pyroclastic flows. Learn more on pages 106–07.
• The danger hasn't passed when the eruption stops. Go to pages 108–09.
• Which were the largest eruptions in history? Find out on pages 116–17.

Ash cloud

Lava erupts through crater

ANATOMY OF A VOLCANO

During an eruption, lava rushes up to the surface. Some erupts through vents and fissures, but some may remain underground, where it pushes into rock layers. These bodies of magma have different names, depending on their shape.

Pyroclastic flow: torrent of hot lava, ash, and gas

Lava rises through central vent

Extinct magma chamber

Magma rises from pool of molten rock called magma chamber

TYPES OF ERUPTIONS

Scientists use the following names to classify different kinds of eruptions.

HAWAIIAN
Fountains and rivers of lava erupt from the crater, vents, and fissures. The lava flows create wide, low shield volcanoes.

STROMBOLIAN
Explosions in partly congealed lava throw rock, ash, and cinders into the air. Falling fragments build tall cones, which may collapse if they become too steep.

VULCANIAN
Violent explosions fire large rocks and lava bombs high into the air. These big blasts occur as a result of a buildup of gas under thick, sticky lava.

PLINIAN
These large explosions empty the volcano's magma chambers and produce immense clouds of ash that may rise 30 miles (48 km) high.

PELÉEAN
A dome of hard lava in the crater collapses, releasing a pyroclastic flow. Rising gases form ash clouds above the flow.

Pumice

Obsidian

Lava bomb

Lava Flows

LAVA IS THE LIFEBLOOD of every eruption. It fuels and builds all volcanoes, whether they are located above collision zones, in rift valleys, on ocean ridges, or over hot spots. But its form varies, depending on the chemicals and gases it contains and the kind of eruption that occurs. Explosive eruptions emit thick, sticky lava that either shoots out as cannonball-like "bombs" or flows slowly, like molasses. Less violent eruptions release streams of runny lava that can travel up to 100 miles (160 km), at speeds of up to 30 miles (48 km) per hour.

As lava flows, it cools and solidifies. Volcanologists use different names to describe the ways in which lava cools. Most of these names come from Hawaii, where there are many volcanoes. Lava that forms a smooth or flowing surface is called pahoehoe. Lava that hardens into sharp lumps is called a'a. Thin strands of lava are called Pelé's hair, for the Hawaiian goddess of volcanoes. Solid droplets are known as Pelé's tears.

Runny lava usually cools to form a rock called basalt. Thicker, sticky lava forms other kinds of rock, such as rhyolite. As gases bubble out of cooling lava, holes form in the rock. Gas-rich forms of basalt and rhyolite are called scoria and pumice. Lava that cools immediately forms volcanic glass. This is called tachylyte if it is a basalt lava, or obsidian if it is rhyolite.

RIVERS OF FIRE

During Hawaiian eruptions, runny lava rises directly from the crater or from vents or fissures. It rushes down the slopes, pouring over ledges and cliffs, and filling valleys. The outside surface of the lava flow is the first part to cool. Sometimes the top and sides solidify, forming a tube through which red-hot lava continues to flow.

Lava tube

PAHOEHOE

When runny but slow-moving lava cools, a thin, rippled skin forms on the surface. This kind of lava is called *pahoehoe* (pronounced *PUH-hoy-hoy*), a Hawaiian word for "runny." Pahoehoe flows usually resemble coiled ropes that end in rounded, toelike lobes. As more lava surges through the coils, it breaks through the lobes, extending the flow. Pahoehoe flows are often less than 3 feet (1 m) thick.

Word Builders

• Certain kinds of lava are named after the Hawaiian goddess of volcanoes, **Pelé**. She is said to live inside Kilauea volcano on the Big Island of Hawaii, U.S.A. When she is in a bad mood, she flings lava out of the crater.

• **A'a** is a Hawaiian word meaning "sharp." It is said to come from the sound you would make if you walked barefoot over this jagged rock!

That's Amazing!

• Between 1983 and 1989, Kilauea volcano in Hawaii produced enough lava to make a road that would circle Earth four times.

• The longest known lava flow came from a volcano that erupted 190,000 years ago at Undara in northeastern Australia. It stretched for more than 100 miles (160 km), and its lava tubes are still visible.

Pathfinder

• Under oceans, erupting lava cools quickly to form mounds called pillow lava. Go to pages 76–77.

• The Hawaiian Islands were formed by an erupting hot spot. Find out about hot spots on pages 82–83.

• Lava may spurt out of craters, spray out of fissures, or trickle out of vents. Learn about different kinds of eruptions on page 103.

• Vast, ancient lava flows cover large parts of the globe. Turn to pages 112–13.

ISLANDS THAT GROW
In Hawaii, lava flows often reach the sea. As the red-hot liquid enters the water, huge clouds of steam billow upward. The lava cools quickly and turns into rock, adding new land to the shore.

HANDS ON
Make a Lava Flow

❶ Take 1 cup of self-rising flour, ½ cup of sugar, 2 heaping tablespoons of cocoa, ½ cup of milk, 2 tablespoons of butter, and ½ teaspoon of salt. Mix the ingredients to form a batter. Pour the batter into a greased cake pan. With your hands, shape the mixture to form a slight peak.

❷ Mix ½ cup of brown sugar with 2 tablespoons of cocoa and sprinkle it on top of the batter. Carefully pour 1 cup of very hot water over the mixture.

❸ Place the cake pan in an oven, preheated to 400°F (220°C). Bake for 30–40 minutes. The cake is ready when the chocolate "lava" starts to flow. Remember, lava is very hot—so wait for it to cool before you try to eat it!

A'A
When a large amount of lava erupts quickly, it cools to form rough lumps called *a'a* (pronounced *AH-ah*). This creates a jagged surface, across or under which fresh lava may flow for some time. Eventually, the entire flow solidifies into a massive rock. If an a'a flow fills a deep valley, it may be up to 330 feet (100 m) thick.

PELÉ'S HAIR
Blobs of lava may be torn into thin strands by the wind or by the force of a volcanic explosion. The strands cool as they fall, forming glassy, hairlike threads.

Gas mask

Helmet and goggles

Ash and Gas

ALL VOLCANOES are driven by gas. Some erupt violently when gas is released from upward-moving magma, either because the pressure underground becomes so great that the rocks above can no longer resist, or because the pressure is suddenly reduced by the collapse of the volcano. The gas carries pulverized rocks, blobs of lava, and fine ash high into the sky.

The most common gases in volcanic eruptions are steam (water vapor), sulfur dioxide, and carbon dioxide. Steam can scald. Large amounts of carbon dioxide can suffocate oxygen-breathing life-forms, including humans. Sulfur dioxide can react with water vapor to form sulfuric acid in the atmosphere. Less common gases are chlorine and fluorine, which are toxic and can corrode metals, and hydrogen sulfide, better known as "rotten-egg gas." Wearing a gas mask, helmet, and goggles may offer some protection.

Gas-powered ash clouds can spell disaster. Falling ash may darken the sky for days and cover a vast area. Ash accumulation can clog roads and waterways, buckle roofs, and corrode machinery. Even more dangerous are pyroclastic flows. These red-hot mixtures of ash and gas sweep down slopes at hundreds of miles per hour, destroying everything in their path.

THE MOUNTAIN THAT ROARED

Soufrière Hills volcano on the island of Montserrat in the Caribbean Sea burst into life in July 1995. Steam and sulfurous gas explosions showered ash over the island. Lava domes bulged above the crater rim. Beginning in July 1996, the domes repeatedly collapsed, sending immense pyroclastic flows all the way to the sea. These flows killed 16 farmers. Many of the island's inhabitants had to flee their homes.

HANDS ON

An Explosive Reaction

Here's a way to see a volcanic eruption without experiencing its bad effects. Make sure you do this experiment with an adult present.

❶ Find an empty squirt bottle and remove the spray nozzle. This container will be your volcano.

❷ Fill the container one-third full of white vinegar mixed with a few drops of red food dye. Place the container in a sink, bath, or open yard. This eruption will be messy!

❸ Now take ½ cup of water, mix in a heaping tablespoon of bicarbonate of soda, and quickly tip the mixture into the container. Stand far back.

A gassy plume will shoot out of the container, just like an explosive eruption. You can repeat the experiment, adding a few drops of dishwashing liquid to the vinegar mixture. This time, when you tip in the bicarbonate mixture, a frothy fluid will bubble out of the container—just like a pyroclastic flow!

DAY TURNS TO NIGHT

In August 1995, heavy ashfalls turned day into night in New Plymouth, the capital of Montserrat. Repeated eruptions continued to rain ash on the city, and finally, in early 1996, it was abandoned. In 1999, the volcano was still erupting and the citizens had not yet been able to return to their homes.

Word Builders

- **Pyroclastic** combines the Greek words *pyros*, meaning "fire," and *klastos*, or "broken." Pyroclastic flows contain fiery pieces of broken pumice.
- **Nuée ardentes** comes from the French *nuée*, meaning "cloud," and *ardente*, or "glowing." Volcanologist Alfred Lacroix first described these pyroclastic flows while studying the eruption of Mount Pelée in Martinique in 1902.

That's Amazing!

- A giant pyroclastic flow released by the eruption of Taupo in New Zealand in AD 186 is estimated to have traveled overland at jet plane speeds of 450 miles (725 km) per hour.
- Pyroclastic flows move so fast that they can skip over water. A prehistoric flow from Kagoshima in Japan traveled 38 miles (60 km), including 6 miles (10 km) over open water.

Pathfinder

- Ash from volcanic eruptions can combine with rain to form destructive mudflows. Go to pages 108–09.
- The biggest eruptions in history spewed out immense amounts of ash and gas. Find out more on pages 116–17.
- In AD 79, pumice and a pyroclastic flow buried the town of Pompeii in Italy. The town remained buried for more than 1,700 years. Turn to pages 118–19.

PYROCLASTIC FLOWS

Pyroclastic flows are the result of sudden, explosive eruptions. They occur in a variety of ways, but there are two main types.

COLLAPSING VERTICAL ERUPTION

The initial eruption thrusts a huge cloud of volcanic material upward. Eventually, part of the column of cloud collapses and falls back toward Earth. Mixtures of ash and gas race down the slopes of the volcano. These flows can radiate out in any direction from the main vent.

DOME COLLAPSE

Thick lava blocking a vent at the top or side of the volcano suddenly gives way or is blown apart by a buildup of gas. The explosion flings ash, gas, and rocks down one side of the volcano. These pyroclastic flows are sometimes called "nuée ardentes."

GOING WITH THE FLOW

In 1991, a dome collapse at Unzen volcano in Kyushu, Japan, unleashed huge pyroclastic flows that killed 41 people and destroyed an elementary school and 705 houses. More than 8,600 people had to be evacuated.

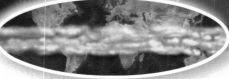

Aftereffects

LAVA, ASH, AND GAS aren't the only dangers from a volcanic eruption. The aftereffects can be just as life-threatening and are often more destructive. Rain from eruption clouds, snow and ice melted by the heat, collapsing crater lakes, and earth tremors can all trigger landslides and mudflows known as lahars. Lava, mud, and pyroclastic flows may also block rivers, causing flooding. In coastal areas, landslides can, in turn, trigger tsunamis.

Communities affected by eruptions may be vulnerable to other threats. If water supplies and sewerage systems are disrupted, diseases may spread quickly. Blocked roads and railways may prevent medical aid from reaching survivors. And if crops are destroyed, people may starve.

Over longer periods, volcanoes can have a significant impact on the local and world climate. The natural aerosols, or pollutants, pumped out by these giant chimneys spread through the atmosphere. Large, sulfur-rich eruptions fill the air with tiny droplets of sulfuric acid that interfere with the Sun's rays and lower the temperature on the ground. Fluorine and chlorine can damage the ozone layer, a thin layer of gases that blocks harmful rays from the Sun. Eventually, however, the volcanic gases thin out, the climate settles, and the ozone layer recovers—at least until the next big blast.

WASHED AWAY
At 11 PM on November 13, 1985, a colossal torrent of mud engulfed the town of Armero in Colombia, killing more than 23,000 people. The mudflow occurred when a small eruption melted snow on top of the Nevado del Ruiz volcano, 28 miles (45 km) away.

INSIDE STORY

Eyes on the Skies

In December 1989, the passengers and crew on a Dutch airliner flying over Alaska got the fright of their lives—courtesy of a volcano. Ash from an eruption at Redoubt clogged all four of the plane's engines, sending it into a silent dive. It plummeted for 2 miles (3.2 km) before the pilots managed to restart the engines and land safely. The scare forced aviation authorities to consider the threat from volcanic ash. Today, the Alaska Volcano Observatory monitors all eruptions in the northern Pacific. It receives regular reports from American and Russian volcanologists and uses satellites to track ash clouds. In an effort to predict eruptions, scientists monitor seismometers, and carry out regular gas surveys on Alaska's 16 most dangerous volcanoes.

THE YEAR WITHOUT A SUMMER

The April 1815 eruption of Tambora in Indonesia was the largest volcanic eruption in history. About 10,000 people were killed immediately, but thousands more suffered from the volcano's aftereffects, including many people living on the other side of the world.

WIDESPREAD FAMINE
The huge Plinian eruption fired about 1.7 million tons of ash into the air and created enormous pyroclastic flows. The ash fell across a vast area of Indonesia, coating soil and plants and leading to widespread crop failures. As a result, more than 80,000 people in the region starved to death.

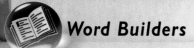

Word Builders

• **Lahar** is the Indonesian word for a volcanic mudflow. Lahars are common in Indonesia, and many volcanologists go there to study these mudflows. This has led to the word being used more widely.
• The word **aerosol** combines two elements. "Aero" comes from the Greek word *aer*, or "air." "Sol" is a substance in which fine particles of one material are suspended in another. In an aerosol, fine droplets and dust are suspended in air.

That's Amazing!

• In 1982, a jumbo jet passed through an ash cloud above Galunggung volcano in Indonesia. All four engines shut down and the plane dropped nearly 5 miles (8 km) before the pilot was able to restart the engines.
• Aerosols and ash particles from major eruptions can cause unusual atmospheric effects. Colored haloes may appear around the Sun, and as the Sun rises, it may first appear green, then blue.

Pathfinder

• The eruption of Mount Pinatubo was one of the largest on record. Find out how it compares with other volcanic eruptions on pages 116–17.
• Learn about the kinds of gases that volcanoes emit on pages 106–07.
• Earthquakes can also cause landslides and mudflows. Go to pages 88–89.
• The 1980 eruption of Mount St. Helens in the U.S.A also produced enormous mudflows. Turn to pages 122–23.

RIVERS OF MUD

The June 15–16, 1991, eruption of Mount Pinatubo in the Philippines killed 320 people and forced 200,000 to leave their homes. But that was just the beginning of trouble. For years afterward, torrential downpours combined with the ash to create enormous lahars. These mudflows killed 600 people—far more than the original eruption. In 1995, one lahar left 100,000 people homeless.

SEVERE WEATHER

Tambora's ash spread around the globe, lowering temperatures in many parts of the world. Some areas of North America and Europe had a particularly severe winter followed by one of the coldest summers ever recorded. As a result, 1816 became known as "the year without a summer."

OPTICAL EFFECTS

Ash particles in the air intensify the yellow and red colors of sunrises and sunsets. After the Tambora eruption, particularly colorful sunrises and sunsets were witnessed around the world. This sunset was painted by the English artist J.M.W. Turner.

Geysers and Hot Springs

THOUSANDS OF YEARS after its last eruption, the area beneath a volcano may still remain hot. In these areas, known as geothermal regions, heat rising from ancient magma chambers encounters water trickling through cracks in the ground. The water deep underground may heat up to 520°F (270°C)—more than twice the temperature of normal boiling water—but the pressure of the cooler water on top prevents it from boiling. However, when water at shallow depths overflows at the surface, the pressure is released and the deeper, hotter water turns to steam and explodes upward. Depending on the amount of pressure, the water and steam may erupt as a giant fountain, called a geyser, or bubble out gently as a hot spring. Sometimes the water and steam rise through soft soil, creating boiling mud pools.

Hot groundwater dissolves minerals in surrounding rocks and carries them to the surface. When the water evaporates, it leaves the minerals on the ground, where they often take on strange shapes and colors.

The most famous geothermal regions are those in Iceland, northern New Zealand, and Yellowstone National Park in the U.S.A. In some places, people use the steam to create electricity and the hot water to heat their homes. For example, geothermal energy, as this is known, provides virtually all of Iceland's power.

A HOT-WATER WONDERLAND
Geothermal regions have dramatic landscapes. Geysers spout amid mineral deposits. Hot water drips from terraces. Pools of all sizes, shapes, and colors bubble in hollows. And everything is shrouded in billowing clouds of steam.

Mineral terraces

Mud pools

KEEPING WARM
Thermal springs bubble throughout the islands of Japan. In the Japan Alps, on the island of Honshu, macaque monkeys have learned to keep warm in the winter by bathing in the hot water.

STEAM POWER
The water in this pool in Iceland comes from hot springs. At the nearby power station, volcanic steam is used to power turbine generators that, in turn, produce electricity.

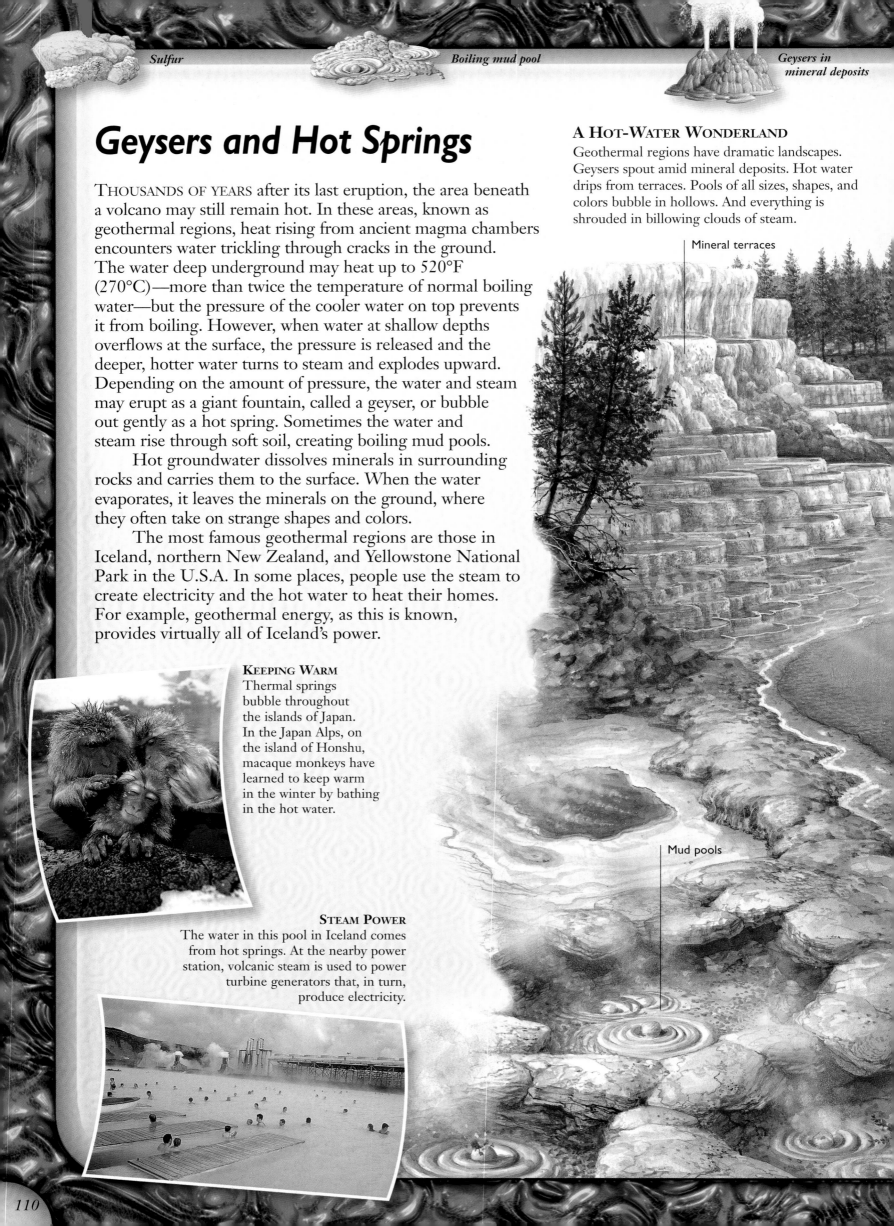

📖 Word Builders

• **Geyser** comes from an Icelandic word, *geysir,* meaning "to spring up" or "to gush." In Iceland, it is also the name of the country's most famous geyser, which lies 50 miles (80 km) north of the capital, Reykjavik.
• **Geothermal** is made up of two Greek terms: *geo,* meaning "Earth," and *thermos,* meaning "hot." Geothermal activity is created by the hot Earth.

✳ That's Amazing!

• The world's tallest active geyser is the Steamboat Geyser in Yellowstone National Park, Wyoming, U.S.A. Its spout has reached a height of 380 feet (115 m)—higher than a 30-story building.
• The highest-spouting geyser ever recorded was the Waimangu (Black Water) Geyser in New Zealand. It erupted between 1900 and 1904, and reached a height of about 1,500 feet (460 m)—as tall as a 125-story building.

⇨ Pathfinder

• The heat that powers hot springs and geysers comes from pockets of magma that have risen from the mantle. Learn more about the mantle on pages 72–73.
• In addition to geysers, Iceland has several active volcanoes and two major rift zones. Find out more on pages 120–21.
• Did you know that there are geysers on other planets? Turn to pages 124–25.

Mineral pool

Geyser

HOW GEYSERS ERUPT

Scientists cannot be exactly sure how geysers work because they cannot visit the hot underground chambers from which geysers emerge. But experiments suggest that an eruption occurs in the following way:

Surface water trickles down through cracks and a main vent into a cavity. Heat rising from a magma chamber warms the water in the cavity, but the downward pressure of the water in the cracks and vent prevents it from boiling.

As the cavity, vent, and cracks fill up, water eventually overflows at the surface. As soon as this happens, the pressure in the cavity is released. The water suddenly boils, and steam and water rush up toward the surface.

✋ HANDS ON
Make Your Own Geyser

You can make your own geyser with a few simple props.

❶ Fill a bowl with water. Place an overturned funnel inside the bowl so that the narrow end of the funnel rises above the water.

❷ Take a bendy straw and place one end under the funnel. The other end should hang over the edge of the container.

❸ Blow into the straw. Watch what happens.

Water erupts from the funnel—just like a geyser! The pressure created by your breath forces the water upward. A geyser functions in a similar way, although the pressure is created by heat from a magma chamber.

The geyser erupts. Big geysers can spout hundreds of feet high. Some erupt at regular intervals and others are erratic. Once the heat source fades, the geyser will die out.

Basalt   Rhyolite   Andesite

Volcanic Landscapes

VOLCANOES CHANGE SHAPE with every eruption. Explosions form new craters, and lava flows add fresh layers of rock. Each event provides a different disguise. Plinian eruptions create the most striking transformations. After these massive explosions empty part of the magma chamber, the volcano collapses, forming a huge crater called a caldera. Domes of lava or new explosive cones may then grow inside the caldera, creating a volcano inside a volcano.

Even after volcanoes become dormant or extinct, they continue to change. Rain, wind, and running water all play a part. Wind and rain scour the rocks, and the rain fills craters. Streams cut deep grooves into slopes. Over millions of years, these elements can erode the volcano's soft exterior to reveal a skeleton of hard lava. This skeleton includes features that originally formed in underground channels and vents, such as plugs and dikes.

Most lava solidifies into basalt, andesite, or rhyolite. Depending on how it cools, the solidified lava may take on strange shapes. Lava that cools quickly in water may form large, pillow-shaped mounds. Some types of lava harden into tall hexagonal columns. Eventually, all lava breaks down into soil that is extremely fertile. That's why people live near active volcanoes, despite the risk of eruptions.

ORGANIC LAVA
These tall columns of volcanic rock in California, U.S.A., look like the pipes of a church organ. They formed when a lava flow cooled. As the lava hardened, it shrank, splitting into regular, six-sided columns.

Plug and dikes formed by lava left in vents of volcano

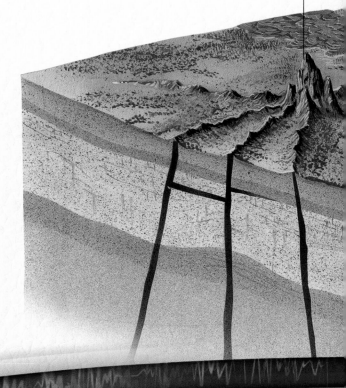

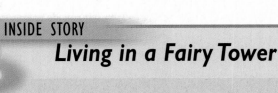

INSIDE STORY
Living in a Fairy Tower

My name is Yashir. I live in Goreme in Turkey. My house is cut into a tall rock spire. The older people call these spires "fairy towers" and say they were once the homes of spirits. But our teacher says they were formed millions of years ago when rivers wore away soft volcanic rock. People began living here about 10,000 years ago. Our house is comfortable. The rock stays cool in the summer and is nice and cozy in the winter. We've got a big living room, a kitchen, and three bedrooms. Recently, my dad decided we needed another room. So he just started digging deeper into the rock.

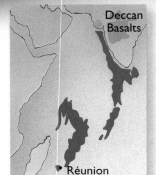

FLOOD BASALTS
Parts of our planet are covered by deep layers of lava called flood basalts. Most formed when a hot spot erupted and poured enormous quantities of molten rock over the surrounding land. Such events are rare, occurring just once every 10 to 20 million years. Among the most famous examples of flood basalts are the Deccan Basalts in central India.

Deccan Basalts

Réunion

HOT-SPOT TRACES
The Deccan Basalts came from a hot spot that was located below India 65 million years ago. Over the course of one million years, lava flows spread over one-third of India. Large areas of volcanic rock have since worn away, but the basalts still cover one-fifth of the country. Since the original eruption, India has drifted away from the hot spot to its current position. A chain of seafloor volcanoes links the Deccan Basalts to the hot spot, now under the island of Réunion in the southern Indian Ocean.

Word Builders

- **Rhyolite** comes from the Greek word *rhyax,* which means "stream of lava."
- **Andesite** is named for the Andes Mountains in South America. The rock is particularly common in the volcanoes of this long mountain range.
- **Caldera** comes from the Spanish word *caldera,* meaning "cauldron." It is also the name of a crater in the Canary Islands.

That's Amazing!

- The world's largest caldera is Toba volcano on the Island of Sumatra in Indonesia. It measures 685 square miles (1,755 sq. km). Driving in a car at 50 miles (80 km) per hour, it would take you an hour to cross it.
- The Binneringe Dike in Western Australia is more than 375 miles (600 km) long. It would take you two days to drive that distance in a car.

Pathfinder

- Plugs, dikes, laccoliths, and sills were all once channels of red-hot molten rock. Turn to pages 102–03.
- When lava flows cool on the surface, they form types of lava called pahoehoe and a'a. Take a look at these lavas and learn about their names on pages 104–05.
- One of the most famous water-filled calderas is Crater Lake in Oregon, U.S.A. Learn more on page 123.

READING THE LANDSCAPE

Volcanic landscapes preserve evidence of the eruption of lava onto the surface. Jagged rims encircle calderas, and flood basalts show up as extensive tablelands with stepped sides. Highly eroded landscapes may expose the underground channels that once fed volcanoes, in the form of ridges (dikes) and towers (plugs).

LAVA WALLS

A dike forms when magma fills a fissure. If the lava is harder than the surrounding rock, eventually the rock will wear away, exposing a long ridge of lava called a dike. This dike is in northwestern Australia.

Plateau made up of many layers of lava, indicating flood basalts

Crater lake filled with and replenished by rainwater

Caldera containing small crater

Sheets of solidified magma called sills visible in rock layers

Layered sedimentary rocks bulge upward above ancient laccolith

Old lava flow

Ancient laccolith exposed at surface

Vertical dikes often feed horizontal sills

LAYERS OF LAVA

The Deccan Basalts form large plateaus more than one mile (1.6 km) thick. In many places, rivers have cut down through the volcanic rock, exposing the layers of lava that created the plateaus. Each layer represents a different eruption. The thickness of the layers varies, depending on how long the eruption lasted and how much lava it produced.

CLOSE STUDY

Scientists study the layers in the basalts to learn about ancient eruptions. They have discovered that soils formed on top of some layers before the next lava flow buried them. Sand, clay, and gravel layers between flows suggest peaceful intervals when rivers and lakes developed.

Volcanology

VOLCANOES HAVE FASCINATED humans for thousands of years. About 2,350 years ago, the Greek philosopher Plato traveled to Sicily to watch Mount Etna erupting, and became the first person to describe cooling lava. Through the 18th century, scholars still disagreed about the origins of volcanic rocks. A group called the Neptunists claimed that many volcanic rocks crystallized from seawater. Their opponents, the Plutonists, argued that all such rocks formed from molten material that came from inside Earth. It was only in the early 19th century that the Plutonists were proved correct.

The scientific study of volcanoes is called volcanology. Today, volcanologists monitor eruptions using aircraft and satellites, and film volcanic activity from afar. To really get to know volcanoes, however, they have to scramble up steep slopes, clamber into craters, and brave the dangers of lava, gases, and landslides. Only then can they collect samples and set up equipment to record tremors and sounds.

Volcanologists work closely with agencies responsible for public safety in a region that might be affected by an eruption from a particular volcano. By studying the volcano's current activity and its history, volcanologists can evaluate the likelihood of a new eruption. Decisions regarding the evacuation of a threatened area are based on this information.

OCCUPATIONAL HAZARDS
As they work, volcanologists must be constantly on the alert for dangers, such as unsteady ground or sudden buildups of lava or gas.

INSIDE STORY

A Dynamic Duo

French scientists Maurice and Katia Krafft are among the most outstanding figures in the history of volcanology. Maurice first became interested in volcanoes at age 7, when he witnessed the 1954 eruption of Stromboli in Italy. By 15, he had joined the French Geological Society and written his first scientific paper. Katia and Maurice met at college. Together, they studied, photographed, and filmed volcanoes all over the world. They took an interest in pyroclastic eruptions because they were "the most dangerous and most deadly." Tragically, at Unzen in Japan, on June 3, 1991, a pyroclastic flow swept the Kraffts and 39 other people away. The world mourned the loss of two intrepid volcanologists, but their important work remains.

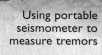

Using portable seismometer to measure tremors

Sampling volcanic gases

Word Builders

- **Neptunists** were named for Neptune, the Roman god of the sea. **Plutonists** were named for Pluto, the Roman god of the underworld. These names relate to the groups' views on the origins of volcanic rocks.
- The word **volcanology** is made up of the Italian name *Volcan*, for the Roman god of fire, and the Greek term *logia*, which means "a branch of knowledge."

That's Amazing!

- The seismometers at the Hawaiian Volcano Observatory are so sensitive that they can detect magma rising from Earth's mantle or from chambers in the crust long before it reaches the surface.
- Aerial surveys using ice-penetrating radar have detected active volcanoes buried 1 mile (1.6 km) below the Antarctic ice sheet.

Pathfinder

- Scientists also use seismometers to monitor earthquakes. Find out more on pages 90–91.
- Read about what happens just before and during an eruption on pages 102–03.
- Warning signs allowed scientists to evacuate many people from around Mount St. Helens in the U.S.A. before it erupted violently in 1980. Find out more on pages 122–23.

IN THE FIELD

Volcanologists work in teams, with each scientist handling a particular task. Some take the temperature of the lava with a thermocouple. Others monitor tremors with portable seismometers. Those who work closest to the lava wear heat-resistant clothing.

Measuring the size of the crater

Measuring the temperature of the lava

LEARNING FROM LAVA

Scientists scoop up lava on long poles bearing prongs. They study lava samples to learn how volcanic rocks form and what they are made of. They can also find out which part of Earth's interior the lava originally came from.

Some lava flows contain pieces of rock from Earth's mantle, which allows scientists to study rocks they could not otherwise obtain. The green pieces in this lava flow are lumps of a rock called peridotite. They formed 25 miles (40 km) underground.

Volcanologists study thin slices of lava under a microscope to find out which minerals make up the rock and therefore what kind of magma lies under the volcano. This provides clues as to how the volcano is likely to behave.

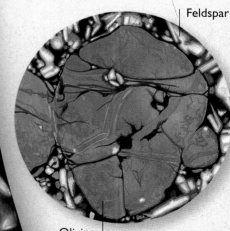

Feldspar

Olivine

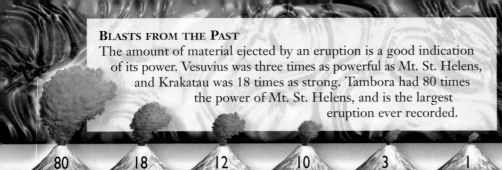

BLASTS FROM THE PAST
The amount of material ejected by an eruption is a good indication of its power. Vesuvius was three times as powerful as Mt. St. Helens, and Krakatau was 18 times as strong. Tambora had 80 times the power of Mt. St. Helens, and is the largest eruption ever recorded.

80	18	12	10	3	1
Tambora 1815	Krakatau 1883	Novarupta 1912	Mt. Pinatubo 1991	Mt. Vesuvius AD 79	Mt. St. Helens 1980

Major Eruptions

THROUGHOUT RECORDED HISTORY, volcanic eruptions have transformed landscapes and affected the lives of large numbers of people all around the world. But some countries have more volcanic activity than others. Most of those countries are located in collision zones—regions where one tectonic plate collides with another. Others lie above hot spots or near major rifts such as the Great Rift Valley in Africa.

Approximately 14,000 volcanoes have erupted in the last 10,000 years. A major eruption is one that explodes with immense power, spews out vast amounts of lava, or causes catastrophic damage. Large explosive eruptions produce an enormous umbrella-shaped cloud of ash and pumice. By measuring the size of these clouds, scientists can estimate the power of different eruptions. They have also used this information to create the Volcanic Explosivity Index, which measures the strength of eruptions on a scale of 0 to 8. Out of 5,000 recorded eruptions, only 160 measured more than 4 on the scale, only 60 were over 5, and just 20 were over 6.

But the size of an eruption does not determine the amount of damage it causes, and even small eruptions can be deadly. In 1985, for example, a small eruption of lava under an icecap on Nevado del Ruiz in Colombia produced a mudflow that killed 22,000 people and destroyed an entire village.

▲ GALUNGGUNG, INDONESIA, 1982
This volcano on the island of Java erupted repeatedly between April 5, 1982, and January 8, 1985, releasing massive ash clouds and pyroclastic flows. More than 80,000 people had to flee, and the homes of 35,000 of them were wiped out.

DANGER ZONES
Like earthquakes, volcanic eruptions tend to occur along plate edges or above hot spots. The greatest concentration of volcanoes occurs in Indonesia—the island of Java alone has 50 active volcanoes. The most dangerous volcanoes are those situated in heavily populated areas such as Indonesia, the Philippines, Japan, Mexico, and Central America.

4 Laki, 1783

EUROPE

Vesuvius, AD 79 5

3   6 Santorini, 1645 BC

Etna, 1669

AFRICA

▲ KRAKATAU, INDONESIA, 1883
The August 28 eruption caused widespread devastation. Volcanic material from the eruption clouds crashed into the sea, setting off tsunamis. The waves killed 36,000 people.

Word Builders

• When Krakatau erupted in 1883, the volcano collapsed, forming a giant caldera in the sea. In 1927, a new volcano rose out of the sea in the center of the caldera. It was soon named **Anak Krakatau**, which in Indonesian means "child of Krakatau."
• **Kilauea** is a Hawaiian word. It means "much spewing," which refers to the many eruptions from this volcano.

That's Amazing!

• The eruption of Krakatau in 1883 was heard 3,000 miles (5,000 km) away and was as powerful as 26 of the largest nuclear bombs ever exploded.
• In 1815, pyroclastic flows surged out of Tambora at the rate of 500 million tons—the weight of 5,000 large ocean liners—every second!

Pathfinder

• Most volcanoes form as a result of collisions between tectonic plates. Turn to pages 78–79.
• Can you imagine what it's like to witness an eruption? Go to pages 102–03.
• Learn more about the eruptions of Nevado del Ruiz and Mount Pinatubo on pages 108–09.

MOUNT PINATUBO, PHILIPPINES, 1991
The June 15 eruption killed 320 people, but many deaths were averted—information provided by volcanologists led to the evacuation of 79,000 people before the mountain blew its top.

KILAUEA, HAWAII, U.S.A., 1983
This eruption on January 8 eventually became the longest and largest side-vent eruption in Kilauea's recorded history. Lava was still flowing in 1999, more than 16 years later.

MOUNT PELÉE, MARTINIQUE, 1902
At 7:52 AM on May 8, Martinique's main town and port, St. Pierre, was engulfed by a white-hot mass of rock, ash, and lava that exploded out of nearby Mount Pelée. About 29,000 people died instantly. Only three people in the town survived.

Bezymianny, 1956 **5**

Novarupta, 1912 **6**

Mount St. Helens, 1980 **5**

ASIA

NORTH AMERICA

Mount Pinatubo, 1991 **6**

Kilauea, 1983

El Chichón, 1982 **5**

Santa Maria, 1902 **6**

Mount Pelée, 1902

Galunggung, 1822 **4**

Tambora, 1815 **7**

Krakatau, 1883 **6**

SOUTH AMERICA

AUSTRALIA

Tarawera Mountain, 1886 **5**

Mount Hudson, 1991 **6**

Taupo, AD 186 **6**

KEY TO SYMBOLS

Volcanic eruption ▲

Major eruption (number on Volcanic Explosivity Index) ▲

TARAWERA, NEW ZEALAND, 1886
Tarawera Mountain exploded suddenly on June 10. Villages, hotels, farms, and forests were buried by rocks and mudflows, and more than 100 people died. A famous thermal feature called the pink terraces vanished instantly.

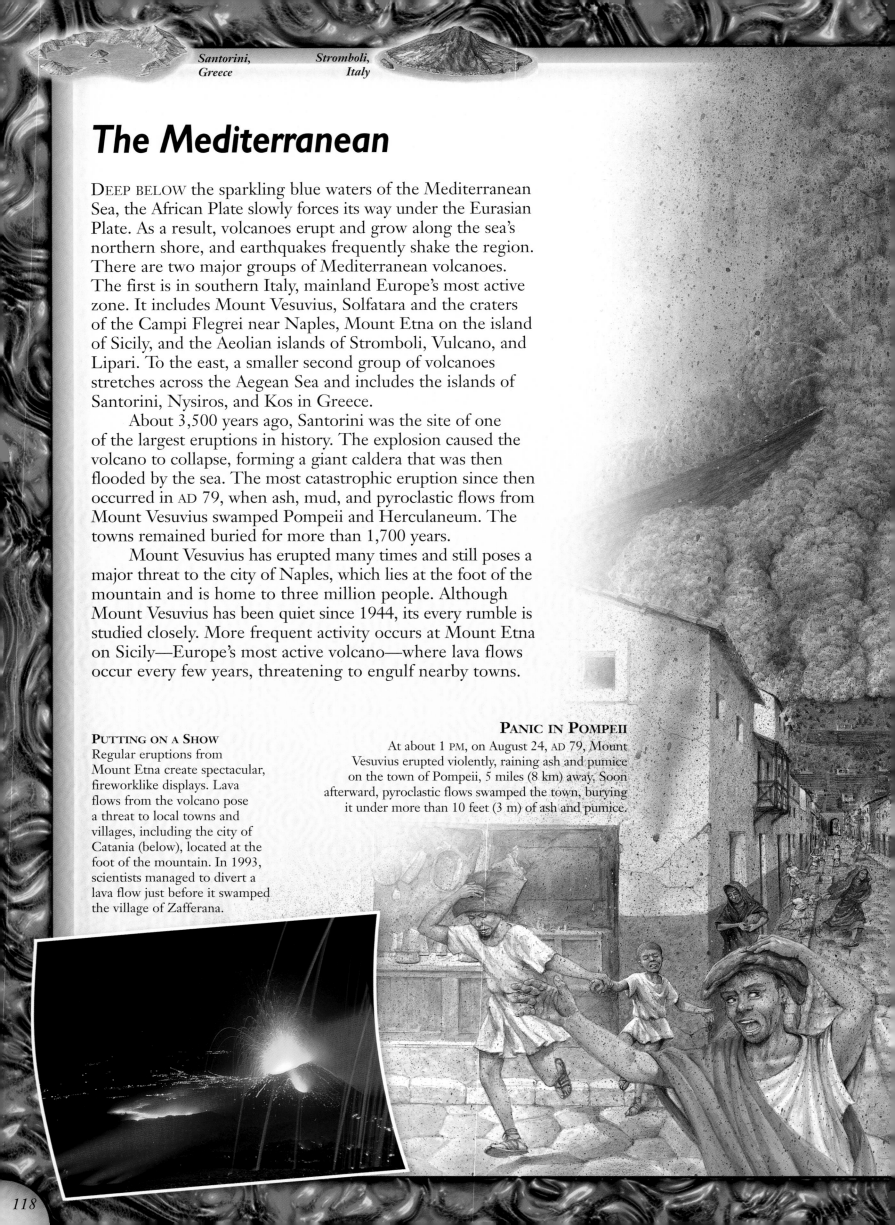

The Mediterranean

DEEP BELOW the sparkling blue waters of the Mediterranean Sea, the African Plate slowly forces its way under the Eurasian Plate. As a result, volcanoes erupt and grow along the sea's northern shore, and earthquakes frequently shake the region. There are two major groups of Mediterranean volcanoes. The first is in southern Italy, mainland Europe's most active zone. It includes Mount Vesuvius, Solfatara and the craters of the Campi Flegrei near Naples, Mount Etna on the island of Sicily, and the Aeolian islands of Stromboli, Vulcano, and Lipari. To the east, a smaller second group of volcanoes stretches across the Aegean Sea and includes the islands of Santorini, Nysiros, and Kos in Greece.

About 3,500 years ago, Santorini was the site of one of the largest eruptions in history. The explosion caused the volcano to collapse, forming a giant caldera that was then flooded by the sea. The most catastrophic eruption since then occurred in AD 79, when ash, mud, and pyroclastic flows from Mount Vesuvius swamped Pompeii and Herculaneum. The towns remained buried for more than 1,700 years.

Mount Vesuvius has erupted many times and still poses a major threat to the city of Naples, which lies at the foot of the mountain and is home to three million people. Although Mount Vesuvius has been quiet since 1944, its every rumble is studied closely. More frequent activity occurs at Mount Etna on Sicily—Europe's most active volcano—where lava flows occur every few years, threatening to engulf nearby towns.

PUTTING ON A SHOW
Regular eruptions from Mount Etna create spectacular, fireworklike displays. Lava flows from the volcano pose a threat to local towns and villages, including the city of Catania (below), located at the foot of the mountain. In 1993, scientists managed to divert a lava flow just before it swamped the village of Zafferana.

PANIC IN POMPEII
At about 1 PM, on August 24, AD 79, Mount Vesuvius erupted violently, raining ash and pumice on the town of Pompeii, 5 miles (8 km) away. Soon afterward, pyroclastic flows swamped the town, burying it under more than 10 feet (3 m) of ash and pumice.

Word Builders

• The name of **Campi Flegrei** near Naples, Italy, combines the Italian words *campi,* meaning "fields," and *flegrei,* for "blazing." It refers to the area's many smoking craters and vents.
• The original Greek name for **Santorini** was Thera. This was the name of a great Spartan leader who ruled the island about 1000 BC. The island was renamed in the Middle Ages for its patron saint, Saint Irene.

That's Amazing!

Before Mount Vesuvius exploded in AD 79, people living nearby had no idea that it was a volcano, because it hadn't erupted for 600 years. After the AD 79 eruption, Pompeii was so deeply buried that local people forgot it had existed. It was only in the 19th century that archeologists dug up the town and rediscovered its name.

Pathfinder

• Take a look at the plate boundaries that run through the Mediterranean on pages 74–75.
• Find out about major earthquakes that occurred in the Mediterranean region on pages 94–95.
• Ash from a volcanic eruption caused inhabitants to abandon the town of Plymouth in Montserrat in 1996. Find out more on pages 106–07.

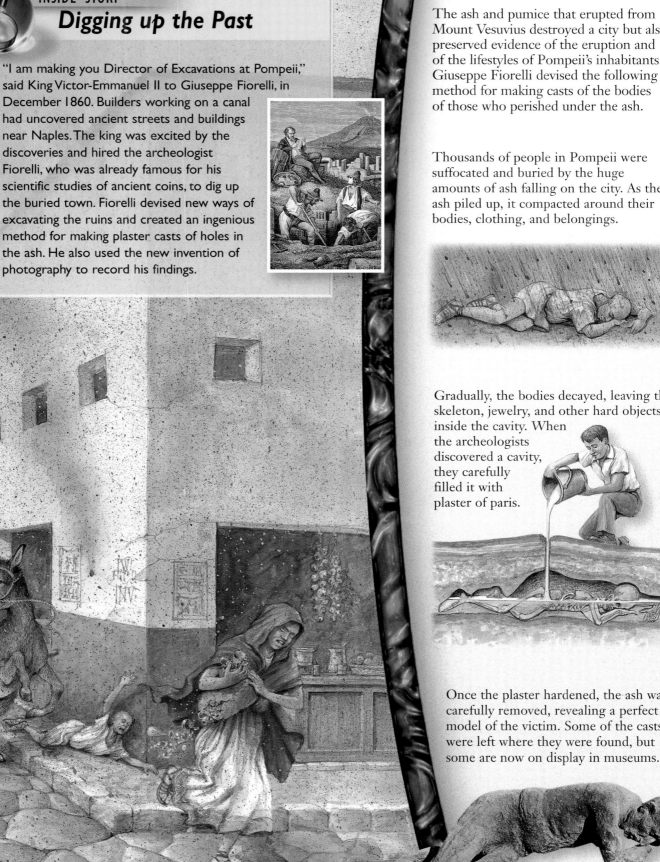

INSIDE STORY
Digging up the Past

"I am making you Director of Excavations at Pompeii," said King Victor-Emmanuel II to Giuseppe Fiorelli, in December 1860. Builders working on a canal had uncovered ancient streets and buildings near Naples. The king was excited by the discoveries and hired the archeologist Fiorelli, who was already famous for his scientific studies of ancient coins, to dig up the buried town. Fiorelli devised new ways of excavating the ruins and created an ingenious method for making plaster casts of holes in the ash. He also used the new invention of photography to record his findings.

TIME CAPSULES

The ash and pumice that erupted from Mount Vesuvius destroyed a city but also preserved evidence of the eruption and of the lifestyles of Pompeii's inhabitants. Giuseppe Fiorelli devised the following method for making casts of the bodies of those who perished under the ash.

Thousands of people in Pompeii were suffocated and buried by the huge amounts of ash falling on the city. As the ash piled up, it compacted around their bodies, clothing, and belongings.

Gradually, the bodies decayed, leaving the skeleton, jewelry, and other hard objects inside the cavity. When the archeologists discovered a cavity, they carefully filled it with plaster of paris.

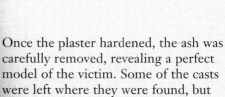

Once the plaster hardened, the ash was carefully removed, revealing a perfect model of the victim. Some of the casts were left where they were found, but some are now on display in museums.

119

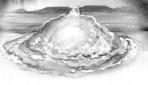

Iceland

ICELAND IS KNOWN as "the land of ice and fire." On the surface it is icy cold for much of the year, but underneath, volcanic fires rage. There are two good reasons for this activity. First, the island lies over a hot spot. Second, it sits on top of the Mid-Atlantic Ridge, a seafloor spreading zone. Together, the hot spot and the spreading ridge produce huge amounts of lava that erupt regularly through vents, fissures, and craters.

The Mid-Atlantic Ridge runs under the middle of the island, from the north to the southwest, forming a strip of rifts and fissures about 40 miles (64 km) wide. Here the land is spreading apart at approximately the rate that your fingernails grow. The hot spot is located under the southeastern part of the island. Krafla, lying on the ridge above the hot spot, has frequent fissure eruptions. The biggest explosive eruptions in Iceland's history occurred at Hekla in 1104, Öraefajökull in 1362, and Askja in 1875. Enormous lava flows followed the eruptions of Eldgja in AD 930 and Laki in 1783.

Icelanders have had to learn to live with dangerous eruptions, but they also benefit from the island's volcanic features. Natural steam heats more than 80 percent of the island's homes, and is used to power turbines that create most of the island's electricity. In addition, the spectacular volcanoes, geysers, and hot springs attract tourists from all over the world.

SPLIT DOWN THE MIDDLE

On Iceland, seafloor spreading occurs on land. As the ocean plates on either side of the Mid-Atlantic Ridge move apart, they push the eastern and western sides of the island in opposite directions. This causes narrow blocks of land to drop downward, forming deep faults like this one near Lake Myvatn in the north of the island.

INSIDE STORY
Halting the Lava

The situation seemed hopeless in January 1973. Lava was advancing across the shore of Vestmannaeyjar, on the island of Heimaey, threatening to block its harbor. Respected volcanologists declared that the island should be abandoned. But physics professor Thorbjorn Sigurgeirsson thought otherwise. He suggested hosing the lava with cold seawater to solidify it. Volunteers used 47 pumps to soak the molten rock. The U.S. Geological Survey called it "the greatest effort ever attempted to control lava flows." Finally, after three months and 6 million tons of water, the lava was halted. Thorbjorn's idea had saved the harbor.

UNDER THE ICECAP

Grimsvötn volcano in southeastern Iceland lies under Vatnajökull icecap, the largest glacier in Europe. In September 1996, a fissure erupted between Grimsvötn and a neighboring volcano, Bardabunga. Hot lava melted a 600-foot (180-m) deep hole in the ice, releasing a billowing plume of ash and steam. The eruption lasted 13 days.

MIXING ICE AND FIRE

Lake Myvatn • • Krafla

Vatnajökull icecap

Bardabunga ▲
Grimsvötn ▲

Subglacial water flow

Heimaey
Surtsey

Word Builders

- A **jokulhlaup** is a flood caused by an eruption under an icecap. This Icelandic term includes the words *jokul,* for "glacier," and *hlaup,* meaning "flood."
- **Surtsey** was named after Surtur, a giant described in Icelandic myths. It was Surtur's job to set the world on fire once the gods had no further use for it.

That's Amazing!

- Iceland has produced one third of all the lava that has erupted on land since AD 1500.
- The eruption at Laki in 1783 was the single largest eruption of lava in history. It poured out 3 cubic miles (13 cubic km) of lava—enough to bury a city 15 miles (24 km) in diameter. Volcanic ash from the eruption fell as far away as China.

Pathfinder

- The western half of Iceland sits on the North American Plate, while the eastern half lies on the Eurasian Plate. Find out about plates on pages 74–75.
- Discover how diverging plates form faults and rift valleys on pages 76–77.
- Iceland's volcanoes have produced vast lava flows. Learn about different kinds of lava flows on pages 104–05.
- Did you know that the word "geyser" comes from Iceland? Go to page 111.

A Town Under Fire

On January 23, 1973, lava erupted from a fissure near Vestmannaeyjar on the island of Heimaey. Many of the town's buildings were buried under a hail of black ash. Others were demolished by a massive lava flow, which added one square mile (2.6 sq. km) of land to the island and threatened to block the entrance to the town's harbor.

Birth of an Island

On November 15, 1963, an eruption occurred under the sea off the south coast of Iceland. Explosions threw up billowing clouds of vapor and towering sprays of lava. The lava piled up on the seafloor, eventually forming a new island called Surtsey.

An Icy Torrent

That October, billions of gallons of meltwater drained into a crater lake beneath the ice. On November 5, the lake overflowed, creating a giant flood, or *jokulhlaup*, which tore off parts of the icecap.

After the Flood

Water poured out at almost 2 million cubic feet (55,000 cubic m) per second—equal to the rate of flow of the Congo, the world's second-largest river. It carried huge boulders and blocks of ice, which destroyed bridges, power lines, and roads. Luckily, the flood lasted just one day.

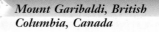

Mount Rainier, Washington, U.S.A.

Mount Garibaldi, British Columbia, Canada

Western North America

ALL ALONG the western side of North America, ocean plates press against the continent. This has created two major chains of volcanoes. One extends through California, Oregon, and Washington into British Columbia. It includes such lofty peaks as Mount St. Helens, Mount Rainier, and Mount Garibaldi. Eruptions occur here as the small Juan de Fuca and Gorda plates thrust under the North American Plate. Another chain stretches along the south coast of Alaska. Volcanoes such as Redoubt, Veniaminoff, and Augustine erupt as the Pacific Plate subducts under the North American Plate.

Enormous eruptions have occurred in both groups during the past 10,000 years. One of the biggest, the eruption of Mount Mazama, which occurred about 6,800 years ago, created Crater Lake in Oregon. In 1912, the eruption of Novarupta in southern Alaska filled a huge valley with an ignimbrite—a pyroclastic flow so hot that the ash fragments fuse. This valley later became known as the Valley of Ten Thousand Smokes.

The most dramatic eruption of recent years occurred at Mount St. Helens in May 1980. Although it was a relatively small eruption, the explosion and its effects were recorded in detail, making people all over the world aware of the immense power of volcanoes.

BAKED ALASKA
Alaskan eruptions are usually small to moderate in size. At Veniaminoff, a typical Alaskan volcano, regular eruptions normally produce only columns of ash. Pyroclastic flows occur occasionally, but lava flows are rare.

WARNING SIGNS
Mount St. Helens sent out a series of warnings that it was about to erupt—including earthquakes, small explosions, and a growing bulge on the mountain's north side caused by magma moving toward the surface. At 8:32 AM on May 18, 1980, an earthquake triggered a landslide that removed the upper part of the volcano.

Magma builds up under north flank

Massive landslide triggers eruption through top and flank of volcano

INSIDE STORY

A Bird's-Eye View

On May 18, 1980, geologists Keith and Dorothy Stoffel flew their small plane over Mount St. Helens. They were eager to take a closer look at the volcano, which had been rumbling and smoking since March. As they neared the peak, they suddenly noticed "landsliding of rock and ice debris inward into the crater…The entire north side of the summit began sliding…A huge explosion blasted out." The plane had to make a steep dive to outrun the mushrooming eruption cloud, but the Stoffels made it to safety with some dramatic photos and an amazing story.

Word Builders

• **The Valley of Ten Thousand Smokes** was named by Robert Griggs, the leader of an expedition sent to investigate the 1912 Novarupta eruption. Griggs named the valley for the many jets of steam rising from the still-hot ignimbrite sheet. Most of the jets died after a few years, but the name remains.
• **Ignimbrite** comes from the Latin words *ignis,* meaning "fire," and *imber,* meaning "shower."

That's Amazing!

• The explosion from the 1912 Novarupta eruption was heard 730 miles (1,200 km) to the east in Juneau, Alaska, U.S.A. But because the wind was blowing eastward, people at Kodiak, 100 miles (160 km) west of the mountain, didn't hear the blast at all.
• The eruption of Mount Mazama blew out 30 times as much ash as the Mount St. Helens eruption.

Pathfinder

• Most of the volcanoes in western North America were formed by subduction. Find out more about subduction on pages 78–79.
• Crater lakes are just one of many features created by volcanic activity. Take a look at some others on pages 112–13.
• The 1980 eruption of Mount St. Helens was a Plinian eruption. Learn about other types of eruption on page 103.

FLOODED CRATER

The blue waters of Crater Lake in Oregon, U.S.A., fill a deep caldera formed by the eruption of Mount Mazama 6,800 years ago. The island in the center of the lake is called Wizard Island. It is a volcanic cone that formed about 4,670 years ago.

SCENES OF DEVASTATION

The Mount St. Helens eruption claimed 60 lives. Most of the victims died in the initial blast, which traveled faster than the speed of sound (745 miles [1,200 km] per hour). The explosion was followed by avalanches, mudflows, and ash clouds.

The blast snapped, flattened, and stripped trees over an area of 230 square miles (600 sq. km), and killed tens of thousands of animals. U.S. Forest Service scientists predicted it would be a century before the environment recovered fully.

The landslide cascaded into nearby Spirit Lake and Toutle River. Lake waters slopped out, forming huge mudflows. These swept down the mountain, destroying houses, bridges, roads, and trees.

Huge column of ash rises high into the air

Rock, hot ash, and lava roar down the mountainside. Melting snow combines with ash to form mudflows.

Winds carried the ash cloud 930 miles (1,500 km) eastward. It blocked out the Sun in some areas, damaged machinery and vehicles, and caused widespread breathing problems. Although it had immediate effects on Earth's atmosphere, it had little permanent impact on the climate.

Extraterrestrial Volcanoes

EARTH IS NOT THE ONLY volcanic body in our solar system. Several rocky planets and moons, including Earth's own moon, display traces of volcanic activity—and some have active volcanoes. Scientists study volcanic activity on other planets and moons by viewing them through telescopes, looking at pictures taken by space probes, and examining space rocks that crash to Earth as meteorites. They've also studied rocks that astronauts have collected from the Moon.

You can see ancient lava flows on the Moon. They form large dark patches within giant impact craters. Samples of moon rocks reveal that these patches are made of a type of basalt similar to the basalt found on Earth. Some glassy grains resemble the lava formations known as Pele's tears, which are found on Hawaii.

Mars has extinct volcanoes, ancient lava flows, and some pyroclastic deposits. Venus has high shield volcanoes and large lava flows, some of which may have formed fairly recently. Farther out in the solar system, Io, one of Jupiter's moons, is a hotbed of volcanic activity. Its giant volcanoes spray out huge clouds of sulfuric steam. The sulfur deposits have colored its surface in shades of yellow and red. Even the gas giants, Saturn and Neptune, and their moons show signs of volcanic activity—marks that suggest these frozen bodies are studded with icy geysers.

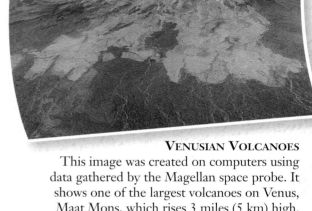

VENUSIAN VOLCANOES
This image was created on computers using data gathered by the Magellan space probe. It shows one of the largest volcanoes on Venus, Maat Mons, which rises 3 miles (5 km) high. It is surrounded by giant lava flows, which show up as bright areas in the photograph.

HANDS ON

Moonwatching

You can take a closer look at the lava plains on the Moon with an ordinary pair of binoculars. The best time to look is between the new moon and a full moon, when shadows make the outlines of lunar features stand out. Use the picture at the lower right to pinpoint the largest maria. (Remember that if you are in the southern hemisphere, the features will be the other way up.) You should be able to see the dark plains and many impact craters quite clearly. The Mare Tranquillitatis is where the *Apollo 11* astronauts landed. Imagine studying volcanoes up there!

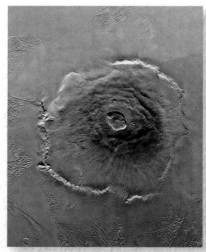

MAMMOTH MARTIAN
One of the most prominent features on Mars is this huge volcano called Olympus Mons. It measures 375 miles (600 km) across, rises 16 miles (25 km) high, and is edged by cliffs 2.5–5 miles (4–8 km) high. All of the Hawaiian Islands could easily fit inside it.

LUNAR LAVA FLOWS

The Moon's surface is studded with huge craters that contain giant lava plains called maria. The plains formed in the following way.

CRASH LANDINGS
About three to four billion years ago, numerous enormous asteroids collided with the Moon. These impacts formed large craters up to 900 miles (1,450 km) in diameter. Shock waves from the collisions fractured the underlying crust.

📖 Word Builders

• **Maat Mons** was named after Maat, the Egyptian goddess of truth and justice. **Olympus Mons** was named after Mount Olympus in Greece, said to be the home of the gods in Greek mythology. *Mons* is a Latin word, meaning "a towering mass or mountain."
• **Mare** is a Latin word, meaning "sea." On the Moon, a mare is a sea of lava. The plural of mare is **maria**.

✶ That's Amazing!

• Olympus Mons on Mars is more than 20 times the size of Earth's largest volcano, Mauna Loa. Earth's crust would probably collapse under the weight of such a mammoth mountain.
• Io is the size of Earth's Moon, but has 20 times the volcanic activity of Earth.
• The Moon's volcanoes have been extinct for more than 1 billion years, but the lava is still visible because there are no plants or water to cover it.

▭ Pathfinder

• To find out how Earth's internal structure compares to those of neighboring planets, turn to page 72.
• Like the volcanoes on Io, some of Earth's volcanoes expel large amounts of sulfur. This can have an effect on our planet's climate. Go to pages 108–09.
• Huge basalt lava flows also cover parts of Earth, although much of the rock is hidden by water and vegetation. Find out more on pages 112–13.

SULFUR PLUMES

Volcanoes and lava flows pockmark the surface of Io, one of Jupiter's moons. The volcanoes eject umbrella-shaped sprays of sulfur and sulfur dioxide up to 180 miles (300 km) high. You can see one at the top of this photo taken by the Voyager probe.

RISING LAVA

The fractures released some of the pressure under the crust. This caused large amounts of molten rock to form and rise toward the surface. Gradually, the molten rock filled the craters, forming seas of lava, or maria.

Mare Serenitatis

Mare Imbrium

Mare Foecunditatis

Mare Tranquillitatis

ON THE FACE OF IT

The lava-filled craters appear as scattered dark patches on the face of the Moon. They contrast with lighter-colored upland rocks. Some of the lava plains are thousands of miles wide. Among the largest is the Mare Imbrium.

Glossary

a'a A type of lava that has a jagged surface.

active volcano A volcano that produces regular eruptions of gas and lava. The bursts may be separated by weeks or many centuries.

aerosol Small particles and liquid droplets introduced by volcanic gases into air.

aftershock A tremor that follows a large earthquake and originates at or near the hypocenter of the initial quake.

ash Fine pieces of rock and lava ejected during volcanic eruptions.

asthenosphere A layer in Earth's upper mantle, so soft that it can flow. It contains pockets of hot, soft rock.

black smoker A vent situated on an ocean ridge that emits hot, mineral-laden water.

caldera A large, circular depression formed when a volcano collapses above its magma chamber.

continent One of Earth's seven main landmasses: Africa, Antarctica, Asia, Australia, Europe, North America, and South America. The landmasses include edges beneath the ocean as well as dry land.

convection current A current that transfers heat through moving material, such as the movement of hot rock in the mantle.

convergent margin A boundary between two tectonic plates that are moving toward each other.

core Earth's center. It consists of a solid inner core and a molten outer core, both of which are made of an iron-nickel alloy.

crater A circular depression formed as a result of a volcanic eruption (volcanic crater) or by the impact of a meteorite (impact crater).

crater lake A water-filled crater. It may be filled on a seasonal or permanent basis.

crust The outermost solid layer of Earth, which varies from a thickness of 3 miles (5 km) under the oceans to 45 miles (72 km) under the continents.

dike A sheet of igneous rock formed when magma rises through a crack.

divergent margin A boundary between two tectonic plates that are moving apart.

dormant volcano A volcano that is not currently active but that could erupt again.

epicenter The point on Earth's surface that is directly above the hypocenter, or starting point, of an earthquake.

eruption The volcanic release of lava and gas from Earth's interior onto the surface and into the atmosphere.

extinct volcano A volcano that has shown no sign of activity for a long period and is considered unlikely to erupt again.

fault margin A crack in rock layers created by the rocks shifting in opposite directions or at different speeds.

fissure A fracture or crack in the ground. In volcanic areas, a fissure may be associated with a line of vents (known as fissure volcanoes).

flood basalt A flow of basalt lava that spreads over a large area. It forms a basalt plateau.

geothermal energy Energy that can be extracted from Earth's interior heat, whether from hot rocks, hot water, or steam.

geyser A surface vent that periodically spouts a fountain of boiling water.

hot spot A persistent zone of melting within Earth's mantle.

hypocenter The place within Earth where energy in strained rocks is suddenly released as earthquake waves.

island arc An arc-shaped chain of volcanic islands that forms above a subducting seafloor.

laccolith A mushroom-shaped body of volcanic rock formed when rising magma pushes rock layers upward.

lahar A mudflow created by a volcanic eruption.

lateral fault A fault along which rocks have moved sideways. It is sometimes called a strike-slip or transform fault.

lava Molten rock that has erupted from a volcano onto Earth's surface.

lava bomb A large lump of lava, usually more than 1.25 inches (32 mm) across, that is thrown out of a volcano.

lava dome A mound of thick, sticky lava that grows at the top of, or on the flanks of, a volcano.

lava flow A stream of lava that erupts from a volcano and runs over surrounding land.

lava tube An underground river of lava formed when the surface of an open lava channel solidifies.

liquefaction The change of sediment or soil into a fluid mass as a result of an earthquake.

lithosphere The rigid outer part of Earth, consisting of the crust and the uppermost part of the mantle.

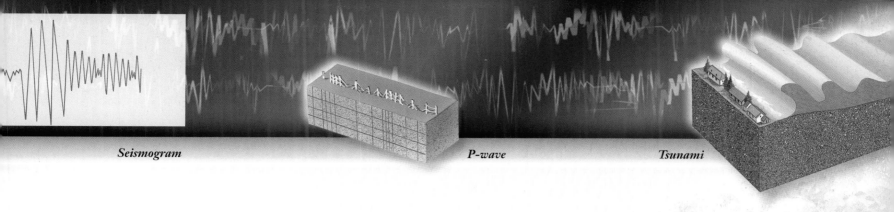

Seismogram *P-wave* *Tsunami*

magma Melted rock found inside Earth. It may solidify inside Earth or erupt at the surface to form lava.

magma chamber A pool of magma in the upper part of the lithosphere from which volcanic materials may erupt.

magnitude The strength of an earthquake, based on the amount of energy released. Seismologists measure magnitude using the Richter Scale, which begins at zero and has no maximum.

mantle The layer between Earth's crust and the outer core. It includes the lower mantle and asthenosphere—the parts of the mantle that flow—and the lithosphere, which is the rigid uppermost part of the mantle.

mare On the Moon, a dark, low-lying, level, and relatively smooth plain of rock formed when lava flooded an impact crater.

meteorite A piece of planetary material from outside Earth that has fallen through the atmosphere onto Earth's surface.

mid-ocean ridge A long, raised ridge formed by volcanic action at the edges of diverging oceanic plates.

mineral A naturally formed solid with an ordered arrangement of atoms found in Earth's crust.

mudflow A river of ash, mud, and water set off by a volcanic eruption or earthquake. Those triggered by volcanoes are also known as lahars.

normal fault A fracture in rock layers, where the upper side has moved downward relative to the other side along a plane inclined between 45 and 90 degrees.

pahoehoe A type of lava with a smooth, ropelike surface.

pillow lava Lava that forms rounded mounds by cooling quickly after erupting under water or flowing into water.

plug A column of volcanic rock formed when lava solidifies inside the vent of a volcano.

plume A rising column of hot rock in the mantle within which melting can take place. The term can also apply to a large column of ash above a volcano.

primary wave A seismic wave, also known as a P-wave, that compresses and expands rocks as it travels through them. It is called a primary wave because it is the wave that arrives first during an earthquake, before the secondary wave.

pumice A light-colored, glassy volcanic rock that contains many cavities. It is so light that it can float in water.

pyroclastic flow A dense, heated mixture of volcanic gas, ash, and rock fragments that travels at great speed down volcanic slopes. It forms as a result of the collapse of an eruption column or a lava dome.

reverse fault A fracture in rock layers, where the top side has moved upward relative to the other side along a plane inclined between 45 and 90 degrees.

rift valley A wide valley that forms when rock layers move apart and a central section drops downward as a result of normal faulting.

secondary wave A seismic wave, also known as an S-wave, that moves rocks from side to side as it passes through them. It is called a secondary wave because it is the second type of wave to arrive during an earthquake.

seismic Related to an earthquake or tremor.

seismogram A graph or computer image that depicts earth tremors as wavy lines.

seismograph An instrument that detects, magnifies, and records Earth's vibrations.

seismology The study of Earth tremors, whether natural or artificially produced.

shield volcano A wide, low volcano formed by slow, continuous lava flows. This type of volcano looks like a shield when viewed from above.

sill A layer of igneous rock formed when magma solidifies between parallel rock layers.

subduction The process in which one tectonic plate descends below another.

surface wave A seismic wave that travels along Earth's surface. It arrives after primary and secondary waves and moves up and down or from side to side.

tectonic plate Rigid pieces of Earth's lithosphere that move over the asthenosphere.

thrust fault A fracture in rock layers, where the upper side rides over the top of the lower side at an angle of less than 45 degrees.

transform fault A fault or plate margin along which rocks move in opposite directions or at different speeds.

tsunami A Japanese word for a sea-wave produced by an earthquake, landslide, or volcanic blast. It reaches its greatest height in shallow waters before crashing onto land.

vent A pipe inside a volcano through which lava and gas erupt.

volcano A typically circular landform from which molten rock and gases erupt.

volcanologist A scientist who studies volcanoes, active as well as inactive.

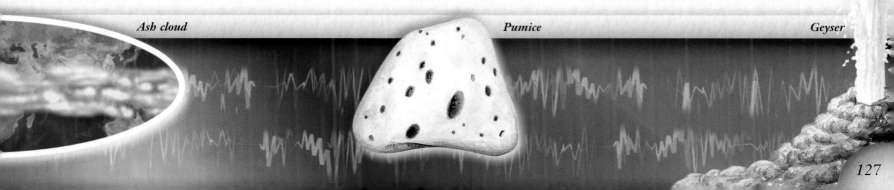

Ash cloud *Pumice* *Geyser*

Index

A

a'a, 104–105, 126
active volcano, 102–103, 126
African Plate, 74, 94, 118
aftereffects of earthquakes, 88–89
aftereffects of volcanoes, 108–109
aftershocks, 88, 126
Alaska, 122–123
Alpine Fault, 81
andesite, 112–113
animal sensitivity, 91, 102
Antarctic Plate, 75
ash, 106–107, 126
ash cloud, 103, 106–109, 123
asteroid, 79, 124
asthenosphere, 74–75, 126
atoll, 83
Australia, 82, 113

B

basalt, 104, 112–113, 124
black smokers, 76–77, 126
buildings, 92–93

C

caldera, 112–113, 123, 126
California, 96–97, 112, 122
Campi Flegrei, 118–119
Cecchi, Filippo, 90
climatic effects, 102, 108–109
collapsing vertical eruption, 107
collisions, 78–79
convection current, 74–75, 126
convergent margin, 74, 79, 126
core, 78–73, 126
crater, 103, 112–113, 124–125, 126
crater lake, 122–123, 126
creepmeter, 90–91
crust, 72–73, 78–79, 126

D

Deccan Basalts, 112–113
dike, 76–77, 102, 112–113, 126
disaster preparation, 92–93
divergent margin, 74, 126
dome collapse, 107
dormant volcano, 103, 112, 126

E

earth's layers, 72
earthquake, 73, 84–99
earthquake aftereffects, 88–89
earthquake monitoring, 90–91, 99
earthquake portrait, 96
earthquake preparation, 92–93
earthquake-proof buildings, 92–93
earthquakes, largest recorded, 94–95
epicenter, 86–87, 97, 126
eruptions, 102–103,
106–109, 116–123, 126
eruptions, largest recorded, 116–117
eruptions, types of, 103, 107
Eurasia, 78–79
Eurasian Plate, 74, 94, 98, 118
extinct volcano, 82, 103, 112, 126
extraterrestrial volcano, 124–125

F

fault, 74, 80–81, 120, 126
feldspar, 115
Fiorelli, Giuseppe, 119
fires, 88, 99
fissure, 95, 102–103, 120, 126
flood, 121
flood basalt, 112–113, 126
folding, 78–79

G

gas, 106–107, 114
geothermal, 110–111, 126
geyser, 110–111, 120–121, 126
Glasshouse Mountains, 82
Global Positioning Systems (GPS), 90–91
Gondwana, 78
graben, 81
Great Rift Valley, 81, 116
Griggs, Robert, 123
growing planet, 72–73

H

Hawaiian Islands, 82, 104–105, 117
Hawaiian Volcano Observatory, 115
Hess, Harry, 76
Himalaya mountain range, 78–79
horst, 81
hot spot, 82–83, 120, 126
hot spring, 110–111, 120
hypocenter, 86–87, 97, 126

I

Iceland, 82, 110, 120–121
ignimbrite, 122–123
India, 78, 112
Indo-Australian Plate, 74, 79
Indonesia, 108–109, 113, 116
Io, 124–125
island arc volcano, 79, 126
Italy, 118–119

J

Japan, 98–99, 107, 110, 114
Japanese safety techniques, 93
jokulhlaup, 121
Jupiter, 124–125

K

Kilauea, 117
Krafft, Maurice and Katia, 114
Krakatau, 116–117

L

laccolith, 102, 113, 126
Lacroix, Alfred, 107
lahar, 108–109, 126
Laki eruption, 121
lateral fault, 80, 126
lava, 73, 76–77, 82–83, 102–105, 112–115, 120, 124–125, 126
lava walls, 113
Lehmann, Inge, 73
liquefaction, 86, 126
lithosphere, 74–75, 126
Loma Prieta, 96–97
Love waves, 91

M

Maat Mons, 124–125
magma, 73, 78–79, 82–83, 102–103, 113, 122–123, 127
magnetic stripes, 77
magnetometer, 90–91
magnitude, 95, 127
major earthquakes, 94–95
major eruptions, 116–117
mantle, 72–73, 82, 127
mapping the seafloor, 76
mare, 124–125, 127
Mariana Trench, 79
Mars, 72, 124–125
Mauna Loa, 83, 125
Mediterranean, 118–119
Mercalli, Giuseppe, 86
Mercalli scale, 86–97
meteorite, 73, 127
Mid-Atlantic Ridge, 76, 120
mid-ocean ridge, 77, 127
Mimatsu, Masao, 102
mineral pool, 111
mineral terrace, 110
monitoring earthquakes, 90–91, 99
Moon, 72, 124–125
Mount Etna, 114, 118
Mount Mazama, 122–123
Mount Pelée, 116–117
Mount St. Helens, 122–123
Mount Vesuvius, 116, 118–119
mud pool, 110
mudflows, 108–109, 123, 127
Mydans, Carl, 98

N

namazu, 98–99
Nazca Plate, 74–75
Neptunists, 114–115
New Madrid earthquake, 88–89
New Zealand, 110, 117
normal fault, 80, 127
normal magnetism, 77
North America, 122–123
North American Plate, 75, 80, 96, 122
Novarupta eruption, 122–123
nuée ardentes, 107

O

obsidian, 104
oceanic plates, 78–79
olivine, 115
Olympus Mons, 124–125

P

Pacific Plate, 74–75, 79–81, 94, 96, 98
pagodas, 93
pahoehoe, 104, 127
Palmeri, Luigi, 90
Pangaea, 75, 78
passing plates, 80
Pelé, 104–105, 124
peridotite, 115
Philippine Plate, 75, 98
Philippines, 109, 117
pillow lava, 77, 127
plate collisions, 78–79, 94
plate movements, 80–81, 83
plug, 112–113, 127
Plutonists, 114–115
Pompeii, 118–119
preparing for earthquakes, 92–93
pumice, 104, 127
P-waves, 90, 127
pyroclastic flow, 103, 106–108, 114, 122, 127

Q

quake-proof buildings, 92–93

R

radar, 76–77, 96
Rayleigh waves, 77
Red Sea, 76, 81
reverse fault, 80, 127
reverse magnetism, 76
rhyolite, 104, 112–113
Richter, Charles, 94
Richter Scale, 94–95
rift, 76
rift valley, 81, 127
Ring of Fire, 98

S

safety techniques, 92–93
San Andreas Fault, 80–81, 96–97
San Francisco earthquake, 96–97
Santorini, 118–119
scoria, 104
seafloor cross section, 76
seafloor mapping, 76
seafloor spreading, 76, 120
seamount, 83
seismic waves, 87, 97
seismogram, 90–91, 127
seismology, 90–91, 127
seismometer, 90–91, 114–115
shake table, 92
shield volcano, 82–83, 127
shifting continents, 74–75
shock waves, 86, 94
Showa-Shinzan, 102
Sigurgeirsson, Thorbjorn, 120
sill, 102, 113, 127

solar system, 72
sonar, 76–77
Soufrière Hills volcano, 106–107
South American Plate, 74–75
space rocks, 73
Stoffel, Keith and Dorothy, 122
subduction, 78–79, 82–83, 98, 127
sulfur, 124–125
Surtsey, 121
survivor stories, 116
S-waves, 90, 127

T

tachylyte, 104
Tambora eruption, 108–109, 116–117
tectonic plates, 74–75, 78–79, 94, 127
tectonics, 75
temblor, 97
thermal springs, 110, 120
thermocouple, 114–115
thrust fault, 81, 127
time capsules, 119
Transamerica Pyramid, 92–93
transform fault, 74, 127
tremor, 87, 90, 94
tsunami, 88–89, 99, 127
Turkey, 112

V

Valley of Ten Thousand Smokes, 122–123
Venus, 72, 124
volcanic eruptions, 103, 106–109, 116–123
volcanic eruptions, largest recorded, 116–117
Volcanic Explosivity Index, 116
volcanic glass, 104
volcanic landscapes, 112–113
volcano, 73, 78–79, 82–83, 98, 100–125
volcano, active, 102–103
volcano, dormant, 103, 112
volcano, extinct, 82, 112
volcano, extraterrestrial, 124–125
volcano aftereffects, 108–109
volcano chain formation, 82–83
volcanologist, 104, 107, 114–115, 127
volcanology, 114–115

W

warning signs, 122
weather patterns, 102, 108–109
Wegener, Alfred, 75

Y

Yellowstone National Park, 110–111
Yellowstone plateau, 82

Insects and Spiders

Contents

Introducing...Insects 132

What Is an Insect? 134
Up Close and Personal 136
Scents and Sense Ability 138
Egg, Nymph, Adult 140
Total Makeover 142
Going Buggy 144
Beetle Mania 146
Flights of Fancy 148
High Society 150
Stings on Wings 152
The Flies Have It 154

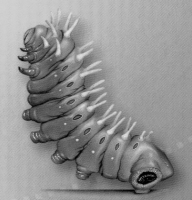

The World's Abuzz 156

Insect-Plant Connection 158
Predators, Etc. 160
Contact! 162
Takeoff 164
On the Move 166
Staying Alive 168
Home, Sweet Home 170

Spider Story 172

Spider Versus Insect 174
Closing In 176
Body Language 178
A Spider's Life 180
Webmasters 182
Spiders Stalking 184
Defensive Action 186

Glossary 188
Index 190

Pick Your Path!

THE WORLD IS TEEMING with animals—some of which live no farther than your backyard or even your own home. Are you ready to learn more about life on the wing? Open the pages of *Insects and Spiders* and prepare to be amazed. Read straight through to find out about insects and spiders from the inside out. Or try something different. Have you always wanted to know more about the "hive mentality"? Sneak a peek at the real thing in "Stings on Wings" and read on from there.

You'll find plenty of other discovery paths to choose from in the special features sections. Get insight into insect and spider behavior in "Inside Story," or meet nature head-on with "Hands On" activities.

INSIDE STORY
World in Miniature

Watch a smart spider at work. Learn from experts who've used one insect to control the population of another. Read more about that summertime scourge, the menacing mosquito. Then look out—a pack of driver ants is ready to hit town! With INSIDE STORY, you'll get an insider's look at the way insects and spiders have affected the world around us. You'll never look at an anthill or a spiderweb in the same way again.

Word Builders

What a strange word! What does it mean? Where did it come from? Find out by reading *Word Builders*.

That's Amazing!

Awesome facts, amazing records, fascinating figures— you'll find them all in *That's Amazing!*

HANDS ON
Create and Make

Use paper and a spoonful of jam to test ants' food-finding faculties. Learn the best techniques for locating and caring for insects. Search your surroundings for cicadas. Find out where to look for your local spiders. The HANDS ON features offer experiments, projects, and activities that will bring the world of insects and spiders to life.

Pathfinder

Use the *Pathfinder* section to find your way from one subject to another. It's all up to you.

Ready! Set!
Start exploring!

page **134** Most crickets have wings, but this one doesn't need them. Why not?

Go to WHAT IS AN INSECT?

page **136** Insects don't breathe through their mouths. What does this caterpillar use?

Go to UP CLOSE AND PERSONAL.

Introducing... Insects

GET READY TO meet some of Earth's smallest inhabitants. Learn how insects work from the inside out—how they live, communicate, change, and grow. Then get acquainted with some of the stars of the insect world. Find out what it takes to be a true bug. After that, meet the beetles—the most numerous insects of all. Admire delicate butterflies and moths, and then go underground with a colony of ants. Take a look inside a beehive before zooming off with the flies. It's time to meet nature head-on. Just turn the page.

page **138** If you have pets, you probably know this critter well. Find out how it knows when your dog or cat is walking by.

Go to SCENTS AND SENSE ABILITY.

page **140** Almost every insect mother must find a special place to lay her eggs. Why?

Go to EGG, NYMPH, ADULT.

page **142** This creature hatched from an egg into a caterpillar and is now a moth. How does that happen?

Go to TOTAL MAKEOVER.

page **144** When is a "bug" really a bug?

Go to GOING BUGGY.

page **146** Why might this insect be brightly colored?

Go to BEETLE MANIA.

page **148** Is this a moth or a butterfly? Learn how you can tell the difference.

Go to FLIGHTS OF FANCY.

page **150** Are these ants eating this plant, or are they helping it survive?

Go to HIGH SOCIETY.

page **152** This bee is carrying honey-making ingredients back to the hive. What happens next?

Go to STINGS ON WINGS.

page **154** This fly likes to drink nectar from flowers. Do its maggot young like the same food?

Go to THE FLIES HAVE IT.

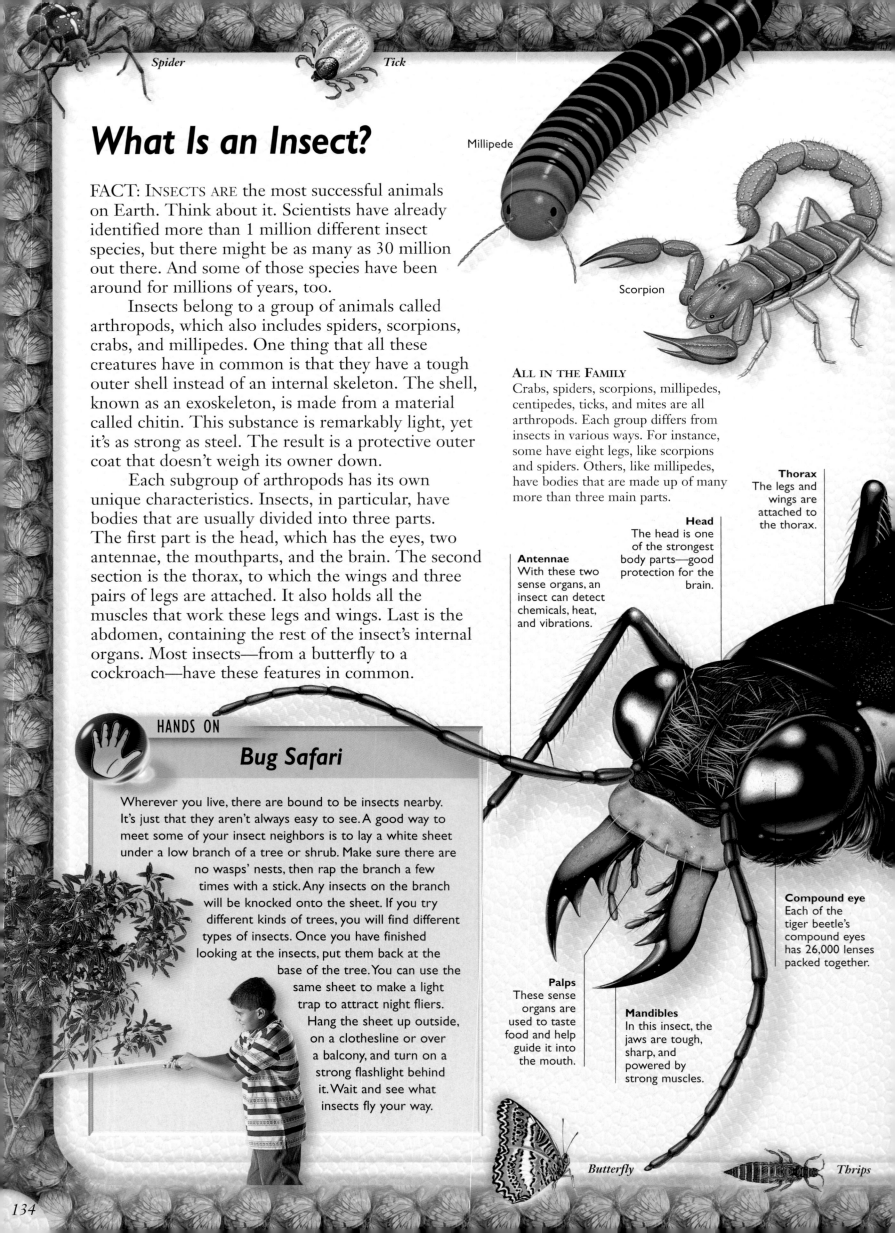

Spider

Tick

Millipede

Scorpion

What Is an Insect?

FACT: INSECTS ARE the most successful animals on Earth. Think about it. Scientists have already identified more than 1 million different insect species, but there might be as many as 30 million out there. And some of those species have been around for millions of years, too.

Insects belong to a group of animals called arthropods, which also includes spiders, scorpions, crabs, and millipedes. One thing that all these creatures have in common is that they have a tough outer shell instead of an internal skeleton. The shell, known as an exoskeleton, is made from a material called chitin. This substance is remarkably light, yet it's as strong as steel. The result is a protective outer coat that doesn't weigh its owner down.

Each subgroup of arthropods has its own unique characteristics. Insects, in particular, have bodies that are usually divided into three parts. The first part is the head, which has the eyes, two antennae, the mouthparts, and the brain. The second section is the thorax, to which the wings and three pairs of legs are attached. It also holds all the muscles that work these legs and wings. Last is the abdomen, containing the rest of the insect's internal organs. Most insects—from a butterfly to a cockroach—have these features in common.

ALL IN THE FAMILY

Crabs, spiders, scorpions, millipedes, centipedes, ticks, and mites are all arthropods. Each group differs from insects in various ways. For instance, some have eight legs, like scorpions and spiders. Others, like millipedes, have bodies that are made up of many more than three main parts.

Antennae
With these two sense organs, an insect can detect chemicals, heat, and vibrations.

Head
The head is one of the strongest body parts—good protection for the brain.

Thorax
The legs and wings are attached to the thorax.

Compound eye
Each of the tiger beetle's compound eyes has 26,000 lenses packed together.

Palps
These sense organs are used to taste food and help guide it into the mouth.

Mandibles
In this insect, the jaws are tough, sharp, and powered by strong muscles.

HANDS ON

Bug Safari

Wherever you live, there are bound to be insects nearby. It's just that they aren't always easy to see. A good way to meet some of your insect neighbors is to lay a white sheet under a low branch of a tree or shrub. Make sure there are no wasps' nests, then rap the branch a few times with a stick. Any insects on the branch will be knocked onto the sheet. If you try different kinds of trees, you will find different types of insects. Once you have finished looking at the insects, put them back at the base of the tree. You can use the same sheet to make a light trap to attract night fliers. Hang the sheet up outside, on a clothesline or over a balcony, and turn on a strong flashlight behind it. Wait and see what insects fly your way.

Butterfly

Thrips

Word Builders

• An **arthropod** has jointed legs and an external skeleton. The word is from the ancient Greek words *arthron*, for "joint," and *podos*, for "foot."
• **Exoskeleton** comes from the ancient Greek: *exo*, meaning "outside," and *skeletos*, meaning "dried up, hard." An insect's skeleton is on the outside. It is made up of plates joined together by more flexible membranes, which let the insect bend and twist.

That's Amazing!

• Some insects live in very harsh habitats and conditions. The petroleum fly lives in puddles of crude oil. It feeds on insects that fall in and get stuck.
• Snow fleas can survive in subzero temperatures. But if you pick one up, the heat from your hand will kill it in seconds.
• The larvae of some midges can be put in boiling water and still survive.

Pathfinder

• To meet more of the beetles, turn to pages 146–47.
• Beetles have elytra. Do other insects have specialized wings? Go to pages 164–65.
• Discover the differences between spiders and insects on pages 174–75.

A TIGER ON SIX LEGS

With its large eyes, razor-sharp jaws, and powerful running legs, this beautiful tiger beetle deserves its name. It is a true predator. Its eyes are able to detect the smallest movements of a potential victim. Its legs can carry it along at speeds that outrun most other insects—either to catch them or avoid being caught by them.

Elytra and wings
A beetle has elytra, or wing cases. They protect the delicate flying wings beneath.

Abdomen
Usually the largest part of an insect's body, the abdomen contains most of the vital organs.

Leg
Most insects have six legs. The legs vary in length and are usually divided into five parts.

Foot
An insect's feet may have hooks, pads, or suckers to help it hold on to surfaces or food.

TRAPPED IN TIME

Fossils of insects date back 400 million years. Insect remains are very fragile, so not much survives to become fossils. Sometimes, though, creatures like this 40-million-year-old grasshopper were trapped in the sticky sap of trees. When the sap fossilized and turned into amber, the grasshopper was perfectly preserved.

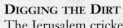

Silverfish   *Lacewing*

THE SUCCESS STORY

Insects occur in almost all the world's habitats, including oceans, polar zones, and mountain peaks. The animals below are all crickets, but each has made adaptations to its individual surroundings.

GREEN CAN'T BE SEEN

Living in forests and grasslands, a great green bush cricket needs good camouflage to avoid predators. Large eyes scan for danger, while long legs and wings help with a quick getaway.

FIELD WORK

The field cricket has strong, multipurpose mouthparts to deal with its varied diet. Its long and powerful back legs help it to hop or push its way through the grass of the meadows where it lives.

DIGGING THE DIRT

The Jerusalem cricket spends most of its life below ground. It has stout, powerful legs for digging. Wings might get in the way, so it has none.

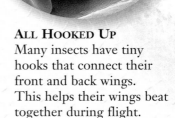

Up Close and Personal

INSECTS HAVE THE SAME basic bodily functions we have—they eat, breathe, move, and have babies. The difference is in how it all happens. Insect blood carries nutrients to body parts and removes wastes just like human blood, but is pumped by a long, thin heart that stretches through the abdomen. Insect blood is yellow or green because it contains certain proteins.

Another difference is that insects have no lungs. Instead, they get oxygen through openings along the sides of their bodies called spiracles. Spiracles are connected to tracheae, which branch out into smaller tubes that carry oxygen to every part of the insect. Functions like this are controlled by the large brain, which is connected to all nerves by a long nerve cord.

To keep all these systems running, an insect needs energy from food. In the case of this wasp (right), the food is mixed with saliva in the mouth. It passes down the throat to the crop, where it is broken down by more saliva and other secretions. Then it heads for the stomach, where special enzymes churn up the food further, making it ready for the insect to use.

ALL HOOKED UP
Many insects have tiny hooks that connect their front and back wings. This helps their wings beat together during flight.

INSIDE OUT
With its external skeleton cut away, this wasp's organs are revealed in color code. The breathing system is light blue. The system for digesting food is green. The blood circulation system is red, and the central nervous system is dark blue.

Heart
An insect has no arteries or veins. The tubelike heart pumps blood around the body.

Air sac
These pocketlike sacs allow the insect to store oxygen.

Ventral nerve cord
This connects series of nerve bundles, or ganglia, which help control many organs.

Stomach
Food goes through its final digestion stage in the stomach.

Spiracle
Insects usually have between 2 and 11 pairs of air holes.

INSIDE STORY
Taking Insect Pics

Insects are small, and that makes it hard to photograph them. The solution: Put a magnifying glass on the camera! With a special macro lens, an insect can be magnified several times. Attach a microscope to a camera, and you can magnify an insect hundreds of times. But the most powerful way to magnify insects is with a scanning electron microscope. The resulting image, called an electron micrograph, isn't really a normal photo at all. It is a computer-generated image created by bouncing electrons off an object so that they strike a sensor. With this machine, it's possible to magnify an insect 20,000 times its normal size, like this picture of a fly.

A THING CALLED STING
The barbed stinger of a honeybee is shown here, threaded through the eye of a needle. When used, the barbs get stuck, causing a deadly injury to the bee when it tries to crawl away. Wasps have smooth stingers that can be used many times.

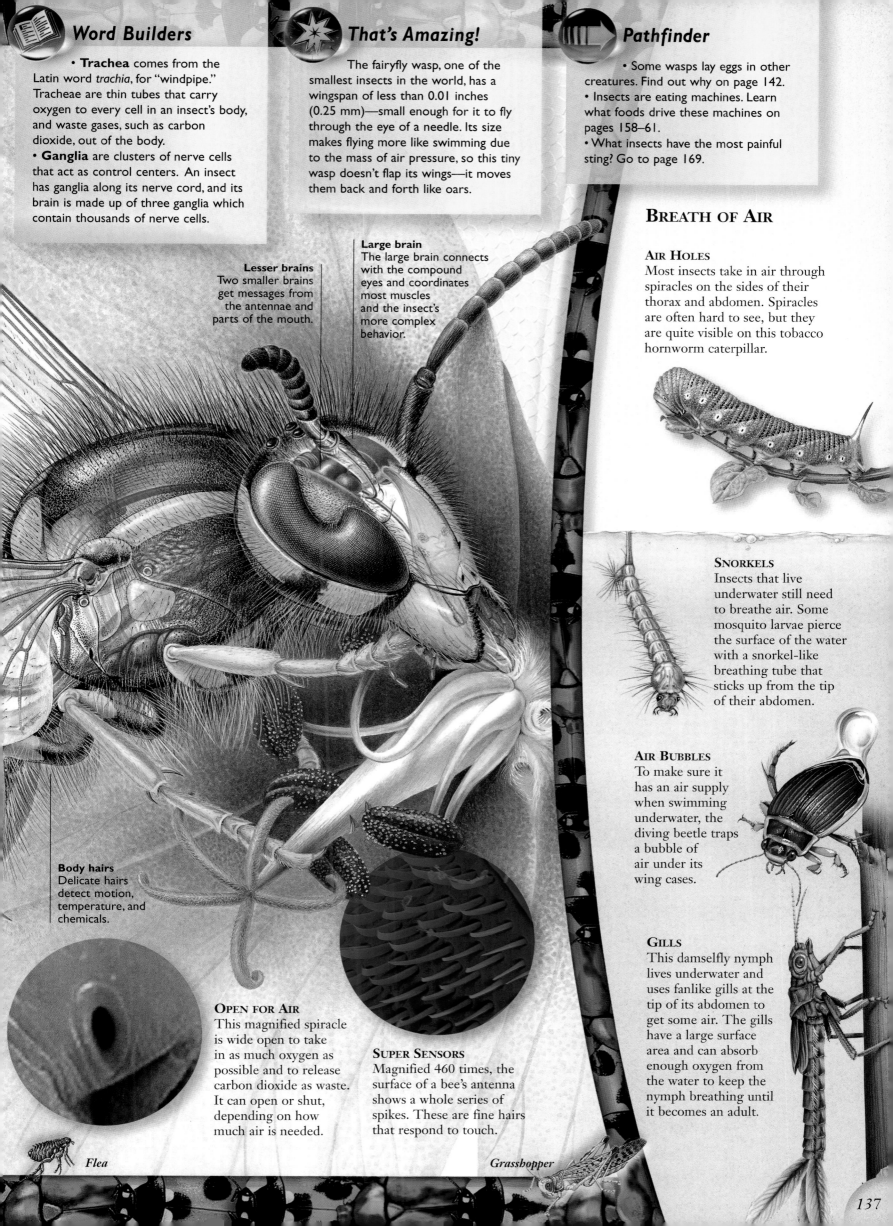

Word Builders

• **Trachea** comes from the Latin word *trachia*, for "windpipe." Tracheae are thin tubes that carry oxygen to every cell in an insect's body, and waste gases, such as carbon dioxide, out of the body.

• **Ganglia** are clusters of nerve cells that act as control centers. An insect has ganglia along its nerve cord, and its brain is made up of three ganglia which contain thousands of nerve cells.

That's Amazing!

The fairyfly wasp, one of the smallest insects in the world, has a wingspan of less than 0.01 inches (0.25 mm)—small enough for it to fly through the eye of a needle. Its size makes flying more like swimming due to the mass of air pressure, so this tiny wasp doesn't flap its wings—it moves them back and forth like oars.

Pathfinder

• Some wasps lay eggs in other creatures. Find out why on page 142.
• Insects are eating machines. Learn what foods drive these machines on pages 158–61.
• What insects have the most painful sting? Go to page 169.

Lesser brains
Two smaller brains get messages from the antennae and parts of the mouth.

Large brain
The large brain connects with the compound eyes and coordinates most muscles and the insect's more complex behavior.

Body hairs
Delicate hairs detect motion, temperature, and chemicals.

OPEN FOR AIR
This magnified spiracle is wide open to take in as much oxygen as possible and to release carbon dioxide as waste. It can open or shut, depending on how much air is needed.

SUPER SENSORS
Magnified 460 times, the surface of a bee's antenna shows a whole series of spikes. These are fine hairs that respond to touch.

Flea

Grasshopper

BREATH OF AIR

AIR HOLES
Most insects take in air through spiracles on the sides of their thorax and abdomen. Spiracles are often hard to see, but they are quite visible on this tobacco hornworm caterpillar.

SNORKELS
Insects that live underwater still need to breathe air. Some mosquito larvae pierce the surface of the water with a snorkel-like breathing tube that sticks up from the tip of their abdomen.

AIR BUBBLES
To make sure it has an air supply when swimming underwater, the diving beetle traps a bubble of air under its wing cases.

GILLS
This damselfly nymph lives underwater and uses fanlike gills at the tip of its abdomen to get some air. The gills have a large surface area and can absorb enough oxygen from the water to keep the nymph breathing until it becomes an adult.

Scents and Sense Ability

LIKE HUMANS, INSECTS use their senses—smell, touch, taste, sight, and hearing—to assemble a picture of the world around them. Much of this information is filtered through their hard-working antennae, which enable insects to smell, touch, and hear.

Sight can be a complicated thing for insects—they rely on compound eyes that may have a total of 56,000 lenses, each one recording a slightly different view! Many insects also have ocelli, a small group of eyes on the top of their heads that help with balance, flight, and light detection.

Insects taste food before they eat it, using sense organs clustered around the mouth. The most important of these are the palps. Flies and butterflies get extra help in this department from sense organs on...their feet! This way, they know when something they land on is good to eat.

Most insects rely on their antennae and the fine hairs that cover the body to help them tune in to sounds. But insects such as grasshoppers have something close to human hearing—they use earlike organs called tympana.

Insect view

Human view

NECTAR AHEAD!

Many insects have eyes that are sensitive to ultraviolet light, so they see things invisible to us. We may see a patch of flowers and nothing more. But nectar-drinkers, such as bees, butterflies, and wasps, see landing patterns that announce: "This way to a good meal!"

EARS ON THEIR BELLIES

Insects have hearing organs on their thorax, abdomen, or front legs instead of their head. The young lubber locusts (below) have tympana on their abdomen. Tympana work like human ears. A thin skin stretches between the sense receptors. When sound waves vibrate against the skin, the receptors relay the vibrations to the brain, which translates them into sound.

HANDS ON

Follow That Scent

Ants use antennae to actually sniff out food. Try this to see ants in action.

❶ Place a 12-inch (30-cm) circle of paper on flat ground near an anthill. Put a spoonful of jam outside the circle, away from the anthill, and wait for the ants to discover it. The first ants will leave a scent trail that tells the others where to find the food.

❷ While some ants are feeding, gently rotate the circle by 90°. The ants on the paper will follow the scent left by the others, but once they reach the ground, the scent and the jam won't be there. Use a magnifying glass to see how their antennae help them rediscover their lost snack.

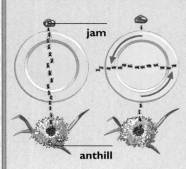

jam

anthill

DOUBLE DUTY

This weevil has thin, clubbed antennae at the end of its snout. When it bores into nuts or grain, the antennae help the insect decide if it's found food or a good place to lay eggs.

BODY HEAT

Adult fleas are sensitive to heat. They use their antennae to sense the body heat of a passing mammal or the presence of carbon dioxide, a gas breathed out by mammals. They then hop on for a meal.

TUNING IN

The most important sense organs that an insect has are the antennae on its head. These multipurpose super sensors let insects smell the world around them, as well as touch and hear it.

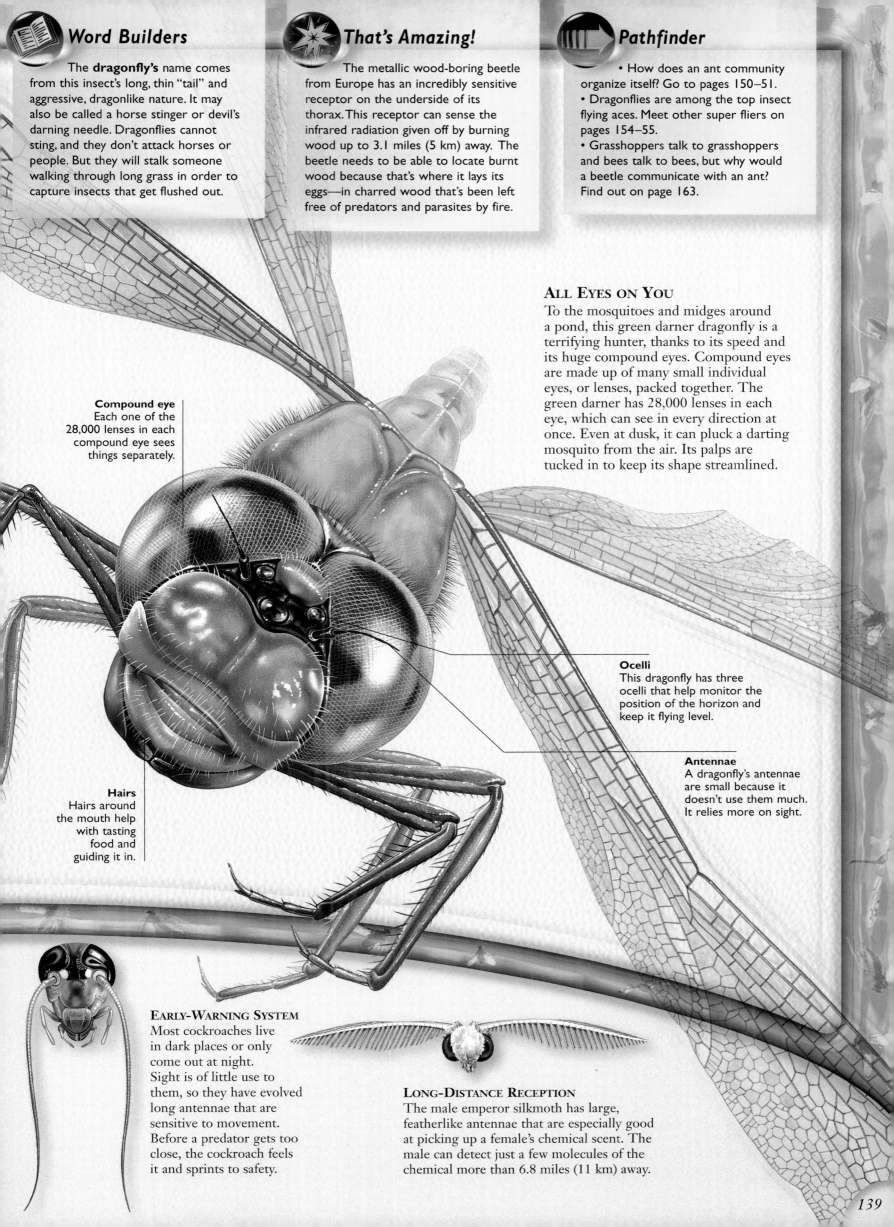

Word Builders

The **dragonfly's** name comes from this insect's long, thin "tail" and aggressive, dragonlike nature. It may also be called a horse stinger or devil's darning needle. Dragonflies cannot sting, and they don't attack horses or people. But they will stalk someone walking through long grass in order to capture insects that get flushed out.

That's Amazing!

The metallic wood-boring beetle from Europe has an incredibly sensitive receptor on the underside of its thorax. This receptor can sense the infrared radiation given off by burning wood up to 3.1 miles (5 km) away. The beetle needs to be able to locate burnt wood because that's where it lays its eggs—in charred wood that's been left free of predators and parasites by fire.

Pathfinder

• How does an ant community organize itself? Go to pages 150–51.
• Dragonflies are among the top insect flying aces. Meet other super fliers on pages 154–55.
• Grasshoppers talk to grasshoppers and bees talk to bees, but why would a beetle communicate with an ant? Find out on page 163.

ALL EYES ON YOU

To the mosquitoes and midges around a pond, this green darner dragonfly is a terrifying hunter, thanks to its speed and its huge compound eyes. Compound eyes are made up of many small individual eyes, or lenses, packed together. The green darner has 28,000 lenses in each eye, which can see in every direction at once. Even at dusk, it can pluck a darting mosquito from the air. Its palps are tucked in to keep its shape streamlined.

Compound eye
Each one of the 28,000 lenses in each compound eye sees things separately.

Hairs
Hairs around the mouth help with tasting food and guiding it in.

Ocelli
This dragonfly has three ocelli that help monitor the position of the horizon and keep it flying level.

Antennae
A dragonfly's antennae are small because it doesn't use them much. It relies more on sight.

EARLY-WARNING SYSTEM
Most cockroaches live in dark places or only come out at night. Sight is of little use to them, so they have evolved long antennae that are sensitive to movement. Before a predator gets too close, the cockroach feels it and sprints to safety.

LONG-DISTANCE RECEPTION
The male emperor silkmoth has large, featherlike antennae that are especially good at picking up a female's chemical scent. The male can detect just a few molecules of the chemical more than 6.8 miles (11 km) away.

Egg, Nymph, Adult

ALL INSECTS start out life as eggs. After mating, many females will try to lay their eggs close to a food source. That way, the young will have plenty to eat when they hatch from the eggs. Like all babies, insect young grow—but their exoskeletons cannot. The insect's solution is to molt, or shed, its exoskeleton. A new exoskeleton has already formed beneath the old one. With each molt, the insect changes size and shape until it becomes an adult. This is called metamorphosis, and in some species, it can take an awfully long time. The periodical cicada takes 17 years!

When some insects hatch, they already look a little like their parents. These young, called nymphs, go through a simple metamorphosis—they change, or mature, gradually until adulthood. Nymphs of some species—like silverfish, bedbugs, and aphids—may look almost exactly like their parents. Others look less like the adults. Dragonfly and damselfly nymphs are so different from their parents that they live underwater before crawling onto land for their final molt into adulthood. Nymphs of some winged insects have wing buds at the top of the thorax. These buds grow larger as the nymph grows, but they aren't ready to use until the insect hits maturity.

CARING PARENT
This shield bug is protecting her young. If a predator comes too close, she will try to scare it away. This is unusual behavior in insects. Most abandon their eggs once they have laid them. The eggs are usually tough and well hidden, so they often don't come to any harm.

A soft-shelled adult leafhopper pulls free of its old exoskeleton.

MALE AND FEMALE
The size difference between males and females is easy to see with these mantids. The male mantid (behind) is usually smaller and lighter, so he can fly around searching for a mate. The female's greater size is needed to make room for her eggs.

A cluster of mosquito eggs floats like a raft on a pond.

EGGS-TRAVAGANZA
Insect eggs come in many shapes, sizes, and colors. The number of eggs also varies among different insects. A female spider-hunting wasp produces between 20 and 40 eggs in her lifetime, while a termite queen can lay more than 10 million.

The females of many cockroach species make a case to protect their eggs.

Word Builders

- **Molt** comes from the Latin word *mutare*, "to change." Molting is a dangerous time for an insect because it can't really defend itself without its hard outer covering. Most hide during this period and finish within an hour. Some timber beetles, though, take several days.
- **Metamorphosis** comes from two ancient Greek words—*meta*, meaning "change," and *morphe*, meaning "form or shape."

That's Amazing!

Some nymphs wear several different disguises on the way to becoming adults. When a young Australian prickly insect hatches, it looks like a fierce bull ant. As it grows and molts, it begins to look like a piece of flaky eucalyptus bark. Eventually, when it is fully grown, it resembles a dead eucalyptus leaf.

Pathfinder

- There are two ways for an insect to get from egg to adult. Simple metamorphosis is one way. What is the other? Go to pages 142–43.
- People call all kinds of insects "bugs," but only certain types really qualify. Find out what it takes to be a true bug on pages 144–45.
- Compare an insect's life cycle with a spider's. Turn to pages 180–81.

The adult leafhopper, with its exoskeleton hardened.

HANDS ON

Cicada Search

If you live in a warm part of the world and you go looking for cicadas in midsummer, you will probably find them. This is when most cicada nymphs emerge from their underground homes, climb up the closest tree, molt one last time, and then start singing to attract a mate. That's the first clue to locating cicadas—their call. Next, look for the molted skins of the nymphs (right), which will be left on trees and shrubs near ground level. You will probably discover some adults nearby. After you have studied your cicada, let it go near where you found it—it won't survive for long in captivity.

A leafhopper nymph gets ready to shed its last exoskeleton.

GROWING PAINS

A leafhopper nymph finds a hiding place to make its final molt. By expanding and contracting its abdomen, the nymph forces air into its body to split the old exoskeleton. In a difficult move, the scarlet-and-green adult leafhopper climbs free and uses the extra air to stretch its new, soft exoskeleton. When this hardens, the air is released and there is space to grow into. Blood pumps through the veins of the leafhopper's wings to stretch them out before they harden.

Lacewing eggs on long stalks stay out of reach of small predators.

A single honeybee egg is laid in each cell of the honeycomb.

A ladybug lays her bright yellow eggs on a leaf.

Total Makeover

SOME INSECT YOUNG look nothing at all like their parents. Unlike insects that start out as nymphs, these insects don't change gradually. They go through a single, drastic makeover called complete metamorphosis. They hatch from eggs as soft-bodied larvae—wingless and often legless. Moth and butterfly young are called caterpillars. Legless fly larvae are called maggots, while many beetle young are called grubs.

The larvae eat constantly, molting several times. Once the larvae are fully grown, they stop eating...and moving, too. They are getting ready to pupate, or change into adults. Many form tough pupal cases, and some build silk or earth cocoons to protect themselves, while others simply find a safe place to hide. The pupal stage can last throughout the cold winter months. During this time, the juvenile body parts break down and the adult features grow. At last, the fully mature adult emerges, complete with wings and reproductive organs. The adults can look vastly different from their larval stages, often eating completely different foods and living in different habitats as well.

A female Indian moon moth lays her eggs on a leaf.

A young caterpillar feeds on the nearby leaves.

GOT IT COVERED
A parasitic wasp has laid its eggs on this living caterpillar. After the eggs hatch, the wasp larvae burrow into the caterpillar host to feed. They then burst out through its skin and turn into pupae that cover its body.

A male Indian moon moth flies off to look for a mate.

CYCLE OF LIFE
A female Indian moon moth starts the cycle of life by laying a few eggs on leaves. The new caterpillars eat their own eggshells, then start on the leaves. Once they are fully grown, the caterpillars stop feeding and find a place to pupate. A few months later, adult moths emerge. They are ready to fly in an hour or two but will wait until dark before taking to the air for the first time.

A new adult moth hangs to stretch and harden its wings.

Stag beetle ———
○ *Egg*

Word Builders

- **Larva** is a Latin word that means "ghost." It is the term used for the young of many insects. This is because larvae are often very pale and so look a little like ghosts.
- **Cocoon** comes from *coco*, a French word for "shell." A cocoon is a shell-like covering of silk, with mud, wood, or leaves, that protects the helpless pupa while it turns into an adult insect.

That's Amazing!

Larvae are born to eat. From the moment they hatch, they feed as much as they can. Some caterpillars grow dramatically over a short period of time. For instance, the oak silk moth caterpillar balloons from just 0.2 inches (5 mm) in length to nearly 5 inches (12.7 cm) in length. That's 12,000 times its original size—all in just three weeks.

Pathfinder

- Where does silk come from? Find out on page 149.
- Learn how a bee goes through a total makeover in the hive on pages 152–53.
- What other kinds of insect parasites are there? Go to pages 160–61.

LARVAE EATING HABITS

FAST FOOD
The diving beetle grub is long and thin so it can zip through water to catch prey. Its long, needle-sharp mandibles are powerful enough to spear small fish.

SAFE HAVEN
After spending seven years as a larva burrowing through the trunk of an oak tree, a young jewel beetle formed a small chamber in which to pupate. It has now emerged as an adult, so its new exoskeleton is soft.

This caterpillar has molted four or five times.

A caterpillar pupates inside a silk cocoon for several months.

HEALTHY SNACK
After a hawk moth larva hatches, it must eat its eggshell or it will die. The shell has chemicals that stimulate the larva to start feeding. Many insect eggshells hold nutrients and make a good first meal.

LEGGY LARVA
The grub of the seven-spot ladybug needs strong legs to climb after the aphids that it feeds on.

ALL YOU CAN EAT
Blowfly maggots don't need legs. They hatch directly on their food—rotting animals—and legs would get in the way. Their streamlined shape lets them burrow quickly into decaying flesh.

HANDS ON

Insect Care and Feeding

It's easy to keep an insect for closer study. Just follow these tips for making your subject feel comfortable.

❶ Use a glass jar or plastic container. Punch holes in the lid so the insect can breathe.

❷ Provide a small dish with damp tissue, so the insect won't dry out. Add twigs or leaves for climbing insects.

❸ For longer stays, identify the insect and find out what it likes to eat. What else does it need?

❹ When you're finished, release the insect where you originally found it.

GET A GRIP
The large caterpillar of the hercules moth has to hang on tight when feeding on leaves high up in trees. Patches of tiny hooks at the tips of its prolegs give it a strong grip.

 Larva   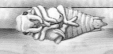 *Pupa*   *Adult*

Going Buggy

WE CALL A LOT of insects and other crawly things "bugs," but that name really refers to only one particular group of insects. The insect world is divided into separate groups called orders, and true bugs—like bedbugs and stinkbugs—belong to the order Hemiptera. Cicadas, aphids, treehoppers, and leafhoppers are in this order, too.

While many of the creatures in this order look quite different from one another, most have one feature in common: their mouthparts. Bugs don't have jaws for biting or chewing—instead they have special mouthparts for piercing and sucking up liquids. These mouthparts, shaped like hollow needles, are contained in a long, thin beak.

True bugs can be found all over the world. Most are terrestrial (land-dwelling), but there are plenty of aquatic (water-dwelling) bugs, too. Many bugs feed on plant juices, while some feed on other insects, making them useful in pest control. Still others suck the blood of animals and people, and some pass on diseases via their mouthparts as they feed.

MOTHER AND YOUNG
Many bugs live in groups, with adults and nymphs mixed in together. The colorful leafhopper bug pictured above is the adult. The white tufted creatures are nymphs. Their spiky appearance and unpleasant taste keep predators away.

NO JOKE
A jester bug uses its needlelike mouthparts to suck nectar from a flower. When the bug is not feeding, its mouthparts stay inside the beak, tucked away in a special groove running along the underside of its body.

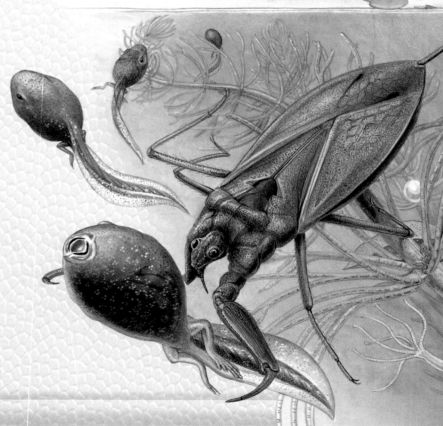

PUTTING INSECTS IN ORDER
Entomologists divide insects into about 30 different orders. The insects in each order have certain features in common, such as sucking mouthparts in bugs. Here are some of the best-known orders.

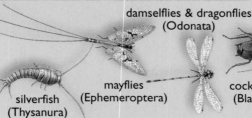

damselflies & dragonflies
(Odonata)

mantids
(Mantodea)

silverfish
(Thysanura)

mayflies
(Ephemeroptera)

cockroaches
(Blattodea)

termites
(Isoptera)

earwigs
(Dermaptera)

Word Builders

Hemiptera comes from the ancient Greek *hemi*, meaning "half," and *ptera*, meaning "wings." Many bugs in this order look "half-winged" because their wingtips are transparent. The true bugs are often split into two subgroups. The Homoptera feed on plants and hold their wings up like a roof over their back. The Heteroptera may feed on insects, animals, and humans, and their wings are held flat.

That's Amazing!

The common aphid is one of the fastest reproducing animals on Earth. When an aphid is born, it already has a baby developing inside. If it were not for insect-eaters such as ladybugs, spiders, and birds, the world would be overrun by aphids. Just one could result in 10 quintillion offspring in as little as six months. That would form a column of aphids 3 feet (1 m) wide from Earth to the Moon.

Pathfinder

• How does a white waxy treehopper nymph turn into a brightly colored treehopper adult? Go to pages 140–41.
• A ladybug is called a bug, but it isn't one. Find out what kind of insect it really is on pages 146–47.
• Discover the trick water striders use to walk on water on page 166.

WATER WORLD

Ponds can teem with bugs living both in and on top of the water's surface. Below, a water scorpion hangs suspended among the weeds, grabbing at a passing tadpole with its powerful front legs. Its long, tail-like breathing tube pierces the surface, providing a ready supply of oxygen. On the right, a water boatman paddles through the water with legs like oars. Immediately above it, two water striders stand on the pond's surface, one making a meal of a hover fly.

INSIDE STORY

Bug-ology

People who study insects are called entomologists. Because there are so many different kinds of insects living in a wide variety of habitats throughout the world, entomologists can find themselves doing lots of different things—from teaching farmers new means of pest control to collecting rainforest specimens that might provide cures for diseases like malaria and cancer. Scientists say there are still millions of animal species out there, just waiting to be identified. Since most of these species are insects, you might say that entomologists have got their work cut out for them.

grasshoppers, crickets & katydids (Orthoptera)

stick insects (Phasmida)

lice (Phthiraptera)

true bugs (Hemiptera)

thrips (Thysanoptera)

lacewings (Neuroptera)

beetles (Coleoptera)

fleas (Siphonaptera)

flies (Diptera)

caddis flies (Trichoptera)

moths & butterflies (Lepidoptera)

ants, bees & wasps (Hymenoptera)

Beetle Mania

IF INSECTS ARE the most successful creatures in the animal world, then beetles have to be the most successful insects. There are more than 350,000 different members of the order Coleoptera, and entomologists think there are still hundreds of thousands more to be identified.

While beetles vary greatly in shape and size, just about all of them have bodies that are heavily armored like little tanks. They have extra-thick exoskeletons as well as elytra—hardened wing cases—that protect delicate body parts like flying wings. The extra weight may slow beetles down a little, but their tough exteriors are good shields against predators.

Beetles have powerful biting and chewing mouthparts that can tackle almost any kind of food. The plant-eaters among them are often extremely picky about what kinds of leaves, flowers, pollen, or bark they will eat. Some beetles are skilled predators that hunt for small animals, including fish and other insects. Still others feed on the bodies of dead animals or on animal droppings. If they didn't, the world would be a much dirtier and smellier place.

THE SWARM
It's the end of summer, and these ladybugs (which are beetles, not bugs) have swarmed to find a sheltered hibernation spot for winter. This behavior is called aggregation. Sometimes, swarms of ladybugs can contain thousands of individuals. But they are harmless—even beneficial—unlike a swarm of locusts.

TAKE A DIVE
This diving beetle, 1.25 inches (3.2 cm) long, has a good grip on a small fish. Though clumsy on land, diving beetles fly and swim very well. In water, they paddle along quickly, pushing their streamlined bodies along with their powerful back legs.

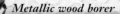

Metallic wood borer

Word Builders

• The word **beetle** comes from the Old English word *bitula*, which means "biter."
• During the Middle Ages in Europe, many crops were destroyed by aphids. Just when the people thought they would starve, swarms of **ladybugs** appeared and ate the aphids. In thanks, the people named them "Our Lady bugs" after Mary, the mother of Jesus.

That's Amazing!

Some of the strongest insects in the world belong to the scarab beetle family. It has been calculated that a rhinoceros beetle can carry 350 times its own weight. In human terms, this is the same as carrying more than 34,000 pounds (15,422 kg), or three bull elephants! Rhinoceros beetles can manage this incredible feat because of their extremely thick exoskeleton and very efficient muscles.

Pathfinder

• Wasps and weevils are also helpful insects. What do they do? Go to pages 152 and 158.
• Some beetles have a taste for dung. Find out which beetles like to eat dead bodies on page 160.

BEETLE BAZAAR

Beetles come in many colors, shapes, and sizes, depending on their lifestyle and needs.

STREAMLINED
This rove beetle is small and slender, just the right shape for squeezing between twigs and leaves as it hunts for food amidst the leaf litter where it lives.

COLOR GUARD
In the creature world, bright colors often warn predators that prey tastes bad or stings. This brightly colored bee-eating beetle fools predators into staying away—even though it is harmless.

HAIR TUFTS
Some beetles have tufts of hair all over their back, like this African jewel beetle. The hairs break up the outline of the beetle's body, and may make it more difficult to spot.

LONG HORNS
The antennae of this South American longhorn beetle are 3 inches (7.5 cm) long. With these antennae, it can locate a mate or food from more than 2 miles (3.2 km) away.

HANDS ON

Make a Pitfall Trap

Small crawling insects can be hard to spot, especially when they are active at night, like many beetles. One way to meet the crawlers in your backyard is to build a pitfall trap to catch them.

❶ Place a layer of damp tissue paper, some leaves, and twigs in an empty can with the top removed.

❷ Dig a hole in the ground and place the can inside the hole so the open end is level with the soil.

❸ Arrange four stones around the can and lay a flat piece of wood on top of the stones. This will let insects in, but keep rain and larger animals out.

❹ Check the trap throughout the day. The insects you catch in the morning will be different from those you'll catch at night. Your catch will change with the seasons, too.

❺ Let the insects go once you've finished looking at them.

ON A ROLL

These male and female dung beetles have shaped some animal droppings into a ball and are rolling it toward their burrow. The female will lay one or more eggs in it, and eventually the new larvae will hatch and eat the dung ball up. These beetles do a very important job. Australia had to import some from Africa because the local dung beetles couldn't cope with all the droppings piling up from the cattle and sheep that had been brought into the country.

Goliath beetle

Vaporer moth caterpillar

Puss moth caterpillar

Monarch caterpillar

LEAVE ME ALONE!
Some caterpillars are not as defenseless as they seem. The vaporer moth caterpillar has hairs that irritate the skin and make a nasty mouthful. Packed with toxic chemicals, the bright monarch caterpillar can kill its predators. The puss moth, when disturbed, raises its head and flicks two rear whips from side to side. As a last resort, it sprays formic acid.

Flights of Fancy

BUTTERFLIES ARE SOME of the insect world's most valued ambassadors to people. Nearly everyone loves their brilliant colors and delicate, fluttering wings. Actually, butterflies are just a small portion of the 150,000-plus species that make up the order Lepidoptera—moths! Moths get much less publicity than their colorful cousins. They are usually small and drab, camouflaged to look like bark or leaves when they rest. Most are nocturnal (active at night) and have developed acute senses of smell and hearing. Still, there are exceptions to the rule. Some moths are diurnal (active during the day) and vibrantly colored. And some butterflies have dull, brown underwings for camouflage so they look like dead leaves when they're sitting still.

Lepidopteran young and adults have different eating habits. Both butterflies and moths start out as soft-bodied caterpillars with strong chewing jaws. The slow-moving caterpillars make easy pickings for predators, so they've evolved ways to protect themselves (see above). During a complete metamorphosis, most caterpillars' mouthparts re-form into a long, thin mouthpart called a proboscis. With the proboscis, an adult usually feeds only on liquids.

MONARCHS ON THE MOVE
These monarch butterflies gather every fall in North America. Then millions of them migrate south to California, U.S.A., and Mexico to avoid the freezing winter. Some travel thousands of miles and cover up to 80 miles (129 km) a day.

THINGS ON WINGS
Looked at under a microscope, the wing of a moth or butterfly—such as this peacock butterfly—reveals thousands of scales, all overlapping like the shingles on a roof. The scales of each species are different shapes, colors, and sizes, allowing the members of a species to identify each other.

WHICH IS WHICH?

ANTENNAE...
If you're trying to tell a butterfly from a moth, look at the antennae first. All butterflies have thin, threadlike antennae that are clubbed at the tips, as seen on this marine blue. They also always have a proboscis, which uncurls to feed on nectar.

PROBOSCISES, TOO
Moths' antennae can be straight or feathery, like those of this ornate tiger moth. Most species also have curled proboscises. Some have short, stabbing mouthparts. Others, which have none at all, cannot eat and only live long enough to breed.

Word Builders

- **Butterfly** comes from the name given to the yellow brimstone butterfly in England between 400 and 500 years ago, when it used to be known as the "butter-colored fly."
- **Migration** comes from the Latin word *migrare*, "to change." It means to travel from one area to another, usually to find a better situation. Some beetles migrate just a few inches, while certain butterflies travel 1,800 miles (2,900 km).

That's Amazing!

Not all butterflies and moths are vegetarians. Several swallowtails suck up the rotting flesh of animals. South American heliconiid butterflies like to sip on urine. And the vampire moth from Asia has a dagger-like proboscis that it uses to suck the blood of its victims, including humans.

Pathfinder

- How does a caterpillar turn into a moth? Go to pages 142–43.
- Why would one butterfly want to look like another? Learn more about it on page 169.
- Find out what humans use spider silk for on page 174.

BATHING BEAUTY

A boldly colored heliconiid mimic butterfly spreads its wings to bask in the sun while feeding on some flowers. The undersides of its wings are surprisingly drab, and in its usual resting position—with wings folded straight up over its back—predators are less likely to take notice. This South American butterfly feeds on liquid nectar, using its uncurled proboscis. It can also eat some solid pollen food.

INSIDE STORY

Wearing Caterpillar Spit

The next time your mother puts on a nice silk blouse, think of this: she's wearing caterpillar spit.

Silk is made from the material that silkworm caterpillars use to make their cocoons. When the caterpillars are ready to pupate, they make a special saliva that solidifies into thread when it hits the air. This thread is the strongest of all natural fibers—a thread of silk can be stronger than the same size thread of some kinds of steel. It takes about three days for the caterpillars to spin their cocoons. Once the cocoons are finished, silk farmers bake them in an oven, killing the insects inside. Next, they drop the cocoons in boiling water. The cocoons unravel into single strands that are then twisted together to make silk thread, ready to weave into cloth.

COLOR CONFUSION

Not all moths are drab. This colorful creature may look like a butterfly, but it is a day-flying moth from Madagascar. Like almost all moths, it rests with wings spread flat. It also has straight antennae.

RESTING POSITION

Very few moths can fold their wings the way this 88 butterfly does. Butterflies rest with wings folded up over their backs. Unlike most, the undersides of the 88's wings are brightly colored, while the upper surfaces are drab.

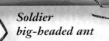

Soldier
big-headed ant

Worker
big-headed ant

Queen
big-headed ant

Male
big-headed ant

High Society

ANTS. YOU SEE THEM everywhere, but do you really know what goes on inside that anthill? Members of the order Hymenoptera, like bees and wasps, ants are social insects—that means they work together for the survival of the colony. The smallest ant colonies have a few dozen members, but the largest can be huge. Japanese wood ants can form groups of more than 300 million individuals in underground nests bigger than 490 football fields! Most ants build nests in wood, on plants, or out of soil—and these can be above or below ground, or even up in trees. But some species, such as driver and army ants, are nomadic and never stay in one place for long.

Nearly every ant colony has two castes, or types, of ants—the queen and the workers, who are all females. The few males in the colony exist only to mate with a new queen to start a new nest. They die soon afterward. The queen's job is to lay eggs, while the workers take care of all other business. Large workers, called majors, or soldiers, defend the nest. Medium-sized ants concentrate on building the nest or foraging for food. Some ant species gather almost anything—dead or alive—while others prefer specific seeds, fungi, or sweet plant and animal secretions. The smallest ants in the colony usually stay inside to nurse the young or clean the nest.

BIG BAD BULLDOG
One of the biggest and toughest of all ants is the Australian bulldog ant. It eats all kinds of plant foods, but it is also a ferocious hunter with huge mandibles that can deliver a painful bite to humans—and a lethal one to insects. After ambushing its katydid prey, this bulldog ant has swiftly killed and butchered it. All that's left of lunch is the katydid's head.

SOUP DU JOUR
The cups formed by the leaves of a pitcher plant are full of digestive juices. Most insects that fall in will drown and be digested by the plant. But some can survive. Here, an ant has dived in, probably to gnaw apart the cricket. Big insects take so long to digest that the plant's juices can turn bad. By removing the cricket, the ant will stop a case of plant indigestion.

GOOD NEIGHBORS

Ants can be social with a variety of different ants as well as other insects—and even plants.

ANT AND APHID
Red ants and aphids know how to keep each other happy. The ants aggressively protect the aphids from predators. The ants reward themselves by feasting on honeydew, a sweet liquid produced by the aphids.

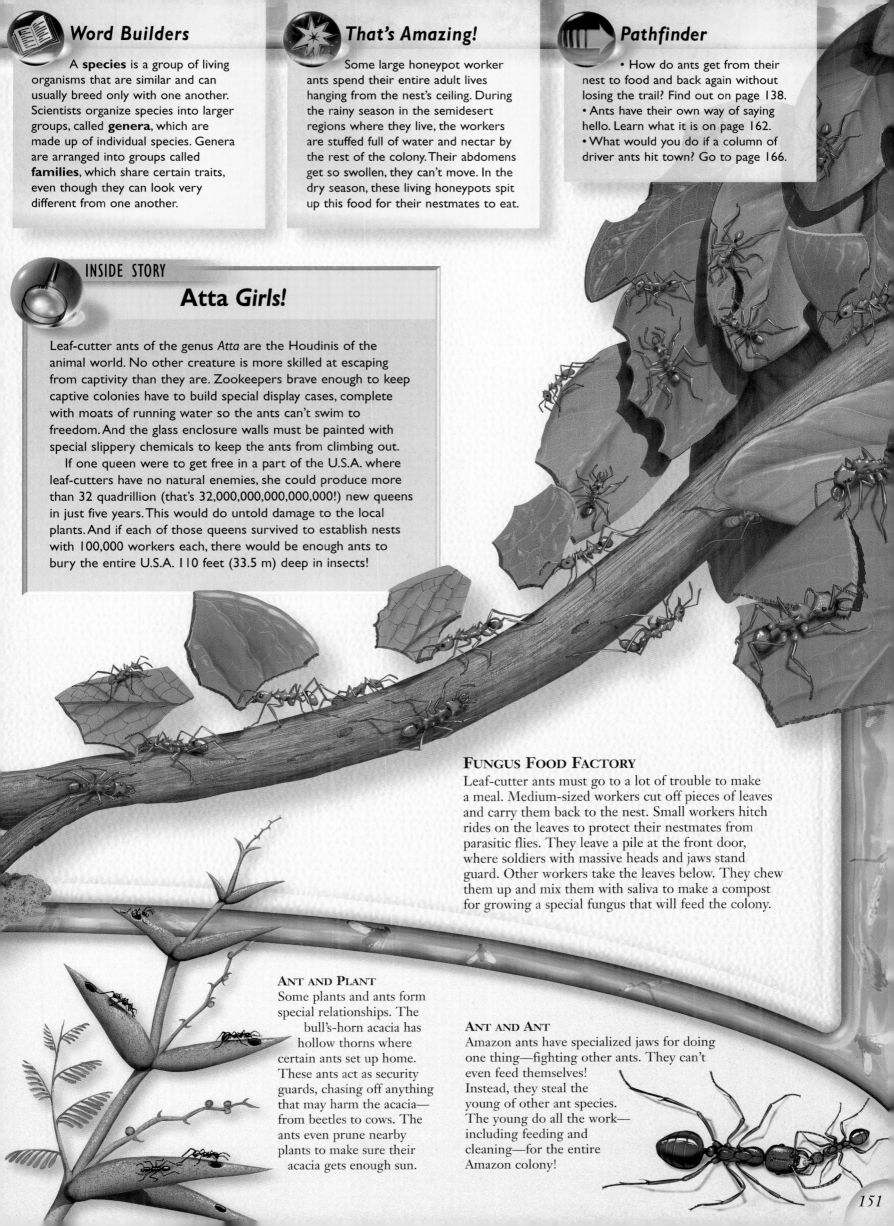

Word Builders

A **species** is a group of living organisms that are similar and can usually breed only with one another. Scientists organize species into larger groups, called **genera**, which are made up of individual species. Genera are arranged into groups called **families**, which share certain traits, even though they can look very different from one another.

That's Amazing!

Some large honeypot worker ants spend their entire adult lives hanging from the nest's ceiling. During the rainy season in the semidesert regions where they live, the workers are stuffed full of water and nectar by the rest of the colony. Their abdomens get so swollen, they can't move. In the dry season, these living honeypots spit up this food for their nestmates to eat.

Pathfinder

• How do ants get from their nest to food and back again without losing the trail? Find out on page 138.
• Ants have their own way of saying hello. Learn what it is on page 162.
• What would you do if a column of driver ants hit town? Go to page 166.

INSIDE STORY

Atta Girls!

Leaf-cutter ants of the genus *Atta* are the Houdinis of the animal world. No other creature is more skilled at escaping from captivity than they are. Zookeepers brave enough to keep captive colonies have to build special display cases, complete with moats of running water so the ants can't swim to freedom. And the glass enclosure walls must be painted with special slippery chemicals to keep the ants from climbing out.

If one queen were to get free in a part of the U.S.A. where leaf-cutters have no natural enemies, she could produce more than 32 quadrillion (that's 32,000,000,000,000,000!) new queens in just five years. This would do untold damage to the local plants. And if each of those queens survived to establish nests with 100,000 workers each, there would be enough ants to bury the entire U.S.A. 110 feet (33.5 m) deep in insects!

FUNGUS FOOD FACTORY

Leaf-cutter ants must go to a lot of trouble to make a meal. Medium-sized workers cut off pieces of leaves and carry them back to the nest. Small workers hitch rides on the leaves to protect their nestmates from parasitic flies. They leave a pile at the front door, where soldiers with massive heads and jaws stand guard. Other workers take the leaves below. They chew them up and mix them with saliva to make a compost for growing a special fungus that will feed the colony.

ANT AND PLANT

Some plants and ants form special relationships. The bull's-horn acacia has hollow thorns where certain ants set up home. These ants act as security guards, chasing off anything that may harm the acacia—from beetles to cows. The ants even prune nearby plants to make sure their acacia gets enough sun.

ANT AND ANT

Amazon ants have specialized jaws for doing one thing—fighting other ants. They can't even feed themselves! Instead, they steal the young of other ant species. The young do all the work—including feeding and cleaning—for the entire Amazon colony!

Stings on Wings

ZZZZZZZ...OUCH! Sound familiar? That may be what your first experience with a bee or wasp was like. Despite the pain they can cause, though, bees and wasps are among the most important members of the insect world. Plants depend on them to pollinate their flowers. If there were no bees to do this, we'd have few fruits or vegetables to eat. And if there were no wasps, our gardens and farms would teem with destructive insects.

Bees evolved from wasps, and they both belong to the order Hymenoptera. Scientists have identified more than 100,000 species, most of which have two pairs of wings, a narrow waist, biting mouthparts, and a pair of compound eyes. It is their highly developed way of life that sets them apart from other insects. While many hymenopterans can be called loners because they dig their own burrows or find holes in rotting trees, some social bees and wasps form incredibly complex societies in their hives and nests, making them among the most advanced of all the insects.

FOOD SOURCE
A solitary parasitic wasp like this sand wasp preys on other insects—normally not for herself but for her larvae! She'll catch an insect, such as a caterpillar, and lay eggs on it with a special organ called an ovipositor. Now the wasp's larvae will have fresh food when they hatch.

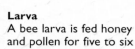

FITTING OUT THE NURSERY
This leaf-cutter bee has cut out a perfect semicircle of leaf, rolled it between her jaws, and now flies it back to her burrow. She uses the leaf as wallpaper to build a cell, then fills it with nectar and pollen, and lays an egg on it.

Larva
A bee larva is fed honey and pollen for five to six days, and molts five times.

Cell
Worker bees produce wax to make or repair cells, which are used to store honey and pollen or to rear young.

Pupa
Its cell capped, a larva spins a cocoon and pupates for several weeks.

Cell capping
A worker bee caps the cell of a mature larva with a wax seal.

INSIDE STORY

Insects on Pest Patrol

Insects reproduce so quickly and in such large numbers that they can easily become pests. One of the best ways to combat pests is to use their natural enemies—including other insects—to keep their numbers in check. The Chinese started using insects for pest control 2,500 years ago, but it has only become common practice worldwide within the last 30 years. After certain insecticides were proven to harm the environment, scientists started looking for safer ways to control pests. Many parasitic wasp species are now bred and sold to farmers to kill insects, such as aphids and scale bugs, that damage crops. Ichneumon wasps like this one (left) are used to kill the larvae of wood-boring wasps, which destroy valuable timber.

Cow killer wasp

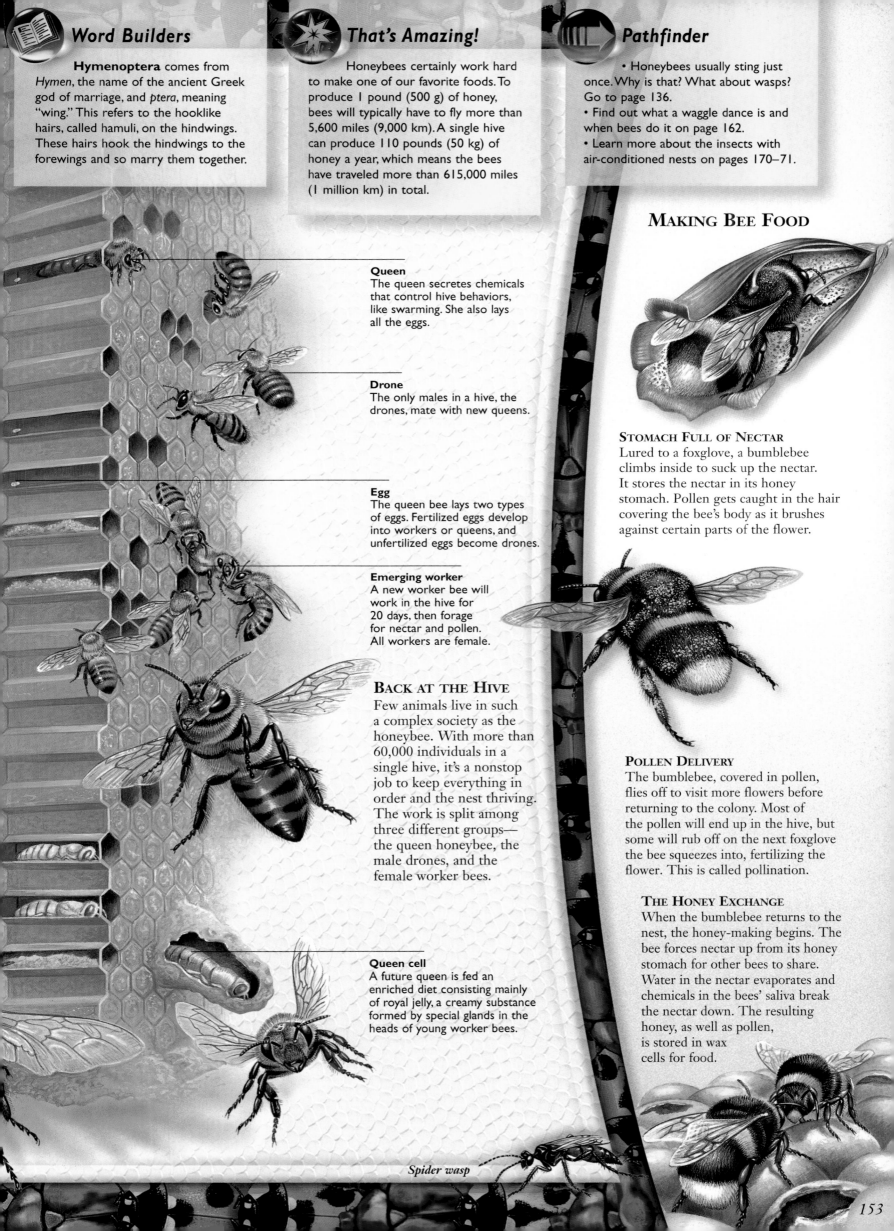

Word Builders

Hymenoptera comes from *Hymen*, the name of the ancient Greek god of marriage, and *ptera*, meaning "wing." This refers to the hooklike hairs, called hamuli, on the hindwings. These hairs hook the hindwings to the forewings and so marry them together.

That's Amazing!

Honeybees certainly work hard to make one of our favorite foods. To produce 1 pound (500 g) of honey, bees will typically have to fly more than 5,600 miles (9,000 km). A single hive can produce 110 pounds (50 kg) of honey a year, which means the bees have traveled more than 615,000 miles (1 million km) in total.

Pathfinder

• Honeybees usually sting just once. Why is that? What about wasps? Go to page 136.
• Find out what a waggle dance is and when bees do it on page 162.
• Learn more about the insects with air-conditioned nests on pages 170–71.

MAKING BEE FOOD

Queen
The queen secretes chemicals that control hive behaviors, like swarming. She also lays all the eggs.

Drone
The only males in a hive, the drones, mate with new queens.

Egg
The queen bee lays two types of eggs. Fertilized eggs develop into workers or queens, and unfertilized eggs become drones.

Emerging worker
A new worker bee will work in the hive for 20 days, then forage for nectar and pollen. All workers are female.

BACK AT THE HIVE

Few animals live in such a complex society as the honeybee. With more than 60,000 individuals in a single hive, it's a nonstop job to keep everything in order and the nest thriving. The work is split among three different groups—the queen honeybee, the male drones, and the female worker bees.

Queen cell
A future queen is fed an enriched diet consisting mainly of royal jelly, a creamy substance formed by special glands in the heads of young worker bees.

STOMACH FULL OF NECTAR

Lured to a foxglove, a bumblebee climbs inside to suck up the nectar. It stores the nectar in its honey stomach. Pollen gets caught in the hair covering the bee's body as it brushes against certain parts of the flower.

POLLEN DELIVERY

The bumblebee, covered in pollen, flies off to visit more flowers before returning to the colony. Most of the pollen will end up in the hive, but some will rub off on the next foxglove the bee squeezes into, fertilizing the flower. This is called pollination.

THE HONEY EXCHANGE

When the bumblebee returns to the nest, the honey-making begins. The bee forces nectar up from its honey stomach for other bees to share. Water in the nectar evaporates and chemicals in the bees' saliva break the nectar down. The resulting honey, as well as pollen, is stored in wax cells for food.

Spider wasp

The Flies Have It

THEY FEAST ON decaying flesh, pierce skin to suck blood, and can spread disease wherever they land. Whatever they're up to—even if they're just pollinating flowers—flies have an enormous impact on our world. About 100,000 different species in the order Diptera have been identified, although we notice only a few of the peskier ones.

Flies usually come in the same basic shape and size. Most are no bigger than a thumbnail, although one, called the Trinidad horse fly, can be as big as a walnut. Not all flies actually fly, but those that do have two wings. What was once the other pair has evolved into little knobs called halteres. These peg-shaped body parts are not used for propulsion but, instead, help flies keep their balance during flight. Some parasitic species don't have any wings at all, so they rely on their hosts to move them around. Because flies can't eat solid food, they have developed mouthparts that act like straws or sponges, sucking up food in a liquid form. Most have excellent eyesight and can spot the smallest movement—which is why they are so hard to swat!

Maggots are the blind and legless larvae of flies. Some eat rotting plants and animals. Some live in ponds and streams, feeding on microscopic organisms in the water. Other maggots like to lunch on the living, and that can include caterpillars, spiders, even humans.

AVIATOR'S INSTRUMENTS
Flies are expert aviators thanks to their stabilizing halteres. These peglike pieces with knobs on the end, seen here on this crane fly, used to be their back wings. The halteres vibrate very fast during flight to keep the fly's body balanced and level. Modern ships use a similar technique to keep them from rolling around too much in storms.

MIDAIR ATTACK
This giant robber fly can accelerate from 0 to 25 miles per hour (40 km/h) in just two seconds to snatch a bee out of midair. Its sharp mouthparts stab into the back of the bee's thorax, killing it instantly. But the robber fly will return to its perch before slurping up its prey—it's difficult to fly and eat at the same time.

INSIDE STORY
Mosquito Menace

Mosquitoes don't actually bite. They pierce the skin and then suck up the blood. Only female mosquitoes are bloodsuckers. The males live on nectar, but females also need blood from animals so their eggs will mature. The itchiness you feel from a bite is an allergic reaction to the chemicals the mosquito injects to make your blood flow better. It's the bite (in particular, the small organisms that live in mosquitoes) that makes these insects some of the most dangerous creatures on Earth—especially if the organism is the parasite that causes malaria. More people have died from malaria than from any other cause, including war. Each year, it kills more than two million people. Billions of dollars have been spent controlling mosquito populations, but the insect is still a menace.

Green bottle fly

- **Diptera** comes from the Greek words *di*, meaning "two," and *ptera*, meaning "wings." While some flies have no wings, most have two.
- **Robber flies** are super speedsters that can even catch fast dragonflies in midair. They get their name from the way they sneak up behind their victims before striking, just like a robber.

Many maggots are disease spreaders, but not all. Doctors in the 1800s learned that some feed only on rotting flesh, leaving healthy tissue behind. The doctors put the maggots on soldiers' infected wounds to eat up the rotting areas and make the wounds clean. These types of maggots are still used on certain wounds today.

- How do fly larvae survive if they can't see and they can't walk? Go to page 143.
- Learn how insects keep the world clean on pages 146–47 and 160–61.
- How do flies fly? To find out, fly on over to pages 164–65.

FLY FOOD

LIQUID SPONGER
All flies eat liquid food—different kinds in different ways. The house fly eats almost anything organic, and that includes decaying flesh and dung. But the fly has to dissolve the food first, so it vomits saliva all over the food and then sops up the mush that's left.

FRUIT FEEDER
Fruit flies—both maggots and adults—favor rotting fruit. They will even feed on fruit that has fermented and become alcoholic (but they don't get drunk).

BLOODSUCKER
The tsetse fly, which feeds on the blood of cattle and people, can gorge itself until its belly is hugely swollen (right). It spreads sleeping sickness, a disease that affects the nervous system of both animals and people.

NECTAR SIPPER
The adult hairy bee fly has long, needlelike mouthparts, which it uses to drink nectar from flowers. But the maggots of the bee fly prefer sewage.

EYE CONTEST
Male stalked-eyed flies have eyes on the tips of long stalks extending from their head. When males meet, they compare eyes. The fly with the widest eyes can mate with the female.

Horse fly

The World's Abuzz

NOW THAT YOU'VE met the cast of characters, watch them in action. Insects lead busy lives just as we do—but on a different scale, because they're smaller. Since there are millions upon millions of insects, though, the things they do have a huge impact on our planet and our lives. Just how do the world's insects find mates, feed themselves, and stay safe? Read on.

page **158** Many insects devour plants. Is that always a bad thing?

Go to INSECT-PLANT CONNECTION.

page **160** Both these insects suck up liquid food, but only one of them is a predator. Which one?

Go to PREDATORS, ETC.

page **162** What happens if these two ants aren't from the same nest? And how can they tell?

Go to CONTACT!

page **164** Flying is as simple as beating your wings up and down. Right? Wrong!

Go to TAKEOFF.

page **166** Why can't this beetle walk in a straight line?

Go to ON THE MOVE.

page **168** Some insects fight back when attacked. Find out how the bloody-nosed beetle defends itself—its name is a clue.

Go to STAYING ALIVE.

page **170** Why do bees swarm? What are they waiting for?

Go to HOME, SWEET HOME.

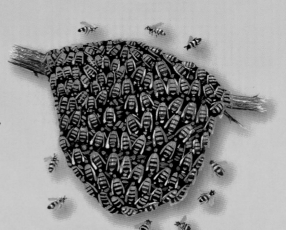

Insect-Plant Connection

PLANTS CAN BE both a home and a meal for insects. In fact, more than half of the world's insects are herbivores, or plant-eaters. But the insect-plant connection is far more complex than this. Insects pollinate flowering plants and help to recycle dead ones, turning them into rich nutrients for new plants. If not for this special give-and-take relationship, we wouldn't have biodiversity—the huge variety of plants and animals now in existence. The process whereby plants and animals help each other to evolve is known as coevolution.

In the wild, populations of plant-eating insects are kept in check by how much food they can find—and by how easily they become food for others. But humans can change this balance, especially when we plant crops. Suddenly, insects such as locusts have unlimited food without any predators to stop them. That's when insects become pests.

Not all plants sit still for the insect onslaught, however. Some species have evolved sharp spines or potent poisons to ward off plant-eaters. Other plants, like the Venus flytrap, have learned to eat the insects that try to eat them.

TRAPPED!
A fly is caught in the clutches of a Venus flytrap from Mexico. The flytrap's bright colors lure the fly, and its spine-rimmed leaves snap shut as soon as the sensitive trigger hairs are touched twice. Over the next few days, the flytrap will digest the fly, absorbing nutrients that it cannot get from the poor soil it grows in.

SPECIAL RELATIONSHIP
Without each other, the yucca moth and the yucca plant might well die out. The yucca plant counts on the moth to pollinate its flowers as the moth lays her eggs on the plant. The plant's seeds provide food for the caterpillars that hatch from the eggs, but they don't eat all the seeds. This way, the surviving seeds grow into the next generation of plants. The next generation of moths grows up too, starting the process all over again.

INSIDE STORY

Weevils to the Rescue

A water fern from Brazil was introduced into Africa, Asia, and Australia, where it had no natural enemies to keep it under control. It grew so fast that it soon choked lakes, reservoirs, and slow rivers like this one in Papua New Guinea (top). Fishermen couldn't use their boats, and mosquitoes started to breed. People tried everything to clear the fern but failed. Eventually, scientists learned about a small Brazilian weevil called *Cyrtobagous*. Its only food was the fern. After being released in the infested areas, the weevils made short work of the weeds. The river in Papua New Guinea was cleared in just three months (bottom).

Before

After

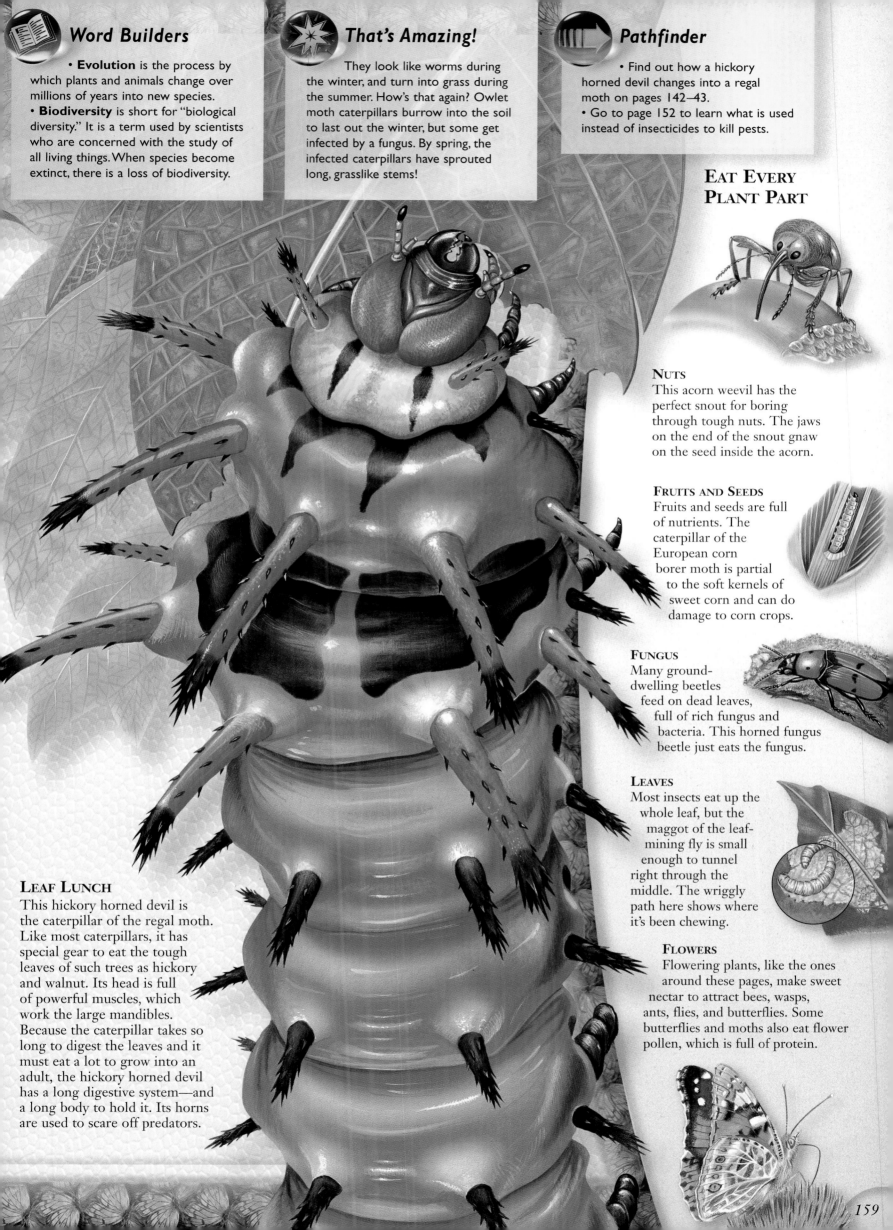

Word Builders

- **Evolution** is the process by which plants and animals change over millions of years into new species.
- **Biodiversity** is short for "biological diversity." It is a term used by scientists who are concerned with the study of all living things. When species become extinct, there is a loss of biodiversity.

That's Amazing!

They look like worms during the winter, and turn into grass during the summer. How's that again? Owlet moth caterpillars burrow into the soil to last out the winter, but some get infected by a fungus. By spring, the infected caterpillars have sprouted long, grasslike stems!

Pathfinder

- Find out how a hickory horned devil changes into a regal moth on pages 142–43.
- Go to page 152 to learn what is used instead of insecticides to kill pests.

EAT EVERY PLANT PART

NUTS
This acorn weevil has the perfect snout for boring through tough nuts. The jaws on the end of the snout gnaw on the seed inside the acorn.

FRUITS AND SEEDS
Fruits and seeds are full of nutrients. The caterpillar of the European corn borer moth is partial to the soft kernels of sweet corn and can do damage to corn crops.

FUNGUS
Many ground-dwelling beetles feed on dead leaves, full of rich fungus and bacteria. This horned fungus beetle just eats the fungus.

LEAVES
Most insects eat up the whole leaf, but the maggot of the leaf-mining fly is small enough to tunnel right through the middle. The wriggly path here shows where it's been chewing.

FLOWERS
Flowering plants, like the ones around these pages, make sweet nectar to attract bees, wasps, ants, flies, and butterflies. Some butterflies and moths also eat flower pollen, which is full of protein.

LEAF LUNCH
This hickory horned devil is the caterpillar of the regal moth. Like most caterpillars, it has special gear to eat the tough leaves of such trees as hickory and walnut. Its head is full of powerful muscles, which work the large mandibles. Because the caterpillar takes so long to digest the leaves and it must eat a lot to grow into an adult, the hickory horned devil has a long digestive system—and a long body to hold it. Its horns are used to scare off predators.

Mosquito

Trapjaw ant

Predators, Etc.

THE WORLD PROVIDES plenty of food for insects who prefer protein—in the form of other insects and small animals such as spiders, snails, and tadpoles—to veggies. Some predators aggressively pursue their prey. Tiger beetles are the fastest hunters on six legs. The less active ground beetles hunt down slower prey like worms and caterpillars. Dragonflies are superswift hunters of the airways, swooping down and occasionally even snacking on prey in midflight.

Other predators wait for home delivery. They can simply blend in with their surroundings and grab prey that wanders within range. Or, like antlion larvae, they can be trappers. This insect lies buried beneath a funnel-shaped sand pit, waiting for an ant to stumble and fall into its huge jaws. Still other species actually attract prey with appealing odors or light sources.

Then there are scavengers, which don't hunt but, instead, live off animal wastes and carrion. Many feed on animal droppings, urine, and shed skin. Maggots and burying beetles feed on corpses, making them some of nature's most efficient recyclers. Still others, like fleas, lice, and some flies, are parasites that feed on the blood and bodily tissues of living victims.

INSECT CLEANERS
The carrion-eating sexton beetle has chewed off some rabbit meat. The female beetle will roll the piece into a ball and drag it into its burrow, ready when its larvae hatch and need a good food supply. Insects such as this beetle—that eat dead bodies or collect them for their young to eat—keep the world from piling up with rotting remains.

CARNIVORE MOUTHPARTS

Mouthparts say a lot about how these meat-eating insects feed. Tiger beetles are hunters with large jaws and teeth to catch, hold, and cut up prey. The house fly survives on liquid foods and uses a spongelike pad on its proboscis to mop them up. Assassin bugs live on liquids, too, but they suck them up with tubelike mouthparts that are tough and sharp—and must pierce prey before sucking them dry.

Tiger beetle

House fly

Assassin bug

Word Builders

• A **parasite**, from the ancient Greek *parasitos*, meaning "one who eats at the table of another," is a plant or animal that lives and feeds off another plant or animal. A parasite doesn't kill its victim but can make it very ill.
• A **parasitoid** slowly eats and kills its host. Larvae of some wasps and flies do this—they are not true parasites.

That's Amazing!

• A predatory katydid from Australia makes sure that its tree frog dinner never gets away. It pins one of the frog's hind legs down, eats the leg first, then starts on the body.
• The flambeau butterfly sips the tears of alligators, while some Asian moths drink the tears of buffaloes and people.

Pathfinder

• Learn how insects find the food they like to eat on pages 138–39.
• What scavenger keeps the world from drowning in dung and droppings? Go to pages 146–47.
• How can other insects defend themselves against predatory insects? Find out on pages 168–69.

DEADLY DECEIVER

An orchid mantis slowly changes color from white to pink and blends in almost perfectly with the flower on which it is living. Petal-shaped parts on its legs help complete the deception. It sits very still, eyeing a katydid that has been attracted to the flower. When the katydid wanders within range, the mantis will lash out, its front legs snapping shut to clamp down on the katydid with sharp spines.

INSIDE STORY

Roaches Rule!

The cockroach has been a successful scavenger for millions of years. It prefers nice warm places with plenty of food, but it can live for weeks at 39°F (4°C) and go without food for months. It will eat any food scraps, and it's also been known to snack on cardboard, the plastic insulation around electrical wire, and even its own offspring. The cockroach rests most of the time but can be very active—swimming underwater for 40 minutes or running up to 3 miles (5 km) in an hour. It can also survive radiation levels that would kill humans.

GRUB FOR A GRUB

This spider-hunting wasp avoids a tarantula's fangs by stabbing it with a long stinger that injects a paralyzing poison. The wasp will drag the victim into its burrow and lay a single egg on it. The grub that hatches will slowly devour the spider. This spider-hunting wasp is called a parasitoid because the hungry grub always kills the spider. True parasites do not actually kill their victim.

Grasshopper

Honeybee

HERBIVORE MOUTHPARTS

Plant-eaters chew or suck up their food, but their mouthparts are different from those of carnivorous insects because of the food they eat. Grasshoppers chew solid plant food. Their jaws are strong, with a sharp edge—perfect for cutting up tough grasses. Honeybees have a long proboscis for taking up nectar, and jaws that shape wax to build cells in the hive.

Contact!

PICTURE THIS: you're very little, but the world around you is huge. How do you find others of your species to let them know you're available to make more of the same? Communication makes it all happen. And insects employ a variety of means to communicate.

Many use sound and vibration. The chirps of male crickets are a familiar sound. Cicadas create an earsplitting buzz—a sign that courting season has arrived. Less obvious are the butterflies that click to each other and the lacewings and treehoppers that stamp messages on the branches they stand on. Backswimmers and water striders feel vibrations through the water with their feet.

Flying beetles, moths, and butterflies release chemicals called pheromones into the air to catch the attention of a possible mate. The male orchid bee from South America can't produce its own scent, so it uses the scent from an orchid—and females, who have special receptors on their antennae, find it irresistible.

Insects also use visual signals to attract a mate. Many butterflies and dragonflies recognize one another's markings—the males are often more colorful than the females. Picture-wing flies use their patterned wings to signal to a mate, while fireflies and glowworms use spectacular light shows for their courtship rituals.

EAU DE MOTH
This female fire-dweller micromoth has special glands on her abdomen, which help spread a male-attracting pheromone through the air. Nearby male micromoths have receptors sensitive enough to pick up just a few molecules of the scent. Most pheromones are too weak to be perceived by human noses, but a few stronger ones smell of vanilla, chocolate, musk, pineapple, or burnt wood.

INSIDE STORY

Singing Pets

You've heard of pet dogs, cats, and even pet snakes. But what about keeping a pet insect? In China, they've been keeping crickets as pets for more than 1,000 years. They do it mainly so they can enjoy the melodic chirping that different crickets produce, and the cages that the crickets live in can be very ornate.

Over the last few hundred years, the Chinese have also raised pet crickets for cricket fighting contests. Two males are placed in a small arena. Because they are very territorial insects, the crickets start to fight and bite at each other. They have powerful jaws, but one will usually run away before there are any serious injuries.

GLOW IN THE DARK
With a mix of special chemicals, this female glowworm, a type of beetle, can "turn on" a light in her abdomen. This is called bioluminescence. She flashes the light on and off in a special pattern, sending a message to a male glowworm, who flashes back as he flies overhead. When lots of these insects get together, they light up whole trees and meadows.

MORE REASONS TO TALK

ANTENNAE CHECK
Every ant nest has its own particular smell, a pheromone produced by the queen ant. When these two red ants meet, they gently touch their antennae together to check smells and see if they are from the same nest. Invading ants are quickly caught and kicked out.

DANCING IN THE DARK
Honeybees tell nestmates where food is with a special dance. In the darkness of the nest, the others must feel the movements to understand. A fast abdomen waggle means lots of nectar. The direction of the dance tells them where to look.

Word Builders

- A **territorial** insect patrols and protects a particular piece of land, or territory, from intruders.
- **Bioluminescence** (formed from the Latin *bio*, "life," and *lumen*, "light") is the ability of certain living organisms to produce light by mixing together chemicals in the body.

That's Amazing!

Deathwatch beetles lay their eggs in old timber so that larvae can end up in wood houses. When an adult beetle emerges, it taps its head on the wood. Another beetle gets the message, and the two home in on each other. In early times, this noise could be heard late at night by people who sat with dying relatives. That's how the insect was given the name "deathwatch" beetle.

Pathfinder

- Find out how insects actually pick up signals and messages from each other on pages 138–39.
- What do bees do after they've done the waggle dance and found the nectar? Go to page 153.
- How does a termite colony work? Learn all about it on pages 170–71.

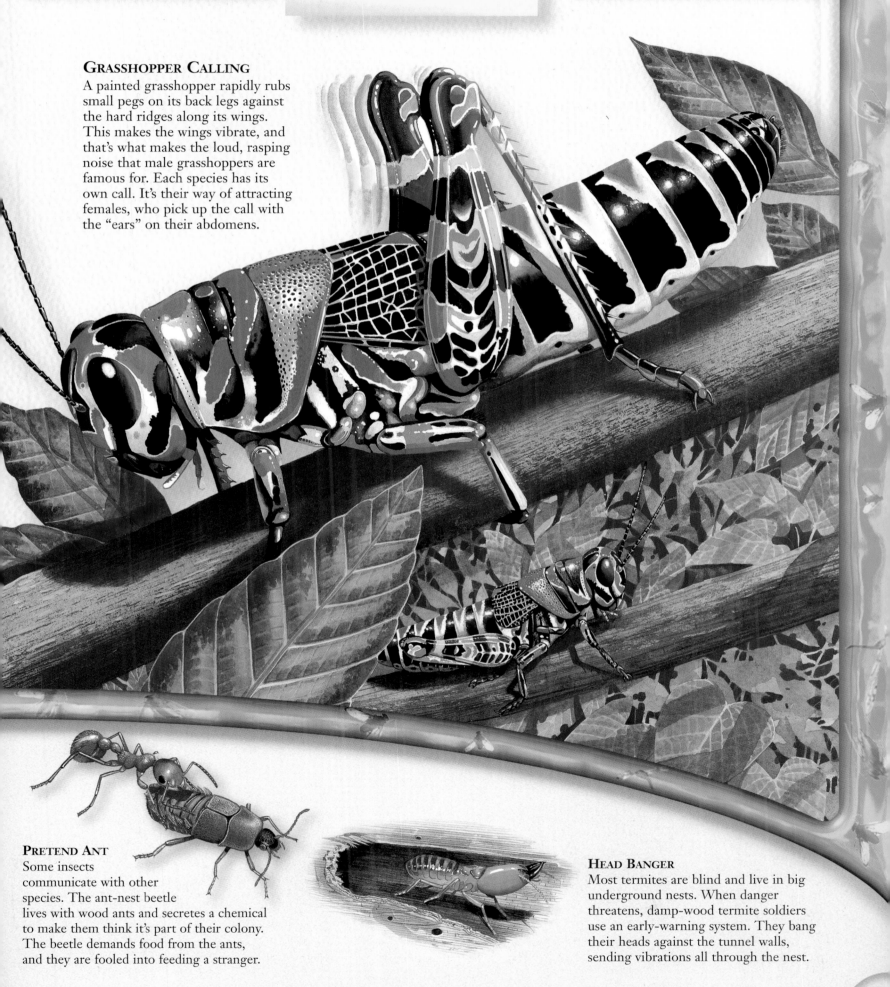

GRASSHOPPER CALLING

A painted grasshopper rapidly rubs small pegs on its back legs against the hard ridges along its wings. This makes the wings vibrate, and that's what makes the loud, rasping noise that male grasshoppers are famous for. Each species has its own call. It's their way of attracting females, who pick up the call with the "ears" on their abdomens.

PRETEND ANT

Some insects communicate with other species. The ant-nest beetle lives with wood ants and secretes a chemical to make them think it's part of their colony. The beetle demands food from the ants, and they are fooled into feeding a stranger.

HEAD BANGER

Most termites are blind and live in big underground nests. When danger threatens, damp-wood termite soldiers use an early-warning system. They bang their heads against the tunnel walls, sending vibrations all through the nest.

Lacewing

Lacewing in flight

Takeoff

INSECTS HAVE BEEN FLYING for more than 300 million years, since wings evolved from gills on aquatic nymphs. The first fliers probably did little more than glide, but as wing design improved, so did flying skills. Some ancient species had three pairs of wings, but most insects today have one or two pairs. Butterflies, dragonflies, bees, and wasps use both pairs as flying wings. Other insects use one pair to fly. In beetles, the other pair has evolved into tough wing cases and in flies, flight-stabilizing halteres.

Some insects are excellent aviators. Hover flies can zoom around or slow down, change direction suddenly, hover in the same spot, and even fly backward! Butterflies beat their large wings slowly, but some can fly continuously for over 100 miles (160 km). Honeybees can fly for only about 15 minutes before they need to refuel.

An insect's wings are powered by strong muscles in the thorax. Each wing connects to the thorax by a tiny plate called a sclerite. With this joint, the wing can move up or down, backward or forward, helping the insect to maneuver. A house fly beats its wings about 200 times per second; some midges make about 1,000 beats in that time.

FLIGHT FOR FOOD
Having stripped an area bare of plants so there is nothing left to eat, this swarm of adult locusts takes to the air to look for more. Insects often use flight to cover large distances when searching for food. But locusts are not strong fliers. They can be blown off course by the wind, and many can drown at sea.

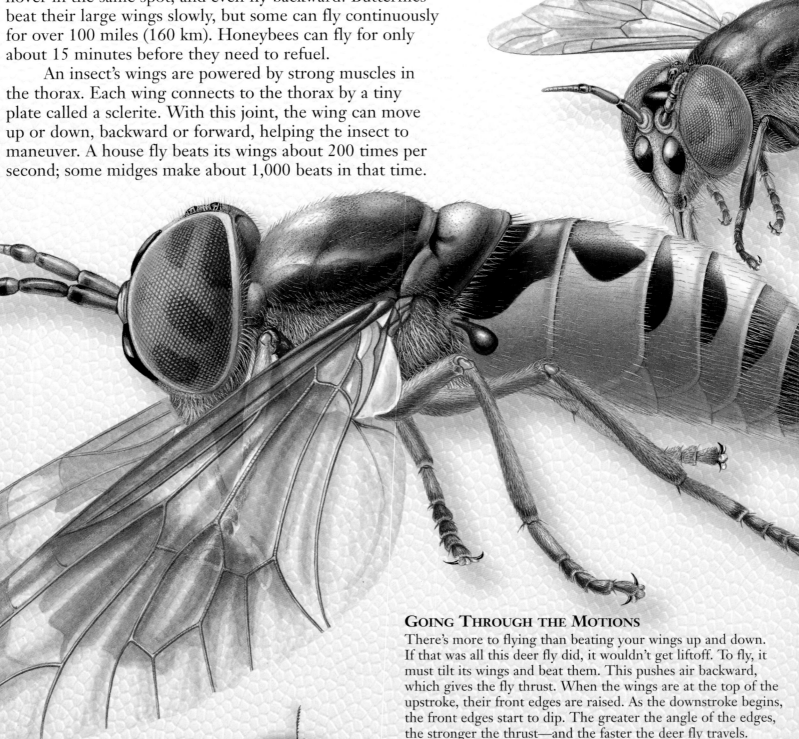

Cardinal beetle

GOING THROUGH THE MOTIONS
There's more to flying than beating your wings up and down. If that was all this deer fly did, it wouldn't get liftoff. To fly, it must tilt its wings and beat them. This pushes air backward, which gives the fly thrust. When the wings are at the top of the upstroke, their front edges are raised. As the downstroke begins, the front edges start to dip. The greater the angle of the edges, the stronger the thrust—and the faster the deer fly travels.

Word Builders

Hawk moths are fast fliers, like the birds of prey they are named after—hawks. The **elephant hawk moth** is named for its caterpillar's long, gray body and false eye spots, which make it look a little like an elephant's head. But the caterpillar is actually mimicking a tiny, sharp-toothed shrew that most predators avoid.

That's Amazing!

When the nymphs of some grasshoppers become too crowded, they start to change color, shape, and behavior, turning into locusts instead of grasshoppers. Once they are adults, they take to the air in huge swarms of as many as 100 billion individuals. This blizzard of insects can cover more than 2,000 miles (3,225 km).

Pathfinder

• Do you see plenty of butterflies fluttering around, but not as many moths? Learn more about it on pages 148–49.
• Why do bees swarm? Find out on page 171.

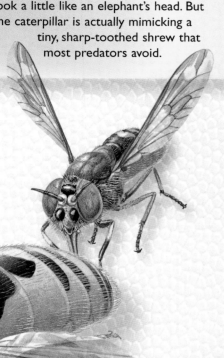

HOVERING HAWK MOTH

This elephant hawk moth is so heavy that it cannot land on some flowers to collect nectar. It has to keep flying in the same spot as it sips from the flower. This is hovering, an action that produces so much heat that the moth would actually cook if it didn't release the heat through its abdomen.

HANDS ON

To Catch a Flier

The best way to catch insects that fly is with a sweep net—a strong, light net with a long handle. Many insects can fly faster than you can run, so you'll improve your chances if you can trap them before they take off. Once they're in flight, the best method is to wave the net from side to side as you walk along through long grass. The second an insect flies into the net, twist your wrist so that the net's mouth points down toward the ground. The insect cannot escape then. After you have studied it, let the insect go quickly—otherwise it will use up energy flapping around, trapped in the net, and will soon become exhausted.

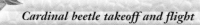

Cardinal beetle takeoff and flight

DIFFERENT WINGS

There are many types of insect wings, but most have a similar structure. Two thin sheets of chitin are sandwiched together. A network of veins running between the sheets gives them support.

UNITED THEY BEAT
Hornets have two pairs of transparent wings. The front and back wings are held together by a series of tiny hooks, so the wings beat in perfect unison.

DOUBLE OR NOTHING
The awkward size and shape of a dragonfly's wings should make it a poor flier. But the back pair beat at a slightly different speed from the front pair, increasing the dragonfly's stability during flight.

AIR PLAY
Few creatures can match the fly's aerial skill. Incredibly agile, flies can even flip themselves over while in midair, ready to land upside down on the ceiling.

GOT IT COVERED
A beetle's tough forewings act mainly as covers for its hindwings. In flight, they also work like the fixed wings of an airplane, keeping the beetle stable and giving it extra lift.

GLIDER
This grasshopper relies on a powerful leap to become airborne. Then large, fanlike hindwings unfold, helping it to glide long distances.

On the Move

NONFLYING INSECTS USE a more pedestrian method of getting around—their legs. Insects have six multijointed legs that make them very stable. They can start fast and stop suddenly without falling over. They are also very light, making it easy for them to maneuver.

Some species have special equipment, like claws or sticky pads on their feet, that allows them to climb walls or windows—or even hang from ceilings. Others have developed appendages made just for jumping. Grasshoppers have such powerful back legs that they can make leaps many times higher than their bodies. Some jumpers don't use legs at all—tiny springtails flick a special "tail," while click beetles use a peglike spring to propel themselves.

Oarlike legs make swimming easy for many aquatic insects. Dragonfly nymphs, for instance, can either paddle around or use jet propulsion. They force water out the tip of their abdomen to push themselves along.

Many kinds of larvae get along fine with no legs at all. Some, like fly larvae, simply wiggle. Others, like ant and bee larvae, have no need for legs because their food is delivered. Still others depend on limo service provided by different insects, such as bees and roaches.

DO THE ZIGZAG
When an insect walks, it moves three legs at a time. The first and third legs on one side and the middle leg on the other side all step forward together. Then it's the turn of the other three legs to step out. The end result is a slightly zigzagging walk.

INSIDE STORY
The Ants Go Marching

When 22 million African driver ants march into town, people know it's time to clear out for a while. Even though they are blind—and each one is only about 0.4 inches (1 cm) long—the insects arrive in a broad, sweeping band, and their vast numbers spell trouble for any small animal that cannot get out of the way. The minute a scout driver ant finds a grasshopper or toad, for example, it releases a chemical, and within seconds, several thousand sharp-jawed workers have completely smothered the doomed victim, pulling it apart into small pieces and carting it back to the main column of ants. In this way, they devour pests like cockroaches, scorpions, and spiders, and send snakes slithering out of their hiding places. Despite the inconvenience of leaving home, villagers in Africa tend not to mind these visits. It's a small price to pay for such a good cleaning service.

WALKING ON WATER
This water strider uses surface tension to skate on the water's surface. Hairs on its feet repel water, and this keeps the strider from piercing the water's surface. Should these hairs absorb water, the insect could no longer stay afloat.

PROTECTING
This koringkriek cricket leg isn't used for jumping away from danger. Its thick armor and spines give the cricket good defense against everything except large predatory birds and lizards.

LEGS GALORE
Insect legs come in so many shapes because they have so many functions. Each species has evolved legs to suit its lifestyle and needs—for walking, swimming, jumping, or catching food.

HUNTING
The spined front legs of a praying mantis shoot out to grab a victim in one-twentieth of a second—too fast for most to see it coming.

Word Builders

- **Surface tension** is the skin on the surface of water, which can support the light weight of leaves, twigs, and even some insects.
- **Appendage**, from the Latin *appendere*, meaning "to hang," is used to describe any body part attached to, or hanging from, one of the main body segments. An insect's antennae, legs, and wings are all appendages.

That's Amazing!

Being legless doesn't mean helpless. Take the legless larva of the stylops. It waits inside a flower's nectar store. A bee drinks the nectar—and the stylops, too. Back at the hive, the bee spits up the nectar for the next batch of bee grubs. The stylops comes too, and tucks into one of the grubs for a meal.

Pathfinder

- Members of this insect order can walk, run, jump, swim, and fly. Read all about them on pages 146–47.
- Mantises have another advantage when they go hunting—they can become invisible. Can you see how on pages 160–61?

IN A SPIN

When this flea beetle makes a jump, it shoots through the air at speeds greater than 9 miles per hour (14 km/h), spinning head-over-claws 70 times in a single second. It does all this and still manages to land feet first. The enlarged back legs hold a special jumping organ—a sliver of chitin with many muscles—that lets the beetle leap at such speeds and always land where it wants.

SWIMMING

Fringed with hairs and powered by strong muscles in the thorax, the two long legs of the diving beetle work like paddles to propel it swiftly through water.

STICKING

Fly legs are simple, but fly feet are special. Each foot has hair pads that secrete oily fluids so the fly can stick to glass and ceilings.

GRASPING

A caterpillar has jointed legs at the front and prolegs, or false legs, at the back. The prolegs have tiny hooks on their tips to help the caterpillar hold on to leaves and twigs.

Velvet ant   *Five-spotted burnet moth*

Staying Alive

INSECTS—THEY'RE ON the lunch menu for many animals worldwide. It's no surprise, really, considering their sheer numbers, availability, and high protein content. But insects have evolved an array of special tricks to avoid becoming lunch. The best method is not to get noticed in the first place. Many insects stay hidden under ground. Others use camouflage to blend in with the leaves, bark, or flowers on which they're resting, or they look like leaves or twigs themselves. Some insects, like moths, may go out only under cover of darkness.

For those insects that don't stay hidden during the day, a painful sting or a toxic poison will ward off many predators. Brilliant warning colors like red, yellow, and orange tell possible attackers that this insect would be an unpleasant mouthful. Some sneaky insects pretend to be dangerous by looking like a species that really is. For example, hover flies are harmless, but they mimic, or look like, stinging yellow jackets. Certain beetles use chemical warfare. They might spray toxic chemicals at an attacker, leak irritating fluids, or even create explosive poisons.

Many insects have simply made themselves too difficult to eat. Caterpillars covered in spines or itchy hairs can't be swallowed comfortably—some have hairs that can actually choke a predator to death. The exoskeletons of several beetles are so tough that predators can't bite into them. These are the tools needed to stay alive in the creature world.

SURPRISE!

These peanut bugs are resting on a tree trunk. They have dull coloration, which helps them go unnoticed by hungry birds. But the lower peanut bug has been spotted. Suddenly it snaps open its wings to flash two huge spots that look like staring eyes. If the bug is lucky, the hungry bird will be startled into leaving it alone.

DOUBLE-DUTY CAMOUFLAGE

A Peruvian lichen mantis waits, almost invisible against the bark of a tree. Its camouflage disguises it from predators and also keeps its prey from seeing it—until it's too late.

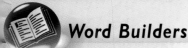
Word Builders

• **Camouflage**, from the French word *camoufler*, "to disguise," lets an animal blend into its surroundings. Insects have patterns and colors to hide against plants, pebbles, or dirt.
• **Mimic** is from the ancient Greek *mimos*, meaning "actor." To mimic is to copy or imitate something. Insects do this to fool their attackers into thinking they are dangerous or poisonous.

That's Amazing!

Since its enemies cannot see warning colors at night, the foul-tasting tiger moth has evolved a different way of letting predators, such as bats, know to beware. It has an organ underneath its thorax that produces sound when it flies, making a distinctive warning call that it tastes bad. Some tasty moths mimic this sound, too.

Pathfinder

• Peanut bugs are true bugs, just like cicadas and aphids. Find out what they have in common on pages 144–45.
• A spider that mimics a bird dropping? Read more about it on page 187.

LINES OF DEFENSE

KATYDID CONFUSION
This photo, right, is actually a katydid (a grasshopper cousin), but it has completely transformed itself by opening its wings. The move is enough to shock or confuse most predators and gives the katydid a chance to make a quick getaway.

TAKE THAT!
When a wasp, bee, or ant wants to get rid of an attacker or immobilize prey, it uses a fearful weapon. The sting of a common wasp is painful, but it's nothing compared to that of a tarantula-hawk wasp or velvet ant, which can be agonizing. Some ants, such as the 24-hour ant from South America, have stings that burn like fire.

BAD BLOOD
When disturbed, the bloody-nosed beetle breaks thin membranes in its mouth and forces out a droplet of its own blood. The blood has chemicals that will make its attacker very sick.

TOXIC SQUIRT
A bombardier beetle that's under attack will secrete chemicals into a chamber in its abdomen. They combine and react, making a hot substance that squirts out of the beetle.

TRUE COLORS
The monarch butterfly (right) is poisonous, as its bold orange colors warn. The viceroy (left) is harmless, but it mimics the monarch so predators will think it, too, is trouble—and will keep away.

SUIT OF ARMOR
All 6 inches (15 cm) of the Malaysian jungle nymph are covered in needle-sharp spines. If that doesn't put off an enemy, it makes a loud, rasping sound and waves its strong, spiny legs before slashing at any persistent attacker.

INSIDE STORY

Tastes Like Chicken?

Birds, frogs, snakes, and other arthropods aren't the only creatures that think insects make tasty treats. Many humans around the world also eat insects, which are an especially important source of protein in areas where people don't farm large animals for meat. Native Australians, for instance, eat sweet-tasting honeypot ants as well as meaty bogong moths—and the fat witchetty grubs shown at right. The witchetty grub is a caterpillar that lives in the roots of certain trees and tastes a little like unsalted peanut butter. In Africa, people collect thousands of tiny midges and make them into burgers. There are plans in China to use minced maggots as a substitute for beef and other meats. And chocolate-coated ants, first eaten in the Americas hundreds of years ago, are now snacked on all over the world.

Blister beetle   *Stink bug*

Home, Sweet Home

HOME MEANS DIFFERENT things to different insects. For some, it's just the underside of a leaf that provides a spot to lay eggs on, or a simple resting place. But many insects go to more trouble, creating structures where their young can eat and grow in relative safety. Solitary bees and wasps may dig burrows or find holes in wood. Many larvae make their own protective apartments to hole up in out of leaves or debris. This way they can pass through their pupal stages in peace. Then there are the insects whose nests are among the most complex in the animal world. Termite mounds, for instance, are rock-solid structures that can be taller than an elephant and hold several million individuals. Scientists think some mounds may have been used for more than 4,000 years!

Insects build their homes from all kinds of materials. Ants mix soil with their own saliva to make a type of cement just right for underground tunneling. Termites add droppings…to make their cement extra-strong. Honeybees produce their building materials differently, secreting wax from a special gland in their abdomens. They use the wax to make the combs where they keep honey and young. Social wasps live in paper houses. They gnaw off wood, chew it into a paste, then work the paste into thin sheets of paper with their jaws. The many layers of paper they use act as insulation, protecting their delicate young in most kinds of weather.

THE TIES THAT BIND
These green tree ants wrestle the edges of two leaves together, preparing their new home to be sewn up with silk from their larvae. Other workers hold the larvae in their jaws and squeeze gently. The larvae dribble out a thin strand of silk—the thread that sews the leaves together. The tree house gets built, but some larvae may die from exhaustion.

Ventilation shaft

INSIDE STORY
The First Papermakers

Legend has it that the inventor of paper, Ts'ai Lun (AD 89–106) of China, learned how to make paper by watching wasps at work. He saw the way wasps used their powerful jaws to chew

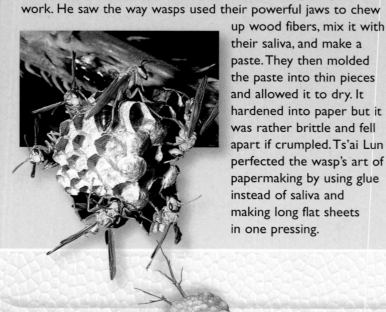

up wood fibers, mix it with their saliva, and make a paste. They then molded the paste into thin pieces and allowed it to dry. It hardened into paper but it was rather brittle and fell apart if crumpled. Ts'ai Lun perfected the wasp's art of papermaking by using glue instead of saliva and making long flat sheets in one pressing.

KEEP IT COOL
Cathedral termites in northern Australia call this huge, hard-as-concrete mound home. It can get very hot in this part of the world, but the mound acts like a cooling tower to keep the nest from overheating. Tunnels on the inside work the same as air-conditioning, letting the heat from the termites escape, while cooler air is sucked in from the ground below.

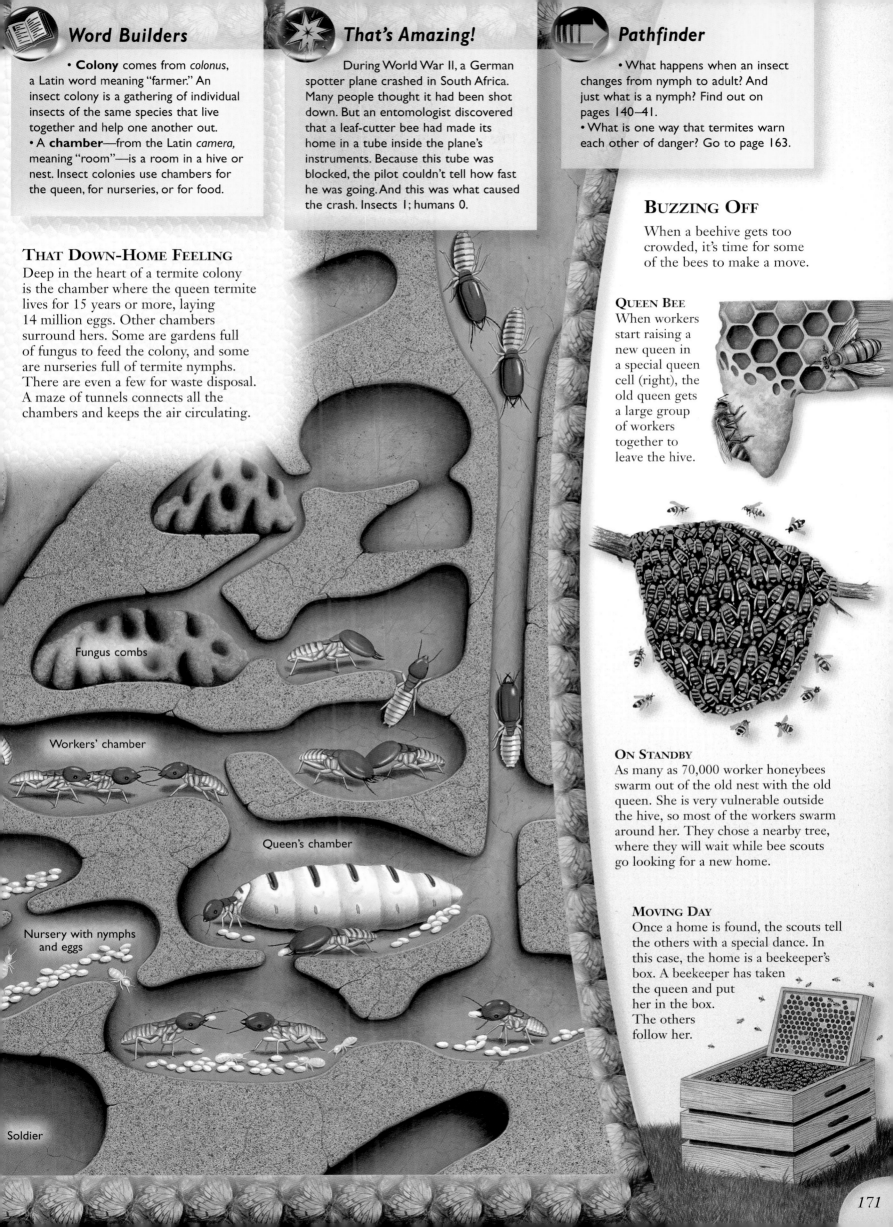

📖 Word Builders

- **Colony** comes from *colonus*, a Latin word meaning "farmer." An insect colony is a gathering of individual insects of the same species that live together and help one another out.
- A **chamber**—from the Latin *camera*, meaning "room"—is a room in a hive or nest. Insect colonies use chambers for the queen, for nurseries, or for food.

✳️ That's Amazing!

During World War II, a German spotter plane crashed in South Africa. Many people thought it had been shot down. But an entomologist discovered that a leaf-cutter bee had made its home in a tube inside the plane's instruments. Because this tube was blocked, the pilot couldn't tell how fast he was going. And this was what caused the crash. Insects 1; humans 0.

🔁 Pathfinder

- What happens when an insect changes from nymph to adult? And just what is a nymph? Find out on pages 140–41.
- What is one way that termites warn each other of danger? Go to page 163.

THAT DOWN-HOME FEELING

Deep in the heart of a termite colony is the chamber where the queen termite lives for 15 years or more, laying 14 million eggs. Other chambers surround hers. Some are gardens full of fungus to feed the colony, and some are nurseries full of termite nymphs. There are even a few for waste disposal. A maze of tunnels connects all the chambers and keeps the air circulating.

Fungus combs

Workers' chamber

Queen's chamber

Nursery with nymphs and eggs

Soldier

BUZZING OFF

When a beehive gets too crowded, it's time for some of the bees to make a move.

QUEEN BEE

When workers start raising a new queen in a special queen cell (right), the old queen gets a large group of workers together to leave the hive.

ON STANDBY

As many as 70,000 worker honeybees swarm out of the old nest with the old queen. She is very vulnerable outside the hive, so most of the workers swarm around her. They chose a nearby tree, where they will wait while bee scouts go looking for a new home.

MOVING DAY

Once a home is found, the scouts tell the others with a special dance. In this case, the home is a beekeeper's box. A beekeeper has taken the queen and put her in the box. The others follow her.

Spider Story

THESE CREATURES HAVE eight legs, but they are constantly mistaken for insects. What are they? They're spiders—and without them we'd be swimming in a virtual sea of insects. How have these amazing animals turned a talent for making silk thread into one of the most successful hunting and trapping tools? You are about to find out—you're going for a spin.

page **174** Is this a spider? Learn what to look for to make an identification.

Go to SPIDER VERSUS INSECT.

page **176** Some spiders come in strange shapes. Why is that?

Go to CLOSING IN.

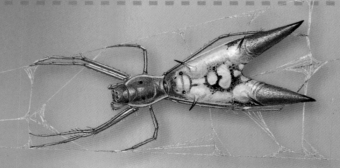

page **178** This spider has huge eyes? Does this mean it has good eyesight?

Go to BODY LANGUAGE.

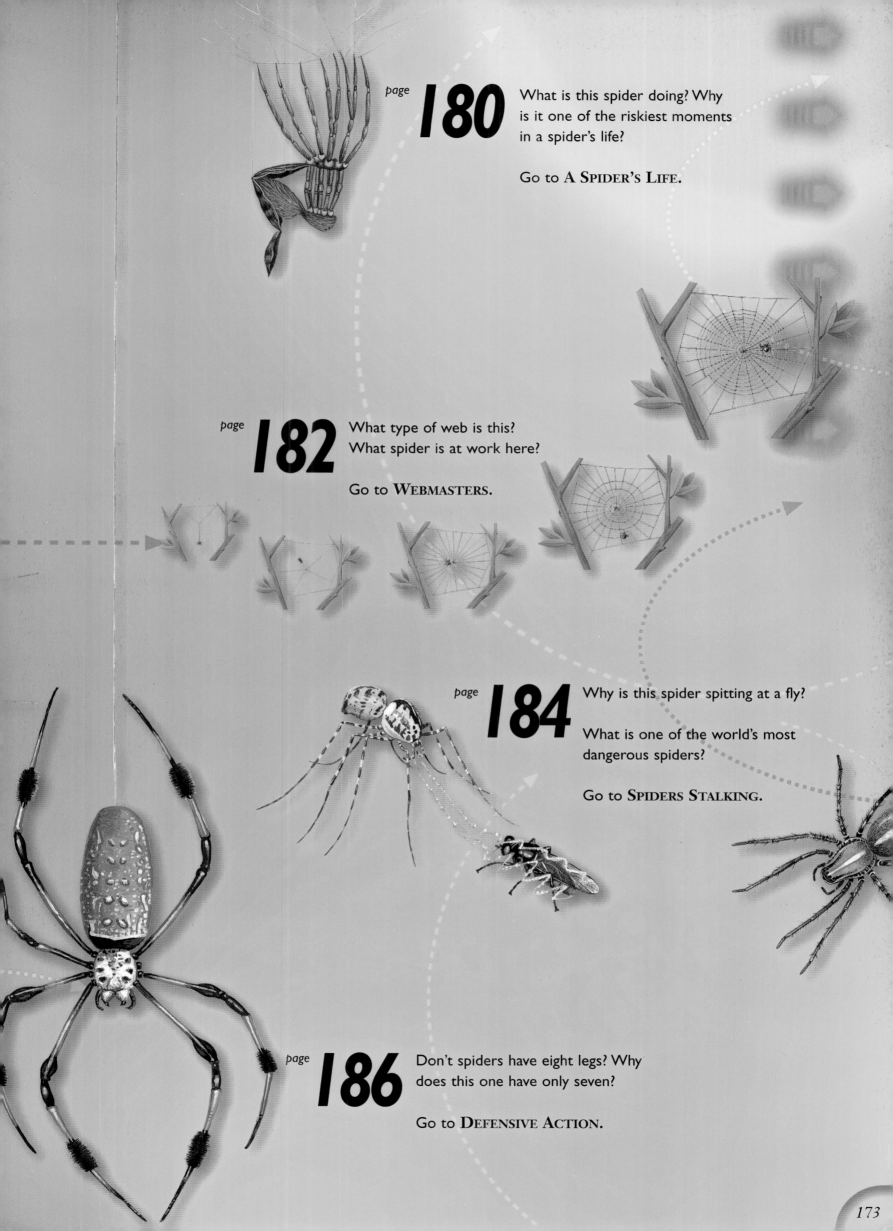

page **180**   What is this spider doing? Why is it one of the riskiest moments in a spider's life?

Go to **A Spider's Life.**

page **182**   What type of web is this? What spider is at work here?

Go to **Webmasters.**

page **184**   Why is this spider spitting at a fly?

What is one of the world's most dangerous spiders?

Go to **Spiders Stalking.**

page **186**   Don't spiders have eight legs? Why does this one have only seven?

Go to **Defensive Action.**

Spider Versus Insect

AT FIRST GLANCE, it can be easy to confuse insects and spiders. Both are arthropods with skeletons on the outside of their body and jointed limbs. But there the resemblance ends. Part of a group of animals called arachnids, spiders have eight legs rather than six. They also have two main body parts—a cephalothorax, consisting of the head and thorax, and an abdomen. Instead of antennae, spiders have two sense organs called pedipalps. They usually have eight simple eyes, although some have no eyes at all. And spiders always have a good set of fangs. In most cases, these fangs are designed to deliver paralyzing venom to their victims.

Like insects, spiders are one of the most abundant animal groups around. They can be found on mountaintops and underwater, in yards and in your home. There are about 36,000 species, including desert tarantulas the size of a dinner plate and tropical spiders smaller than a pinhead. But no matter how big or small, all spiders are predators and what they eat depends mainly on their size and strength. The really big ones can tackle large insects, scorpions, lizards, small mammals, and birds. Most spiders prefer small insects and other spiders. Without these creatures, pests such as flies and cockroaches would simply overrun Earth.

FANGS AT WORK
There are two main types of spiders, each using their fangs differently. The hairy mygalomorphs have fangs that hinge downward (above left). The fangs of more typical spiders, the araneomorphs, hinge together and sideways (right). Both methods allow the spiders to grab and hold their prey close.

DIVING BELL
This aquatic spider lives underwater. To be able to breathe down there, it builds a diving bell out of silk and fills it with bubbles of air from the surface. It stays inside the bell during the day, leaving only at night to find food.

INSIDE STORY

Spider People

Scientists who study spiders are called arachnologists. Some work with extremely dangerous spiders, carefully collecting venom to help make cures for a spider's toxic bite or to develop medicines for illnesses such as cancer and heart disease. Others study spider silk and have come up with ways to use it, such as making incredibly fine thread for sewing up wounds or better protective clothing like bulletproof vests. Conservation is another area where arachnologists are hard at work. As more natural habitats are destroyed, hundreds of spider species are in danger of becoming extinct. Many rare spiders are now bred in captivity so they can be released into the wild when their habitats are safe again.

SPIDER WANNABES
Some arachnids look a lot like spiders, but don't let them fool you.

CHECK OUT THOSE SEGMENTS
A solpugid might look like a hairy spider, but it has the segmented abdomen that is common in scorpions. Solpugids have the most powerful jaws, in proportion to size, of any animal. They slice up mice, birds, and lizards into a pulp, then eat the pieces.

Word Builders

In an ancient Greek myth, Arachne was a woman who challenged the goddess Athena to a weaving contest. This angered Athena, so she decided to change Arachne into a spider who would have to weave forever. The **arachnids**—including spiders—are named for her.

That's Amazing!

The first time you see a black widow or redback spider, it's hard to believe that something so small can be so dangerous. In fact, these pea-size spiders can inject a venom that is 15 times more toxic than that of a rattlesnake. Fortunately, they are shy creatures and prefer to hide.

Pathfinder

• How does a spider survive if it can't see very well? Go to pages 178–79.
• Molting is one of the most dangerous moments in a spider's life. Find out why on pages 180–81.
• A spider that spits? Stand back and flip to page 184 to see it in action.

Eye
Some spiders have excellent eyesight. Others are blind.

Abdomen
This contains the silk-making glands, lungs, and other vital organs.

Pedipalp
The pedipalps, or palps, are used as sense organs or to manipulate food. Males also use them to transfer sperm during mating.

Chelicera
Two fangs are attached to the chelicerae, or jaws. In most species, they contain venom ducts.

Claw
Many spiders have toothed claws plus hairs that help grip their webs.

Cephalothorax
This includes the head and thorax, and also has the jaws and legs attached to it.

Leg
All spiders have eight jointed legs. The back legs sometimes have special claws to wrap prey in silk.

GOOD-GUY SPIDER

This marbled orb weaver isn't a danger to humans. In fact, it's a big help. It will eat more than 350 flies and wasps in its lifetime, getting rid of some pesky insects. Despite their bad reputation, spiders are valuable natural pest controllers, helping to limit populations of cockroaches, flies, and even scorpions.

TARANTULA TIMES TWO

Spiders have exoskeletons, so they have to molt to get bigger, just like insects. This red-kneed tarantula has just wriggled out of its old exoskeleton (left).

COUNT THE BODY PARTS

Mites appear to have one body part, but they actually have two. Most are microscopic, but this red velvet mite is large enough to see unaided. Mites are found almost anywhere—from the nostrils of seals to the "ears" of moths—and there are probably more of them on Earth than any other arthropod.

LOOK PAST THE LEGS

Although this harvestman—or daddy long legs as it is also called—looks a lot like a spider, it appears to have only one body section, much like mites. Despite their name, some in this group have short legs.

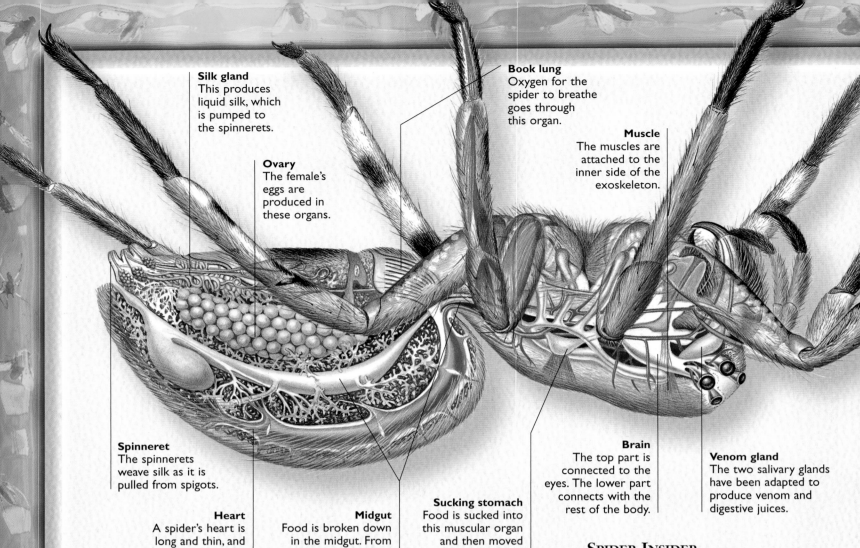

Silk gland
This produces liquid silk, which is pumped to the spinnerets.

Ovary
The female's eggs are produced in these organs.

Book lung
Oxygen for the spider to breathe goes through this organ.

Muscle
The muscles are attached to the inner side of the exoskeleton.

Spinneret
The spinnerets weave silk as it is pulled from spigots.

Heart
A spider's heart is long and thin, and runs along the top of the abdomen.

Midgut
Food is broken down in the midgut. From there, it passes into the bloodstream.

Sucking stomach
Food is sucked into this muscular organ and then moved along to the rest of the digestive tract.

Brain
The top part is connected to the eyes. The lower part connects with the rest of the body.

Venom gland
The two salivary glands have been adapted to produce venom and digestive juices.

Closing In

A QUICK LOOK inside a spider's body shows that it has a number of body systems in common with other animals. It has a brain, which is the body's main control center. It has a heart that pumps nutrient-rich blood to vital organs. It has lungs for breathing air. And it has a system for breaking down food into usable nutrients. As with insects, though, these systems work a little differently than in vertebrates.

Most spiders actually have two ways to get oxygen. Air filters through slits in the abdomen into the book lung chambers, where it seeps into the blood and is then carried to the body parts. Many species also have a few tracheae, or breathing tubes, that are connected to breathing holes, just as insects have. Some spiders have no tracheae and two sets of book lungs.

The only way spiders can eat is to slurp up fluids. So, while some have mouthparts that can mash prey, all spiders must partly digest, or liquefy, their food before they can eat it. Most inject paralyzing venom into their prey, and then spit digestive juices into the victim to dissolve the tissues. The liquid results are vacuumed up by the sucking stomach into the digestive tract.

Another important body system is not exactly unique to spiders. Other arthropod species make silk, but only spiders have perfected the system and to such deadly effect.

SPIDER INSIDER

To get a clearer idea of how a spider functions, take a look inside the body of a brown badge huntsman. This fast-moving predator, with a telltale dark-brown patch on the cephalothorax, is a typical spider.

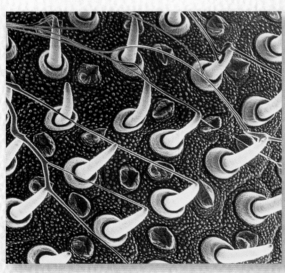

SPIGOTS AND SILKS

Special glands inside a spider's abdomen make liquid silk. This is secreted to the spider's spinnerets, where it is pulled out of hairlike cones called spigots, magnified here 170 times. Spiders have between one and three pairs of spinnerets, and each spinneret has different types of spigots for different types of silk.

Tarantula

Lynx spider

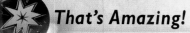

• Insect innards work a bit differently from a spider's. Find out about insect systems on pages 136–37.
• Learn how spiders keep from getting stuck in their own silk webs on page 182.

ODD ARACHNIDS

SPINES AND SHARP PARTS
Some spiders do not come in the standard spider shape. Scientists don't know why the curved spined spider (right) looks the way it does, but there's good reason for the arrow-shaped spiny orb weaver (below) to have sharp protrusions that stick out from its abdomen. They make it very unpleasant for a small bird to swallow.

BELLY-UP
The underside of this common garden spider, seen hanging from its web, provides a very different view of a spider. You can see its fangs folded into their grooves in the chelicerae, and where its legs join the cephalothorax. The spinnerets are also visible on the tip of the abdomen.

BREAK UP
The peculiar knob on the wheel web spider's abdomen breaks up the pattern of its body, making it difficult for a predator to see.

THE HIGH VIEW
This minute spider has eyes high up on its cephalothorax. Some scientists think this helps it spot prey. Others think the long jaws may help in grabbing food.

LONG AND THIN
With its narrow body, the long-jawed orb weaver can hide from predators by lying flat along a grass stem.

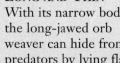

 **HANDS ON**

Spider Watching: Part 1

Most spiders are very secretive and like to hide out. But no matter where you look, there's bound to be a spider lurking nearby.

❶ Never touch a spider unless you know it is completely harmless. Few species are dangerous, but many can give painful nips.

❷ Never put your fingers where you cannot see them, whether it's inside a hole or under a log or rock.

❸ It's a good idea to take an adult along for advice.

❹ Indoors: Look for orb weavers on window-sills. They'll be in the middle of their webs or tucked up in a corner of the window.

❺ Dark, dry attics (right): When you find a house spider web, tap it very gently. The spider should scuttle out to see if it has food.

❻ Outdoors: Spiders may be tricky to find—they tend to hide under stones or pieces of wood.

Trapdoor spider   *Comb-footed spider*

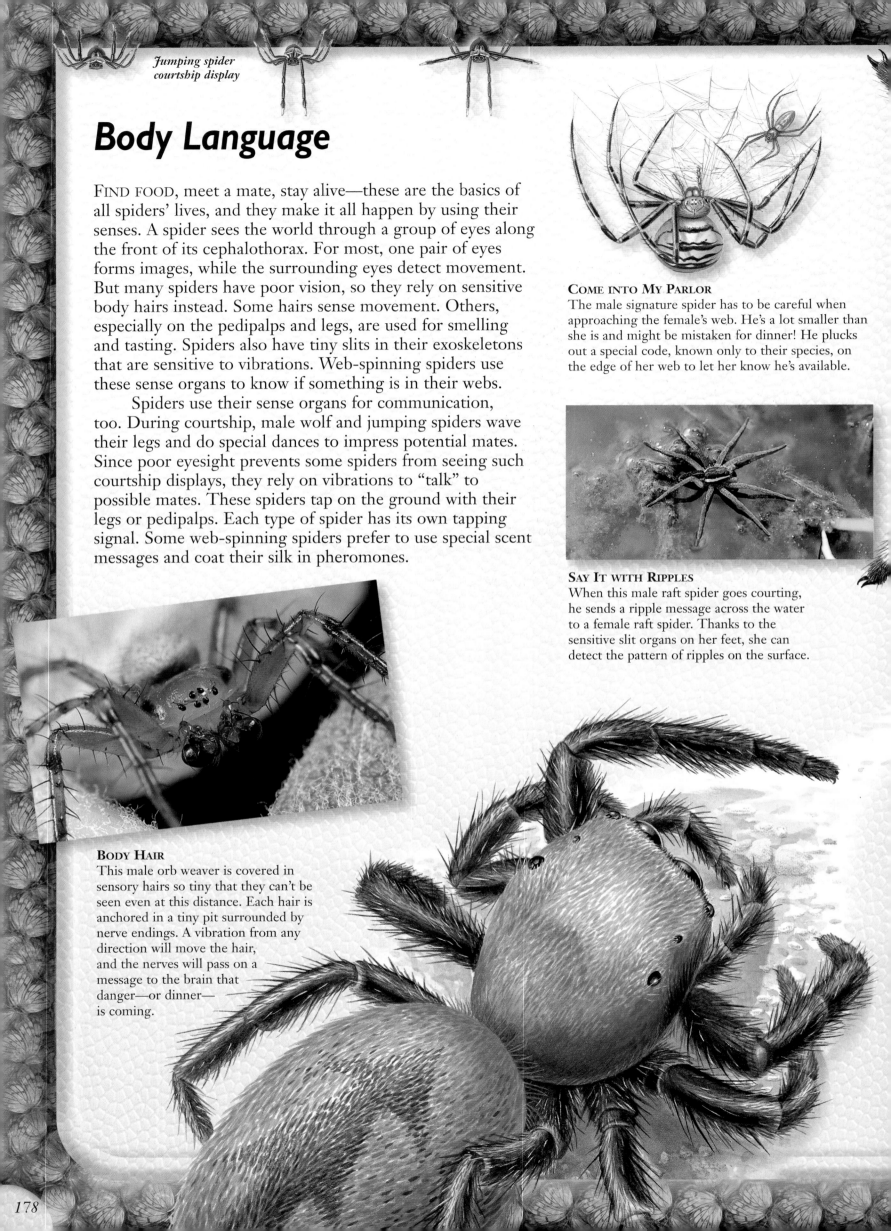

Body Language

FIND FOOD, meet a mate, stay alive—these are the basics of all spiders' lives, and they make it all happen by using their senses. A spider sees the world through a group of eyes along the front of its cephalothorax. For most, one pair of eyes forms images, while the surrounding eyes detect movement. But many spiders have poor vision, so they rely on sensitive body hairs instead. Some hairs sense movement. Others, especially on the pedipalps and legs, are used for smelling and tasting. Spiders also have tiny slits in their exoskeletons that are sensitive to vibrations. Web-spinning spiders use these sense organs to know if something is in their webs.

Spiders use their sense organs for communication, too. During courtship, male wolf and jumping spiders wave their legs and do special dances to impress potential mates. Since poor eyesight prevents some spiders from seeing such courtship displays, they rely on vibrations to "talk" to possible mates. These spiders tap on the ground with their legs or pedipalps. Each type of spider has its own tapping signal. Some web-spinning spiders prefer to use special scent messages and coat their silk in pheromones.

COME INTO MY PARLOR
The male signature spider has to be careful when approaching the female's web. He's a lot smaller than she is and might be mistaken for dinner! He plucks out a special code, known only to their species, on the edge of her web to let her know he's available.

SAY IT WITH RIPPLES
When this male raft spider goes courting, he sends a ripple message across the water to a female raft spider. Thanks to the sensitive slit organs on her feet, she can detect the pattern of ripples on the surface.

BODY HAIR
This male orb weaver is covered in sensory hairs so tiny that they can't be seen even at this distance. Each hair is anchored in a tiny pit surrounded by nerve endings. A vibration from any direction will move the hair, and the nerves will pass on a message to the brain that danger—or dinner— is coming.

Word Builders

Dandy jumper aside (see below), almost all spider and insect behavior is instinctive. **Instinctive behavior** is behavior passed on via genes. For example, a human baby will automatically hold her breath when underwater. Learned behavior is different—a baby has to learn not to touch a hot oven, by being told or getting burned.

That's Amazing!

A female spider usually eats her mate only if he's clumsy or if she gets distracted. Not so with the six-humped dome spider. The tiny male must leap and grab hold of the female. But he can't hold on and mate at the same time. To keep him from falling off, the female buries her fangs in him, then consumes his bodily fluids.

Pathfinder

• Find out about the multipurpose sense organ that insects have but spiders don't on pages 138–39.
• What does it usually mean when a spider's web gets disturbed? Go to pages 182–83.

EYES OF THE SPIDER

To understand how a spider lives and how it gets its food, take a look at its eyes.

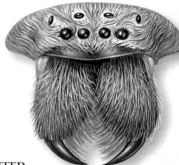

FARSIGHTED

As its name suggests, the huntsman spider actively hunts its food. The huntsman's eyes are spread out to give it fairly good all-around vision for spotting prey.

SIT AND WAIT

The crab spider's super vibration sensors help it detect prey from a distance. Its keen vision kicks in as the prey nears.

SIX EYES

The woodlouse-eating spider has six very small eyes instead of eight. This nighthunter uses its sense of touch to uncover prey under stones and bark.

NIGHT VISION

The ogre-faced spider has two huge eyes that are hundreds of times more sensitive to light than human eyes. It can see prey in near total darkness.

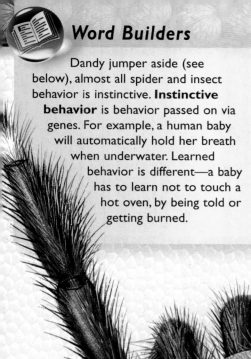

SHALL WE DANCE?

This male jumping spider has spotted a female. Immediately he'll start waving his front legs in the air to show off his colors and patterns, which are unique to his species and help the female recognize him as a potential mate. Once he gets her attention, he'll sashay up to her in a zigzag maneuver and gently stroke her. If she's interested, the two will mate.

INSIDE STORY

Smart Spider

Most spiders use the same hunting method, no matter what kind of prey they're pursuing. This is called instinctive behavior. But the dandy jumper changes the way it hunts depending on the type of spider it is hunting. When it comes across a new web, it taps gently, pretending to be a courting male tapping out a greeting. After trial and error, it taps out the correct message, and the female spider comes over to meet her mate—but gets gobbled up instead. The dandy jumper memorizes the message for use in the future whenever it comes across the same type of web.

Wolf spider courtship display

A Spider's Life

FEMALE SPIDERS LAY their eggs within a few weeks of mating. Some spiders produce a few eggs at a time, but others can lay 1,000 or more. All spider mothers wrap up their eggs in silk to keep them moist and safe from parasites. Many mothers die soon after laying their eggs, leaving the babies to hatch on their own. But trapdoor spiders guard their eggs in their burrows, while wolf spiders and nursery-web spiders carry their egg sacs everywhere until hatching time several months later.

Hatching babies must first break out of their eggs, then fight their way out of the egg sac. They don't eat for the first few days, living instead off the last of their yolk sac, and usually stay clustered together. Some spiderlings have mothers that protect and feed them—the window lace-weaver spider even sacrifices herself as her babies' first meal! But most have to fend for themselves. Once they start to grow, they must leave the nest, or they'll start eating one another. They either scuttle off or balloon away to find themselves a good spot for a new home. Like all arthropods, spider young must shed their old exoskeletons in order to grow. Depending on the species, a spider can molt six to 30 times during its life.

SPIDER SPOUSES
Spiders mate in many different ways. The female green lynx spider is on the left. The female will attach a line of silk to the leaf on which she is standing, then leap into the air. The male will follow her on his line of silk, so they can mate in midair, hanging from their draglines.

HANDS ON

Spider Watching: Part 2

WARNING: If you live near poisonous spiders, do not attempt this activity. The best thing to take with you on a spider hunt is a clear plastic container. Place the bottom section of the plastic container over the spider, being careful to avoid trapping its legs—remember that spiders, with their long legs and soft bodies, are very easy to injure or even squash and kill if you handle them roughly. Slowly drag the container back over the lid. Close it up and the spider will be inside, ready for inspection with a magnifying glass. Once you have finished, let the spider go where you found it.

You can also examine the molted skins of spiders. They are very fragile, so use tweezers to pick them up carefully, and a magnifying glass to get a closer look.

PIGGYBACK
This female wolf spider carried her egg sac on her spinnerets for weeks. She cut open the egg sac to help her young during hatching, and now she's giving her spiderlings a ride. They'll stay with her until their first molt. Then they're on their own.

THE SPIDER'S NEW CLOTHES

Shedding skin is hard to do—and dangerous! If the weather is too dry, for instance, a spider can get stuck in its old exoskeleton and die. The new exoskeleton can stay soft for more than a day, leaving the spider especially vulnerable to attack. Males usually stop molting when they reach adulthood.

SPLIT START
A female giant wood spider hangs from her web as her old exoskeleton splits along the edge of her cephalothorax.

BIG BREAK
The old skin covering her abdomen tears apart and starts to come away as she tries to pull her legs free.

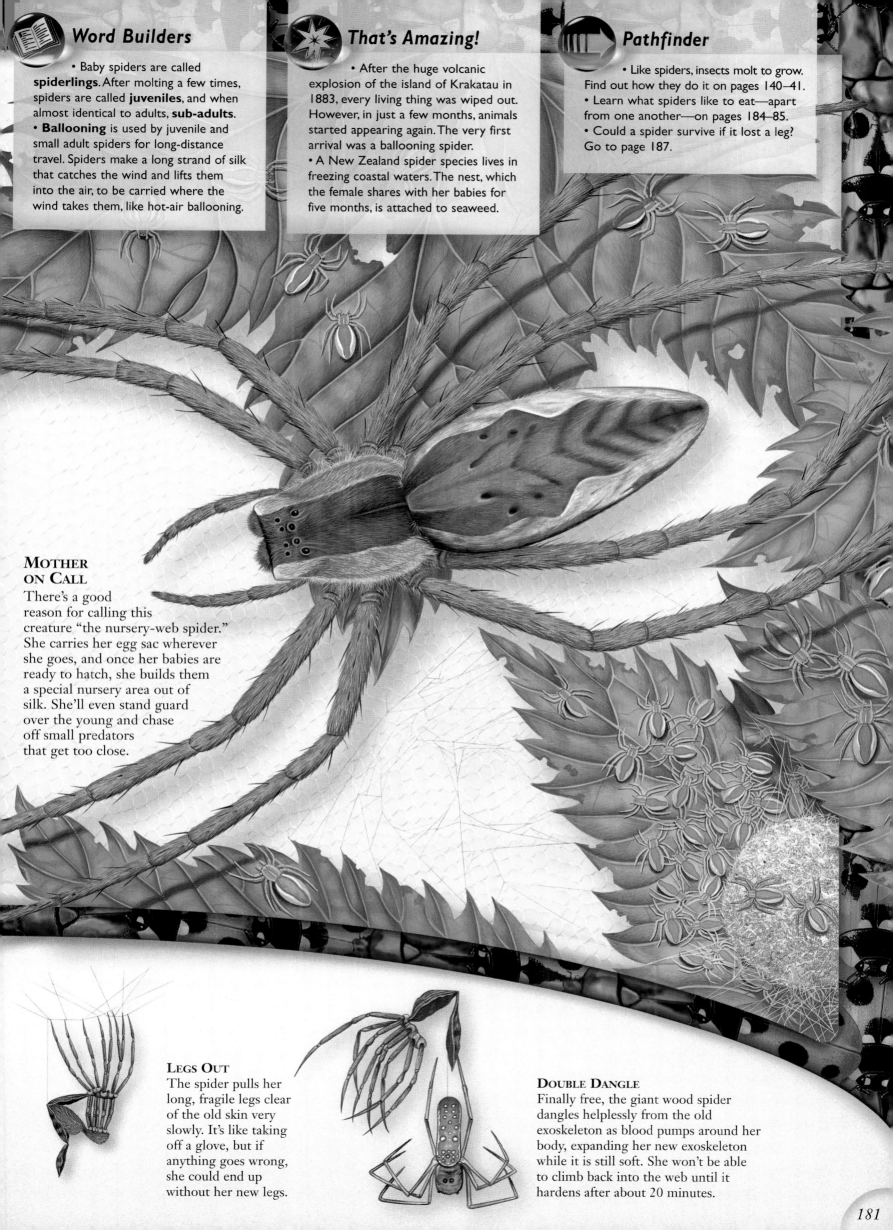

Word Builders

• Baby spiders are called **spiderlings**. After molting a few times, spiders are called **juveniles**, and when almost identical to adults, **sub-adults**.
• **Ballooning** is used by juvenile and small adult spiders for long-distance travel. Spiders make a long strand of silk that catches the wind and lifts them into the air, to be carried where the wind takes them, like hot-air ballooning.

That's Amazing!

• After the huge volcanic explosion of the island of Krakatau in 1883, every living thing was wiped out. However, in just a few months, animals started appearing again. The very first arrival was a ballooning spider.
• A New Zealand spider species lives in freezing coastal waters. The nest, which the female shares with her babies for five months, is attached to seaweed.

Pathfinder

• Like spiders, insects molt to grow. Find out how they do it on pages 140–41.
• Learn what spiders like to eat—apart from one another—on pages 184–85.
• Could a spider survive if it lost a leg? Go to page 187.

MOTHER ON CALL

There's a good reason for calling this creature "the nursery-web spider." She carries her egg sac wherever she goes, and once her babies are ready to hatch, she builds them a special nursery area out of silk. She'll even stand guard over the young and chase off small predators that get too close.

LEGS OUT

The spider pulls her long, fragile legs clear of the old skin very slowly. It's like taking off a glove, but if anything goes wrong, she could end up without her new legs.

DOUBLE DANGLE

Finally free, the giant wood spider dangles helplessly from the old exoskeleton as blood pumps around her body, expanding her new exoskeleton while it is still soft. She won't be able to climb back into the web until it hardens after about 20 minutes.

Webmasters

SPIDERS ARE the most versatile silk-makers of the animal world, making silk that has several uses. Scientists think that spiders first used silk to wrap up their eggs. But spiders have evolved so they can make up to seven different kinds of silk—to wrap prey as well as eggs, to line burrows, and to make draglines for traveling, trip wires, sticky traplines, and, of course, basic webs. Silk can even come in handy during mating. The male stone spider uses it to wrap up the female so she can't eat him!

Webs are as varied as the spiders that weave them. Garden spiders create the familiar, circular orb webs, while house spiders are responsible for the filmy cobwebs found in your attic or cellar. Others make two-tiered webs that cover low bushes or meadow grasses, sheet webs with funnel-shaped retreats where the makers can hide until lunch arrives, or simple traps fashioned with a few trip wires outside burrows. Active hunters don't make webs at all. They make silk draglines to use as a rock climber would—to anchor them to surfaces while they hunt down prey.

Spider silk is a liquid made in abdominal glands and is secreted from spigots on the spinnerets. The spider pulls out several strands at once. The tension causes the silk to harden. Spider silk is almost as strong as steel and twice as elastic as nylon. Because the silk is full of protein, many spiders gobble their webs up when they're not usable anymore. Waste not, want not!

SILK SOURCE
Strands of silk are pulled into a single thread from a spider's spinnerets, which work like fingers to manipulate the silk into whatever the spider wants to make with it. The silk for wrapping prey comes out in broad bands.

THE WAITING GAME
An African signature spider waits in its web for an insect to blunder in. The spider will then dash across the web to grab its victim. The prey gets stuck, but not the spider, which built the web with a frame of nonstick silk that it always steps on. The rest of the web is a different silk with a sticky coating, just right for gluing insects to the spot.

Word Builders

- The word **spider** comes from the Old English word *spinnan*, "to spin."
- **Secretion** is the process whereby a plant or animal releases a special substance. Spiders secrete silk from silk glands, while humans secrete tears from tear glands.
- **Ultraviolet light** is at the far end of the light spectrum. Humans cannot see it, but spiders and insects can.

That's Amazing!

Some giant orb-weaving spiders from tropical countries make webs that are so strong they can catch small birds in them. In Papua New Guinea, where the largest of these spiders are found, the local people use giant wood spiders' webs, which are 9 feet (2.7 m) across, as fishing nets.

Pathfinder

- What does a bee see when it looks at a flower? Find out on page 138.
- Silk clothing is made from insect spit. Say what? Learn more on page 149.

WEB DESIGN

The way a web looks depends on the spider that has spun it. Spiderwebs range from careful constructions to tangled masses. Some spiders make a new web every night. Others just do repairs, spinning a new web only if they really have to because the old web has lost its stickiness.

HAMMOCK WEB

The hammock web spun by a money spider over low bushes may look messy, but any insect caught in its fine lattice weave usually falls into another web suspended below.

TOUCHY TRIP-UP

Having spread a series of silken trip wires in front of its silk-lined burrow, this funnel-web spider sits and waits. When an insect walks across a trip wire, the spider will feel the vibrations—and strike.

TRAP AND WRAP

This garden spider moves fast to wrap up dinner. But the insect trapped in its web is a wasp, so it must first immobilize the struggling wasp in a straitjacket of silk. That keeps the wasp from stinging. Only then will the spider inject its venom.

LACE-SHEET WEB

The trap spun by a lace-web weaver is made of fine, woolly silk. It may not be sticky, but insects soon get tangled up in it.

SCAFFOLD WEB

A scaffold web has stretched traplines with sticky ends attached to the ground. If a crawling insect walks into a trapline, the line snaps back, with the victim dangling in the air.

INSIDE STORY

The Visible Web

Insects can see webs because they can see ultraviolet light, which webs reflect. So why don't they fly around them? Scientists think that some webs look like the ultraviolet patterns made by flowers. Butterflies and bees think they're flying toward flowers full of nectar instead of a sticky web. Other webs may appear as a bright source of light and attract moths the way candles do. Signature spiders often strengthen the center of their webs with zigzag patterns called stabilimenta. Each species has its own pattern—perhaps to lure insects or to act as a visual warning to birds (and humans!) to detour. The stabilimenta may give the spider shade from the hot sun, like an umbrella, or a safe place to molt.

TRIANGLE WEB

The triangle spider holds its web in its front legs while anchored by a thread to the twig behind it. When an insect hits the web, the spider releases it and the web collapses, entangling the prey.

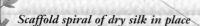

Scaffold spiral of dry silk in place   *Spiral of sticky silk added*

Spiders Stalking

ALL SPIDERS are meat-eaters. While most are trappers, there are 18,000 species that no longer use silk webs to ensnare prey. These are spiders that actively hunt for food or wait in ambush for it.

Spiders that hunt stake out their own territory. Some wolf spiders will chase off any intruder that tries to move in on their turf. Jumping spiders are more free roaming and can often be seen close to each other, leaping after prey with silk draglines sailing out behind them. Bolas spiders use silk to hunt with, but not to make webs. They actually go fishing for their prey, casting out a silken thread with a sticky blob at the end to reel in flying insects. Most hunters eat ants, beetles, and other spiders, but larger individuals—like some tarantulas and huntsmen—can sometimes snag lizards, frogs, rodents, fish, and even birds.

Ambushers wait quietly until lunch comes close enough for them to grab. Trapdoor spiders wait in their tunnels, just beneath trapdoors made from silk, ready to rush out the second they detect vibrations caused by prey. Others simply blend in with the flowers, leaves, or bark of their surroundings, biding their time until some unsuspecting insect wanders within range.

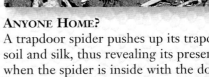

Jumping spider leaps   *Bolas spider with moth*

ANYONE HOME?
A trapdoor spider pushes up its trapdoor of soil and silk, thus revealing its presence. But when the spider is inside with the door shut, you wouldn't know it was there. The hinged trapdoor blends in perfectly with the ground.

SPITTING DISTANCE
This spitting spider is too slow to actually catch a fly, so it delivers its paralyzing venom from a distance. When it gets within a body length of its victim, it shoots streams of sticky venom from its venom glands all over the fly, which roots it to the spot.

INSIDE STORY

Tale of the Tarantula

The large European wolf spider, *Lycosa narbonensis*, was the original tarantula. It got this name because it lived around Taranto, a town in southern Italy. During the 14th century, lots of people were suddenly bitten by spiders, and these tarantulas got the blame. People thought that if they danced wildly until they collapsed from exhaustion, they would not die from the tarantula's bite. This became known as "tarantism," and the dance and music it inspired were called the tarantella. But the relatively harmless European wolf spider wasn't the problem—it was almost certainly the European black widow spider. When Europeans moved to the Americas, they called the large hairy spiders there "tarantulas." Now "tarantula" refers to these New World spiders only.

FUNNEL-WEB SPIDER
With its large fangs, potent venom, and aggressive attitude, the Sydney funnel-web spider is one to avoid. Male funnel-webs are the only male spiders with venomous bites that are dangerous to humans.

VIOLIN SPIDER
The venom of the violin spider rarely kills people, but it can destroy flesh. A single bite can eat into the skin and cause a wound 5 inches (12.7 cm) wide and more than 1 inch (2.5 cm) deep.

THE POISON PACK

Out of the 35,000 known species of spiders, only 30 have venom that is really harmful to humans. Some of these are vigorous ambushers or hunters, but others are quiet web-spinners. And most live in areas of tropical countries where very few people live. There are medicines, called antivenins, to offset spiders' venom, so most people survive their bites.

Word Builders

The **bolas spider** gets its name from a tool used by South American cowboys to trip up cattle. A *bolas* is a long rope with a weight attached to the ends. The scientists who gave the bolas spider its common name thought that its method of catching food looked similar to the way the herdsmen used their bolas.

That's Amazing!

Most spiders live alone, but one social spider species lives in huge colonies in the rain forests of Peru. The webs of a colony can cover 256 square feet (25 sq m) and be home to thousands of spiders. Although they are each no wider than 0.8 inch (2 cm), they can capture prey as large as small birds by working as a team.

Pathfinder

• Who's a better hunter—an insect or a spider? Turn to pages 160–61 to compare notes.
• Sneak a peek at a Mexican red-kneed tarantula just after it has molted on page 175.
• Find out why scientists collect venom from deadly spiders on page 187.

READY AND WAITING

As it's doing here in a cluster of white flowers, a crab spider can change its coloring to match surrounding flowers. The crab spider's venom is very toxic to insects, allowing this very small spider to kill bees twice its size.

TARANTULA ATTACK

This large Mexican red-kneed tarantula can either wait in its burrow for lunch to walk its way, or it can go out hunting. But it has very poor eyesight for a hunter, so it uses sense organs on its legs to pick up the vibrations made by a passing lizard. It rears up, ready to strike faster than the eye can see. Then it sinks its fangs—all 0.4 inch (1 cm) of them—into its victim. That's usually enough to make the kill. But this lizard is larger, so the tarantula might have to inject some venom to stop the struggling.

WANDERING SPIDER

The Brazilian wandering spider is one of the most dangerous spiders in the world. It is big and aggressive, with a fast-acting venom that can kill in 15 minutes. Luckily, it's not common in heavily populated cities.

BLACK WIDOW

The southern black widow is one of the most feared spiders in the world. Yet it is a small, shy spider that will only bite a human if it is provoked.

Defensive Action

SPIDERS ARE ON the lunch menus of
many different animals. Birds are
probably spider enemy #1, but they are
closely followed by assorted lizards,
toads, and small mammals. Spiders are
also vulnerable to attack from parasitic
insects, such as the ichneumon
wasp...and even from their own kind!

But they have developed
strategies to avoid being eaten. Some
spiders simply hide—like common
house spiders, for example, lurking
in their burrows, six-eyed crab spiders
burrowing into sand, or woodlouse-
eating spiders staying tucked away
under rocks. A few will suddenly drop
out of the web, hoping that an attacker
won't spot them dangling from their safety
line. Small size is especially useful with this move.
Others escape notice by camouflaging themselves or by
looking like a more dangerous animal.

Then there are spiders that make such an unpleasant
mouthful that they can afford to stand and fight. Brazilian
wandering spiders are very poisonous, and they have
bright red markings to warn off potential predators.
Large South American tarantulas are known to flick
barbed hairs at attackers, literally driving them away.

NO ONE HOME

Living underground
can have big
advantages, except
when it rains and the
burrow floods. But this
trapdoor spider builds
a flood barrier of twigs
around the entrance to
keep the rain from ruining
its silk-lined home. If a predator
such as this giant centipede barges in,
the spider retreats into a secret chamber
in the side wall and pulls the door shut.
When it's clear that no one is home, the
centipede soon gets bored and leaves.

Word Builders

Antivenin is also known as antivenom. It is from the Latin words for "against poison." It is a substance that works against the effects of the bite or sting of a venomous creature. Each type of venomous spider requires its own antivenin. For example, a person bitten by a widow must be treated with widow antivenin.

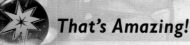

That's Amazing!

Though large South American tarantulas have fearsome jaws, their venom is less than deadly. But the hairs on their abdomens have barbed ends. If a tarantula is disturbed, it brushes off clouds of these hairs at its attacker with quick kicks of its back legs. If the hairs get into the eyes or nose, the pain can stop the attacker in its tracks.

Pathfinder

• Find out how wasps lunch on tarantulas on page 161.
• How do insects use camouflage? Go to pages 168–69.
• Having an odd shape helps some spiders protect themselves. Learn more on page 177.

LOOK-ALIKES

DEAD-LEAF DISGUISE
A scorpion spider hangs in the air imitating a dried-up leaf. Why? Because no predator is going to want to eat a dead leaf. Other times, this spider curls the tip of its abdomen and resembles a dangerous scorpion.

HIDE AND SEEK
As long as she stays very still, it's unlikely that this female lichen spider will be seen. Predators are usually on the lookout for a spider's familiar shape, but her outline is almost invisible against the bark of a tree. Many spiders camouflage their egg sacs, too, with moss, leaves, and twigs.

ON A ROLL
When the South African white lady spider spots trouble, it's out of there! It curls its legs up under its body and rolls down sand dunes, cartwheeling out of danger at amazing speeds.

ANT ANTICS
Several spider species mimic ants, because predators stay away from ant bites and stings. But one Brazilian ant-mimicking spider uses its disguise to get up close to the ants it looks like—then eats them!

SHORT A LEG
How many legs does this spider have? In a last-ditch attempt to escape a predator that had it by its eighth leg, this spider has shed the leg and run away. Many spiders will cut off their own legs in response to danger, and there is no limit as to how many legs they can lose and survive, as long as they manage to eat. The legs are often completely regrown if the spider has more molts to go through.

DUNG BY DAY
This female bird-dung spider spends her day pretending to be a bird dropping—not a popular food choice. But at night she releases a chemical that tricks male moths into thinking she's a female moth. When they arrive, she quickly gobbles them up.

INSIDE STORY

Poison Protection

Up until the late 19th century, if you got bitten by a really venomous spider, there wasn't much that could be done to help you. Then scientists discovered how to create a cure, called antivenin. First, a sample of the venom must be collected. Scientists do this by giving a spider a small electric shock, which causes the venom glands to contract and squirt out the venom. Small amounts of the substance are then injected into a mammal, which develops antibodies that fight the venom's effects. These antibodies are removed from the animal's blood and injected into a spider-bite victim...and the cure begins.

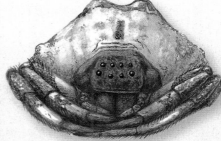

WHICH WAY THE WASP?
Few predators will attack an Asian mutillid wasp because of its painful sting. So this jumping spider from Borneo has evolved into an almost perfect wasp mimic, but backwards. Its long, wiggly spinnerets look just like an insect's antennae.

Northern black widow   *Redback spider*

Rove beetle

Huntsman spider chelicerae and fangs

Glossary

abdomen The rear part of an insect's or spider's body. It holds the organs of the digestive, respiratory, and reproductive systems, as well as the heart.

adaptation Changes an animal or plant makes to help it survive in a particular environment or under certain conditions. Crab spiders have developed the ability to change color to match the flower they are standing on as an adaptation to help them ambush prey.

antenna A delicate sense organ on an insect's head, which it uses to smell, touch, or hear the world. Insects have two antennae, which can be long or short, thin, branched, or featherlike.

arachnid An arthropod with eight legs. Spiders and their relatives—including ticks, mites, solpugids, and scorpions— are all arachnids.

arachnologist A scientist who studies spiders and their relatives.

arthropod An animal with jointed legs and a body divided into segments covered by an exoskeleton. The arthropods are an extremely varied group of animals that includes insects and spiders as well as crabs, scorpions, centipedes, millipedes, ticks, and mites.

ballooning A method used by spiderlings and small adult spiders to travel long distances. They are carried on the wind as they dangle from a long strand of silk.

camouflage Colors or patterns that help disguise an animal so that it blends with and remains hidden in its environment. Insects and spiders camouflage themselves as leaves, bark, or flowers to avoid being seen by predators or prey.

caste A social group that carries out certain tasks. Ants and social bees are divided into two main castes—the queen and the workers.

caterpillar The larva of a moth or butterfly.

cephalothorax The head and thorax of a spider combined in one body segment. The mouthparts, palps, and the eight legs are attached to it, and it also holds the spider's brain, venom glands, and sucking stomach.

chelicerae A spider's mouthparts, used for grabbing and sometimes crushing its prey. A sharp fang hinges from each chelicera, allowing most species to inject venom into prey, killing or paralyzing it.

chitin The light yet tough material that makes up an insect's exoskeleton and wings.

cocoon A protective case, usually made of silk. Insects such as moths, butterflies, some wasps, antlions, lacewings, and many others make cocoons to keep themselves safe while they go through the pupal stage and turn into adults.

colony A group of animals of the same species that live and work together to survive. The inhabitants of an ant nest, termite mound, and beehive are all examples of an insect colony.

complete metamorphosis One of two main ways in which an insect develops. It changes from an egg to a larva to a pupa to a mature insect adult. The larva looks very different from the adult, and the change in appearance is sudden, as can be witnessed in butterflies, moths, beetles, flies, bees, wasps, and ants.

compound eye An insect's main pair of eyes, made up of many smaller eyes, or lenses, each one of which sees movement separately.

dragline A line of silk that a spider will trail behind it as it moves around, occasionally attaching to surfaces. This allows the spider to hunt, find a mate, or drop out of its web suddenly, and always be able to find the way back home.

egg sac A silk covering woven by a female spider to wrap up her eggs, to protect them, and keep them from drying out.

elytra A beetle's forewings. These two wings are hard and provide a protective covering for the beetle's delicate pair of flying wings, which are underneath. They also keep the beetle stable when it is flying.

entomologist A scientist who studies insects.

evolution The gradual change that occurs in plants and animals over many years as they adapt to changing environments and conditions.

exoskeleton The hard, outer skeleton of an arthropod. It is a tough, jointed shell made of chitin, which supports the muscles and soft internal organs.

grub The larva of an ant, bee, wasp, or beetle. It can look a little like a caterpillar.

haltere One of a pair of knoblike structures. The halteres are the modified back wings of flies and allow them to keep their bodies balanced and level during flight.

hibernation The practice of remaining inactive during the cold winter months. Like bears, many insects hibernate, either as eggs, larvae, pupae, or adults.

invertebrate An animal that has no backbone. Some invertebrates, such as worms and jellyfish, have soft bodies, but others, like the arthropods, are protected by their hard exoskeletons.

larva The immature stage of insects that look completely different from their parents and undergo complete metamorphosis to become adults. Caterpillars, maggots, and grubs are all larvae.

maggot The legless larva of some flies.

Tiger beetle head and mandibles

Southern black widow

mandibles The jaws of an insect.

metamorphosis The process of changing form. Insects develop from young to adults either by simple or complete metamorphosis.

migration A group of animals traveling from one region to another, usually to breed or to find enough food to eat during winter or summer. Some butterflies travel thousands of miles as part of their annual migration, while some tiny beetles and springtails will migrate just a few inches to avoid cold soil temperatures.

mimicry A survival tool, with which an animal copies or imitates another animal. Insects and spiders are able to fool attackers into thinking they are dangerous or poisonous when they are not, and thus avoid being eaten.

molt The process of shedding an outer layer of the body. Insects and spiders molt their old exoskeletons so they can grow bigger.

nymph The young stage of insects that look similar to their parents and, through a series of molts, undergo simple metamorphosis to become adults.

ocelli Small, light-sensitive eyes. Many insects have three ocelli on the top of their head, which help flying insects stay level in flight, or tell insects that come out at night when it's getting dark.

order A large group of related plants or animals. Insects are divided into about 30 different orders, each with certain features in common. Spiders belong to only one order within the arachnids. An order is divided into smaller groups, from suborders, families, and genera, down to species.

ovipositor A tube at the tip of a female insect's abdomen used for laying eggs. The ovipositor of a wasp or bee has evolved into its stinger.

parasite A plant or animal that lives or feeds off another plant or animal, called a host. A parasitic insect will feed on the blood or body tissue of its living host, usually without killing the host but still making it very ill.

pedipalp A spider sense organ. A spider has two pedipalps, or palps—appendages at the front of its cephalothorax that it uses to touch, taste, and smell. A male spider also uses modified pedipalps to transfer sperm to the female during mating.

pheromone A chemical message or signal, used by many animals to communicate, usually with the same species—to attract a mate, find food, or warn others of danger.

predator An animal that hunts or preys on other animals for its food.

proboscis A tubelike mouthpart used by moths and butterflies to suck up liquid food.

pupa The stage in development that an insect undergoes to finish complete metamorphosis. Inside a tough pupal case, it changes dramatically as its juvenile body parts break down and adult features emerge.

scavenger An animal that feeds on food scraps or on rotting organic matter, such as corpses, dung, and shed skin.

simple metamorphosis One of two main ways in which an insect develops. The change is gradual, from an egg to a nymph to an adult. Grasshoppers, cockroaches, bugs, and dragonflies all go through this process of change to become an adult.

social insect An insect that lives with insects from the same species, caring for the young and finding food. Ants, termites, and some bees and wasps are social insects.

species A group of plants or animals that have certain features in common and usually breed only with one another.

spigots Tubes that spin spider silk into strands.

spinnerets Two to six fingerlike organs at the tip of a spider's abdomen. Various types of silk made by the spider emerge from the spinnerets.

spiracle A breathing hole in the side of an insect that takes oxygen into the body and expels waste gases, such as carbon dioxide. Insects have between two and eleven pairs of spiracles. Spiders may also have one to two pairs of these breathing holes.

stabilimenta Lines of thick silk in zigzag patterns. They protect and strengthen a spider's web.

swarm A mass of insects, such as bees or locusts, that collect or move around together for eating, mating, or finding a new nest site.

thorax The middle section of an insect's body. It is full of muscles that drive the insect's one to two pairs of wings and three pairs of legs, all of which are attached to it.

trachea A breathing tube. Humans and other vertebrates have only one trachea, which leads to the lungs. Insects and some spiders have a whole network of tracheae that carry oxygen to every organ and cell.

tympana Membranes that act like ears in crickets, grasshoppers, and cicadas. The tympana vibrate when they receive sounds, and this information is carried to the brain via the nervous system, so the insect can hear.

venom A chemical that is injected into another animal to kill or paralyze it or to deter it from attacking. The venom of spiders and some insects also helps liquify the prey so it can be sucked up.

vertebrate An animal that has a backbone, such as fishes, birds, reptiles, and mammals.

Index

A

abdomen, 134–135, 175, 188
antennae, 134, 137, 138–139, 148, 162, 188
antivenin, 187
ants, 138, 145, 150–151, 166, 170
aphid, 145, 150
appendage, 167
aquatic spider, 174
arachnids, 174–175, 188
arachnologist, 174, 188
arthropod, 134–135, 169, 174, 188

B

ballooning, 181, 188
bee, 145, 152–153, 162, 164
beehive, 152–153, 171
beetle, 134–135, 137–13, 143, 145, 146–147, 159–160, 162–165, 167
biodiversity, 159
bioluminescence, 163
black widow spider, 175, 185, 188
Blattodea, 144
bloody-nosed beetle, 169
body language of spiders, 178–179
body parts of insect, 134–139
body parts of spider, 175–177
bolas spider, 184–185
book lung, 176–177
brain, 136–137, 176
bugs, 144–145
bulldog ant, 150
bumblebee, 153
butterfly, 134, 145, 148–149, 162, 164, 169

C

caddis fly, 142, 145, 170
camouflage, 168–169, 186–187, 188
carnivore mouthparts, 160
catching flying insects, 165
caterpillar, 137, 142–143, 148, 152, 159, 166–167
cephalothorax, 175, 177–178, 188
chamber, 171
chelicera, 175, 188
chitin, 134, 188
cicada, 141, 162
claw, 175
cockroach, 134, 139–140, 144, 161
cocoon, 142–143, 188
Coleoptera, 145, 146–147
colony, 171, 188
communication between insects, 162–163
communication between spiders, 178–179
compound eye, 134, 139, 188

crab spider, 174, 179, 185
cricket, 135, 145, 162, 166

D

daddy long legs, 175
damselfly, 137, 144
deathwatch beetle, 163
deer fly, 164–165
defensive action, 168–169, 186–187
Dermaptera, 144
Diptera, 145, 154–155
diving beetle, 137, 143, 146, 167
dragonfly, 136, 139, 144, 162, 164–166
drone bee, 153
dung beetle, 146–147

E

earwig, 140, 144
eggs, 140–142, 153, 180–181
elephant hawk moth, 165
elytra, 135, 146, 188
entomologist, 144–145, 188
Ephemeroptera, 144
evolution, 159, 188
exoskeleton, 134–135, 140–141, 175, 180–181, 188
eyes of spiders, 179

F

fangs, 174–175
flea, 137–138, 145
flea beetle, 167
flowers, 158–159
fly, 145, 154–155, 164–165, 167
flying insects, 164–165
food of insects, 158–161
food of spiders, 183–185
fossil grasshopper, 135
fruit fly, 155
funnel-web spider, 183–184

G

ganglia, 137
genera, 151
glowworm, 162
grasshopper, 145, 161, 163, 165–166
grub, 142–143, 188

H

halteres, 154, 164, 188
hammock web, 183
hawk moth, 165
heart, 136, 176
Hemiptera, 144–145
herbivore mouthparts, 161
hive, 152–153
homes, 170–171
honeybee, 161–162, 164, 170
honeypot worker ant, 151, 169
hornet, 165
huntsman spider, 174, 176, 180, 189

Hymenoptera, 145, 150–153

I

ichneumon wasp, 152, 186
insect care and feeding, 143
insects eaten by humans, 169
insects and plants, 158–159
instinctive behavior, 179
internal organs of insect, 136–137
internal organs of spider, 176
Isoptera, 144

J

jumping spider, 174, 178–179, 184
juvenile, 181

K

katydid, 145, 150, 161, 169

L

lace-sheet web, 183
lacewing, 135, 141, 145, 162, 164
ladybug, 136, 15, 143, 145, 147
larvae, 142–143, 152, 166, 188
leaf-cutter ant, 150–151
leafhopper, 140–141, 144
legs, 135, 166–167, 187
Lepidoptera, 145, 148–149
lice, 145
life cycle of insects, 140–143
life cycle of spiders, 180–181
locust, 138, 158, 164–165
locust swarm, 164

M

maggot, 142–143, 154, 155, 188
malaria, 154
mandibles, 134, 189
mantid, 140, 18, 161
Mantodea, 144
mating of spiders, 180
mayfly, 144
metallic wood-boring beetle, 139, 146
metamorphosis, 140–143, 189
micromoth, 162
midge, 154, 164
midgut, 176
migration, 149, 189
mimicry, 169, 189
mite, 134, 175
molt, 140–141, 180–181, 189
monarch butterfly, 148, 169
mosquito, 140, 154
moth, 145, 148–149, 162, 168

N

nectar, 153
Neuroptera, 145
non-flying insects, 166–167

nursery for bees, 152
nursery-web spider, 181
nymph, 140–141, 189

O

ocelli, 12–13, 189
Odonata, 144
orb weaver spiders, 177–178, 183
orchid mantis, 160–161
orders of insects, 144–155
Orthoptera, 145
ovary, 176
ovipositor, 152, 189

P

palps, 134, 138, 175
papermakers, 170
parasite, 161, 189
parasitic wasp, 142, 152
parasitoid, 161
pedipalp, 175, 189
Peruvian lichen mantis, 168
pest control, 152, 166, 175
pet insects, 162
Phasmida, 145
pheromone, 162, 189
photographing insects, 136
Phthiraptera, 145
picture-wing fly, 162
pitfall trap, 147
plants and insects, 158–159
poison protection, 187
poisonous spiders, 184–185
pollination, 153
predators, 160–161, 189
pretend ant, 163
proboscis, 148, 189
protection, 168–169, 186–187
pupa, 142–143, 152, 189

Q

queen bee, 153, 171

R

raft spider, 178
redback spider, 175, 187
robber fly, 154–155

S

scaffold web, 183
scarab beetle family, 147
scavengers, 160, 189
sclerite, 164
secretion, 183
senses of insects, 138–139
senses of spiders, 178–179
sheep moth, 162
sight, 138–139
signature spider, 178, 182
silk, 149, 176, 182–183
silk gland, 176
silverfish, 139, 144
singing insects, 162
Siphonaptera, 145
social insects, 150–153, 189
social spider, 185
solpugid, 174
species, 151, 189

spider behavior, 178–179
spider watching, 177, 180
spider webs, 182–183
spider-hunting wasp, 161
spiderling, 181
spigot, 176, 182, 189
spined spider, 177
spinneret, 176, 182, 189
spinning webs, 182–183
spiracles, 136–137, 189
stabilimenta, 182–183
stalked-eyed fly, 155
stalking, 184–185
stick insect, 145
sting, 136, 169
stomach, 136, 176
stylops, 167
sub-adults, 181
surface tension, 166–167
surprise tactics, 168–169
swarm, 146, 189

T

tarantula, 161, 174–176, 184–187
tarantula-hawk wasp, 169
termite, 144, 163, 170–171
territorial insects, 163
thorax, 134, 164, 189
thrips, 134, 145
Thysanoptera, 145
Thysanura, 144
tiger beetle, 134–135, 160, 189
toxic squirt, 169
trachea, 137, 189
trapdoor spider, 177, 184, 186
triangle web, 183
Trichoptera, 145
tsetse fly, 155
tympana, 138, 189

U

ultraviolet light, 138, 183

V

venom, 174–176, 187, 189
Venus flytrap, 158
viceroy butterfly, 169
violin spider, 184

W

walking insects, 166–167
wandering spider, 185–186
warning colors, 168–169
wasp, 136–137, 142, 145, 152–153, 164, 169–170, 183
water strider, 162, 166
web building, 182–183
weevil, 138, 158–159
wings, 145, 148–149, 164–165
witchetty grub, 169
worker bee, 152–153, 171

Y

yucca moth, 158
yucca plant, 158

Acknowledgements

Dinosaurs

The publishers would like to thank the following people for their assistance in the preparation of this book: Barbara Bakowski, James Clark, Dina Rubin, and Jennifer Themel.
Our special thanks to the following children who feature in the photographs: Michelle Burk, Elliot Burton, Lisa Chan, Anton Crowden and Henry (dog), Gemma Smith, Gerard Smith, Andrew Tout, Lucy Vaux.

PICTURE CREDITS (t=top, b=bottom, l=left, r=right, c=center, e=extreme, f=flap, F=Front, C=Cover, B=Back) (NHM=Natural History Museum, TPL=The Photo Library, Sydney, SPL=Science Photo Library, UOC=University of Chicago.)
Ad-Libitum 7b, 11br, 16l, 18l, 21tr, 24r, 29l, 30l, 35tr, 35b, 39cr, 41b, 46b, 54l, 55tr (M. Kaniewski).
American Museum of Natural History 17c. Ardea London Ltd 15c (P. Morris), 33tl, 8l (F. Gohier). Auscape 58l (D. Parer & E. Parer-Cook), 12l, 39tr, 40tl, 40tr, 42r, 48c, 55br, 62l (F. Gohier), 50l (S. Wilby & C. Ciantar). Australian Museum 49tl (Nature Focus). Brigham Young University 41c (M.A. Philbrick). Dinosaur National Monument, Utah, 54bc. Everett Collection 14c, 26l. James Farlow 45r. David Gillette 32bl. The Granger Collection 53tr. Jeff Foott Prod.BC 34bl. Museum of the Rockies 24bl (B. Selyem). National Geographic Society 57b (J. Amos). NHM 27tl, 30c, 30r, 33tr, 34tr, 36c, 44bl, 45br, 50r, 50t, 53c, 53r, 53br, 55bl, 57t, 58bl. Palaontologisches Museum Universtat Zu Berlin 38bl. Peabody Museum of Natural History 20bl, 54cl. TPL 10tl (A. Evrard), 52t (Hulton-Deutsch), 11r (SPL/P. Plailly), 36t (K. Schaffer). Dr. Robert Reid, UK 20br, 21bl, 21br. UOC 13c (P. Sereno) US Geological Survey, 60l. Wave Productions 47tr, 58r (O. Strewe). Paul Willis 23tr.

ILLUSTRATION CREDITS
Anne Bowman 46t, 48tl, 48tr, 62tl. Jimmy Chan 42l, 61tl. Simone End 8ebr, 11tc, 15tr, 15c, 15r, 18tr, 26br, 57c, 57r, 44tl, 44tc. John Francis/Bernard Thornton Artists UK 22br. Murray

Frederick 46r, 50/51c, 50t, 50bl, 50br, 51tl, 51r, 51bl, 64tr. Lee Gibbons/Wildlife Art Ltd 47c, 60/61c, 60r, 61r. Ray Grinaway 15c, 15br, 49tr. Jim Harter (ed.) Animals (Dover, 2199) 58br, 59bl. Gino Hasler 7r, 28cr, 29r, 32bl, 32br, 33bl, 33bc, 33br, 42tl, 42tc, 42tr, 42bl, 42br, 43tr, 43cr, 43br, 65tc. Tim Hayward/Bernard Thornton Artists UK 60bl. David Kirshner 9tl, 9c, 18/19c, 18etr, 18tl, 18r, 18b, 19t, 19r, 19bl, 19br, 20/21c, 20tr, 21br, 28r, 29l, 34/35c, 34tl, 34tc, 34tr, 34b, 35r, 35br, 40/41c, 40r, 47l, 47br, 58/59c, 58tl, 58tr, 59r, 59br, 60tr, 60br, 61bl, 62er, 65bl. Frank Knight 6tr, 8tr, 11tl, 12bl, 12br, 13bc, 13br, 22r, 26tl, 27bc, 27bl, 42c, 48/49b. David McAllister 54/55c, 54br. James McKinnon 6cr, 8r, 8br, 12/13c, 12tl, 12tr, 13cr, 13tr, 13bl, 14/15c, 14tl, 14tc, 14tr, 29tl, 29tr, 38tl, 38tc, 38tr, 38bl, 38br, 39c, 39bl, 39bc, 39br, 39eb, 46c, 52tl, 52tr, 52l, 52bl, 52br, 53tl, 53c, 53b, 65tr, 65br. Stuart McVicar (digital manipulation) 8cr, 12r, 14r, 16r. Colin Newman/Bernard Thornton Artists UK 12tr, 25t, 60br. Luis Rey/Wildlife Art Ltd 9cl, 16/17c, 16tl, 16bl, 16br, 17cr, 17br, 22/23c, 22tl, 22tc, 22tr, 22b, 23r, 23bl, 23br, 29c, 30/31c, 30tl, 30tr, 30bl, 30br, 31r, 31bl, 43c, 64bl, 64br. Peter Schouten 6r, 10c, 10/12c, 10/12b, 14bl, 14br, 16tr, 17b, 20tl, 28tr, 29br, 31tr, 31br, 32/33c, 32tl, 32tc, 32tr, 32r, 44c, 64tl. Peter Scott/Wildlife Art Ltd 9br, 24tl, 24tc, 24tr, 24br, 25c, 25bl, 25br, 28br, 29bl, 36/37c, 36tl, 36tc, 36tr, 36bl, 37l, 37cr, 37bl, 37bc, 37br, 44/45c, 44tr, 44l, 44bl, 44br, 45bl, 47bl, 62c, 62c, 62r, 62bl, 62br, 63t, 63r, 63bl. Marco Sparaciari 6br, 47tl, 56tl, 56tc, 56tr, 56c, 56bl, 57r, 57bl, 57br. Kevin Stead 7l, 7bl, 15cr, 26/27c, 26tc, 26tr, 26c, 26r, 26bl, 27tr, 27r, 27br, 48/49c, 60tl, 64tc. Ann Winterbotham 17tr.

Earthquakes and Volcanoes

The publishers would like to thank the following people for their assistance in the preparation of this book: James Clark, Renee Clark, Richard S. Fiske, Susan Garcia, Malcolm Johnston, Saburo Mimatsu, Doug Myren, William Prescott, Carolyn Rebbert, Tom Simkin, Mary Wilkinson.
Our special thanks to the following children who feature in the photographs: Sienna Berney, Irene Finkelde, Lewis Nicholson, Jeremy Sequeira, and Julian Sequeira.

PICTURE CREDITS (t=top, b=bottom, l=left, r=right, c=center, f=flap, F=Front, C=Cover, B=Back)
AAP Image 86tr, 94t, 95b, 95tc, 98/99c, 101tl, 106b, 117tl. AdLibitum 71tr, 71bl, 79tc, 81br, 83b, 87br, 90bl, 92bl, 106bl, 124bl (Mihal K). AKG London 97br (A.L. Murat), 97bl (Houston & Harding), 117tr. Ardea 112tr (John Mason). Auscape 123t (F. Gohier), 118bl (Otto Hahn/Peter Arnold). Black Star 95tr (B. Schalkwijk). Bridgeman Art Library 109br (Agnew & Sons, London). Bruce Coleman Ltd. 116tr (A. Compost) Circus World Museum 116bl (Mihal K). Robert Coenraads 80bl. Corbis 121br, 122tr. Mary Evans Picture Library 72l, 75tr, 119c. The Granger Collection 88bl, 94b, 119br. NASA 124tr. National Geographic Society 81tr (E. Kristof), 108tr (S. Raymer). Nordfoto 73cr (A. Moe). Oxford Scientific Films 109bl (R. Packwood). Pacific Tsunami Museum 89br. Panos Pictures 106/107c (R. Huibers). Picture Media 93bc (Kurita Kaku/WADA), 99b (K. Kurita/M.Batsu), 88l (Press Telegram/Liaison), 99tr, 120bl (E. C. Hrafnsson). Planet Earth Pictures 117tl (Bourseiller-I & V), 102b, 114c, 114tr, 120c (Krafft-I & V). Princeton University/Dept. of Geosciences 76bl. Rotorua Museum of Art and History 117b. Jeff Scovil 71tr. Smithsonian Institute 116br (National Museum of Natural History). Tom Stack and Assoc. 76c (NOAA), 78tr (S. Swanger). F.L. Sutherland 113tr. The Photo Library 112bl (A.G.E. Fotostock), 73c, 105tr (G. Brad Lewis), 109cl (T. Davis), 102tr (E. R. Degginger), 120tr (R. Halin), 122b (Stewart Lowther/SPL), 96tr (Massonnet ET AL/CNES/SPL), 77r (NASA/ SPL), 107b (S&D O'Heara/PRI), 98tr, 98cl (Sipa Press), 82tr (K. Stepnell), 124cr (SPL), 98bl (US Geological Survey/SPL). University of California 95tl. USGS 91br, 91c, 91cr, 91tr, 91tl, 125c. Roger Viollet 96br. Wildlight 77tr (J. Danks)

ILLUSTRATION CREDITS
Susanna Addario 72tc. Richard Bonson/Wildlife Art Ltd 68tr, 71br, 68b, 71br, 76br, 76/77c, 76bl, 76t, 77bl, 77br, 82/83c, 82tl, 82tc, 82tr, 83cr, 83tr, 83br, 100crb, 100tl, 101c, 102/103c, 102cl (Mimatsu Masao Memorial Museum) 103r, 109/110c, 109t, 110bl, 110r, 118/119c 118tc, 118tl, 119tr, 119cr, 127br. Chris Forsey 70cr, 70c, 70tl, 71tl, 71cr, 71cl, 72bl, 72tr, 72br, 73bl, 73br, 74br, 74bl, 74tr, 75bc, 78/79c, 78bl, 78br, 78tc, 78tl, 79bl, 79br, 80/81b, 80/81c, 80tl, 80tr, 84crb, 85bl, 85c, 85cl, 90/91c , 90br, 90bl, 90c, 90t, 91bl, 91br, 96/97c, 96cr, 96tl, 96tc, 96c, 97cl, 97cr, 97tr, 98tc, 98br, 100br, 100crt, 100tr, 101cl, 101cr, 104/105c, 104tr, 105br, 105cr, 106tl, 107br, 107tr, 112bc, 112tc, 112tl, 113br, 113c, 113bl, 120/121c, 120br, 120tc, 120tl, 120tr, 121bc, 122/123c, 122l, 122tl, 122tr, 123br, 123cr, 123tr, 124bl, 124br, 124tc, 124tl, 124tr, 125b, 126bl, 126bl, 127tc. Ray Grinaway 4tr, 20cr, 20crt, 21tl, 21tr, 22bc, 22br, 23b, 22tl, 24tl, 24tr, 24tc, 25tr, 25tc, 28bc, 28bl, 28c, 28tc, 28tl, 28tr 93tc 93br, 93cr, 93tr, 101tr, 104tl, 108bl, 108br, 109bl, 114tl, 114tr, 115cr, 115br, 115tr, 116tl, 126bc, 126tl, 127tr. James McKinnon, 108/109c, 126c. Stuart McVicar/Geocart 10/11c, 11r, 94/95c, 100cr, 108tl, 108tr, 116/117c, 126br. John Richards 86/87c, 88/89c, 114/115c. Michael Saunders 72tc, 85br, 98tl. Ann Winterbotham 72tl.

Insects and Spiders

The publishers would like to thank the following people for their assistance in the preparation of this book: Barbara Bakowski, James Clark, Renee Clark, and Lynn Strong.
Our special thanks to the following children who feature in the photographs: Sienna Berney, Irene Finkelde, Lewis Nicholson, Jeremy Sequeira, and Julian Sequeira.

PICTURE CREDITS (t=top, b=bottom, l=left, r=right, c=center, f=flap, F=Front, C=Cover, B=Back)
AdLibitum 131b, 134bl, 141cr, 143bc, 165bc, 157bl, 180t (M. Kaniewski). Auscape 187b (K. Atkinson), 144tl (J.Cancalosi), 168br (M. Doolittle-Peter Arnold), 140cl, 175c, 182t (P. Goetgheluck-Pho.n.e), 137bc (C.A. Henley), 170cr (J. Shaw), 164cr (J. Sierra-OSF). Bruce Coleman Ltd. 146cl (J. Burton), 145br (R.P. Carr), 146tr, 163b, 187c (M. P. L. Fogden), 14tr, 141/2c (K.Taylor), 143tc (P . Zabransky). CSIRO 160bl (R. Moran/M. Robertson). E.T. Archive 144165 (Private Collection, Naples). Image Library-State Library of New South Wales 164l. Frank Lane Picture Agency 180c (B. Borrell), 164tr (S.C. Brown), 174cr (Silvestris). Minden Pictures 150l (M. Moffett). Nature Focus 174bl (C. Bento), 179b (R. Mascord). NHPA 164tr (G. I. Bernard). Oxford Scientific Films 144tr (C.Bromhall), 15765 (S. Camazine), 1187 (M. Fogden), 180t (J. Mitchell), 184tr (S. Morris), 154tr (R.Packwood), 170tr (P. Parks), 183tl (V. Sinha). The Photo Library 149cr (P. Cheskey), 148c (Eye of Science/SPL), 148tr (R.R. Hansen), 148tr (C. Krebs), 165tc (Nuridsany & Perennou/SPL), 136bl, 176r (D. Scharf/SPL), 169b (R. Smith), 136bc, 136tr, 137bl (A. Syred/SPL), 135c (Dr, Paul Zahl). Photo Researchers Inc. 138ctr, 138tr (L. Lessin). Planet Earth Pictures 143c (G. du Feu), 178l, 183c, 185tr (S. Hopkin), 177tl (W.B. Irwin), 150tr, 163c, (D.P. Maitland), 178r (P. Palmer). Premaphotos Wildlife 155t, 166l, 169c, 170bl, 18t (K. G. Preston-Mafham). Tom Stack and Associates 160tr, 166r (D.M. Dennis), 152bl (J. Shaw).

ILLUSTRATION CREDITS
Susanna Addario 136tc. Anne Bowman 156cr, 162b, 163b, 163b, 186bc, 186t, 187b, 187r, 188bl. Sandra Doyle/Wildlife Art 130br, 131tr, 132tr, 133tl, 136/137c, 137c, 137tr, 144/145c, 144b, 144cl, 145b, 157tl, 164b, 164c, 164t, 165b, 165c, 165tr, 172cr, 172br, 173br, 173bc, 176b, 176t, 177b, 177c, 177tr, 178/179c, 178t, 179b, 179r, 179tr, 188tr, 188bl, 188br, 189br. Simone End 156bl, 137bl. Christer Eriksson 134tl, 154/155c. Ray Grinaway 132tl, 134/135c, 134r, 135cr, 135tr, 136tl, 154t, 154b, 155r, 155bc, 157cr, 170/171c, 170b, 170t, 171r, 173tl, 180b, 180t, 181b, 181c. Ian Jackson/Wildlife Art 132cr, 132br, 138b, 138cl, 138tl, 138tl, 139b, 139c, 140/141c, 140b, 141b. Frank Knight 142br, 142tc, 142tl, 143bl, 143r. David Kirshner 134tc, 135bl. Rob Mancini 130tr, 133c, 148br, 148l, 149br, 149c, 152tl, 172tr, 173c, 174bl, 174t, 175b, 175c, 182c, 182t, 183b, 183cb, 183r, 189tl. James McKinnon 130crb, 157cl, 162/163c, 162r, 162tl, 168c, 168t, 169b, 169l, 169r, 169tr, 186c, 187l, 189bl. Steve Roberts/Wildlife Art 133r, 133cl, 146/147c, 147r, 147tl, 152/153c, 152bc, 152t, 153b, 153cr, 153t, 156tr, 157tr, 160bc, 160bl, 160t, 161tr, 161c, 166b, 166t, 165b, 165c, 188tl, 189tr. Trevor Ruth 8bc. Claudia Saraceni 154b, 154t, 155b, 155r. Chris Shields/Wildlife Art 156br, 164b, 164t, 165b, 165c, 184bl, 184cl, 184t, 185b, 185c. Kevin Stead 130crt, 133cr, 133tr, 135br, 136bl, 137br, 137bc, 137cr, 140tl, 140tr, 142/143c, 142bl, 150/151c, 150b, 150tc, 150tl, 150tr, 151b, 186bl.

Don't miss these other
Pathfinders science collections:

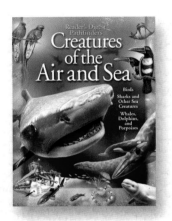

Creatures of the Air and Sea

Did you know that hummingbirds can fly backward? That there is a shark so small it can fit into the palm of your hands? Or that some dolpins are pink? Facts like these are at your fingertips every time you open this collection of three complete Reader's Digest Pathfinders—*Birds*, *Sharks and Other Sea Creatures*, and *Whales, Dolphins, and Porpoises*.

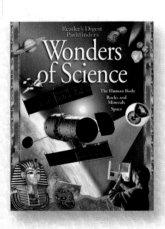

Wonders of Science

Did you know that billions of one-celled creatures live on your skin? That the planet you are standing on is actually a giant ball of rock? Or that astronauts grow slightly taller in space? You'll discover fascinating facts like these every time you open the this collection of three complete Reader's Digest Pathfinders—*The Human Body*, *Rocks and Minerals*, and *Space*.

Reader's Digest

Pathfinders COLLECTION

Wonders
of Science

Creatures
of the
Air and Sea

Marvels of
Nature

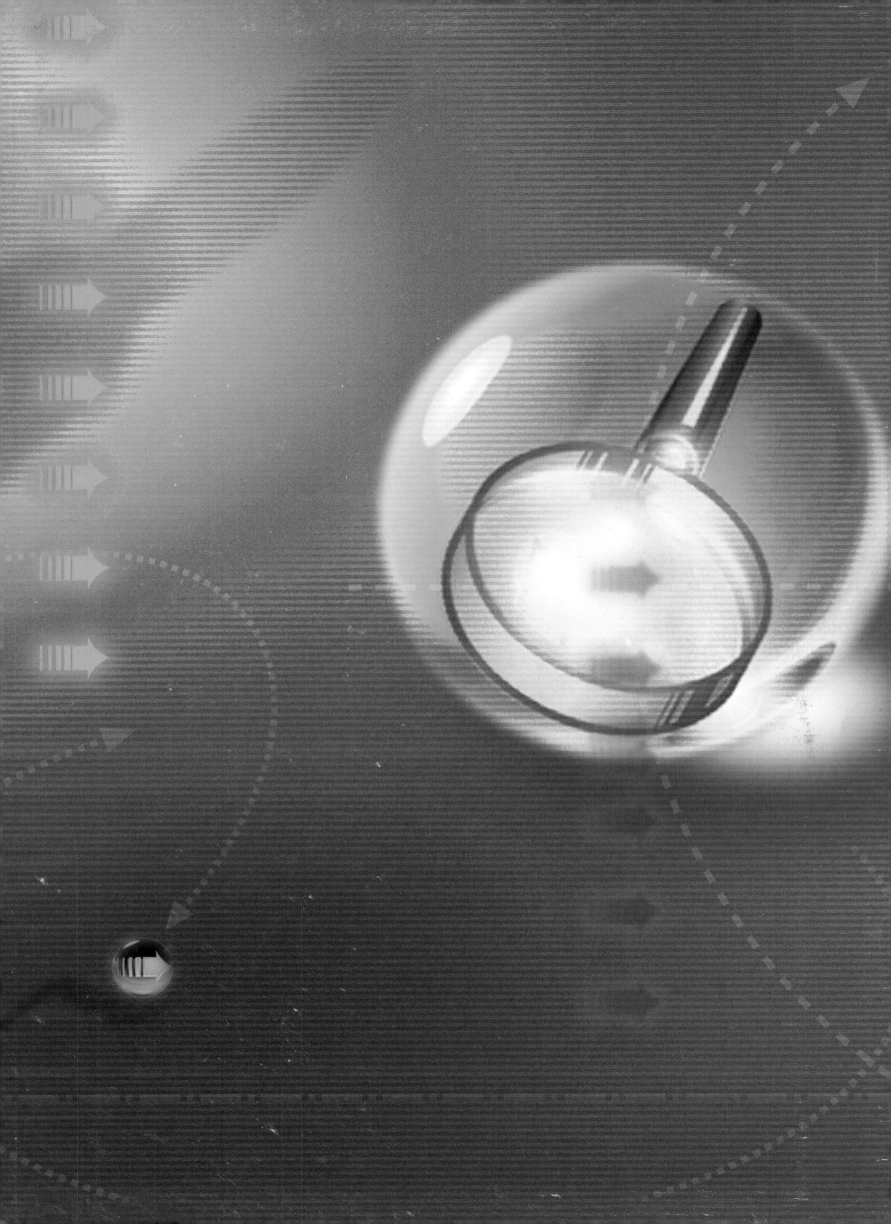